D0948661

CLASSICS
OF
ANCIENT
CHINA

The Analects of Confucius:
A Philosophical Translation

Roger T. Ames
Henry Rosemont, Jr.

BALLANTINE BOOKS
THE BALLANTINE PUBLISHING GROUP
NEW YORK

A Ballantine Book
The Ballantine Publishing Group

English translation, Preface, Introduction, Notes to the Translation, and Appendices
Copyright ©1998 by Roger T. Ames and Henry Rosemont, Jr.

http://www.randomhouse.com / BB

Library of Congress-Cataloging-in-Publication Data

Confucius.
    [Lun yü. English]
    The analects of confucius : a philosophical translation / Roger T.
Ames, Henry Rosemont, Jr.
      p. cm.
    "Ballantine books."
    Includes bibliographical references.
    ISBN 0-345-40154-9 (alk. paper)
    I. Ames, Roger I., 1947- . II. Rosemont, Henry, 1934- .
III. Title.
PL2478.L328 1998
181'. 112—dc21   98-27104
                                   CIP

Manufactured in the United States of America

First Edition: September 1998

10 9 8 7 6 5 4 3 2 1

To the Memory of

Angus C. Graham

distinguished scholar, unorthodox gentleman, friend.

CONTENTS

To read the *Analects (Lunyu* 論語) is to take some initial steps along the Confucian way, or path (*dao* 道). It is an ancient and well-worn way: countless millions of human beings have traveled on it for over two thousand years. But in our opinion it is still highly navigable, eminently capable of guiding explorers, searchers, and other citizens of the world from their present state to a better one.

As a consequence, many readers might simply begin reading the translated text proffered herein, allowing Confucius and his disciples to lead the reader directly to the *dao*. For others unfamiliar with the terrain, however, we fear the signposts may not be clearly discernible. Unlike many of his Western counterparts who have attempted to philosophize in an ahistorical and acultural manner, Confucius was deeply concerned about the pressing problems of his day, and therefore the *Analects* is replete with references to people, places, and events with which the contemporary Western reader will very probably be unfamiliar.

For this reason, we have provided an introductory historical background for the text, against which it might be more easily read, and we will be pleased if it serves that purpose. This is not to say that we have described all the people, places, and events mentioned in the text, either in the historical introduction or in the endnotes; to have done so would have made for a multivolume work, much of which might not contribute to illuminating the way of Confucius. The reader who wishes greater detail on ancient Chinese history is directed to our bibliography, and those more historically oriented translations that take such contextualization as their primary contribution.

We have thought it important to include as well a philosophical introduction to the text, because the Confucian way is a path through a world that differs significantly from ours in important respects. It is surely a habitable world, in our opinion, but it *is* a very different one, and we have attempted to describe that world, its human inhabitants, and their language, in the hope that the signposts for the Confucian way will come into sharper relief for the contemporary Western reader.

Our advice is that readers attend to the philosophical materials in conjunction with their own careful reading of the text. In fact, the purpose of our philosophical introduction is to enable the sensitive reader, in whatever degree possible, to take the Confucian way on its own terms without overwriting it with cultural interests and importances that are not its own. An image may help. As we mature within the milieu of a given culture, we are provided with a worldview—a range of beliefs and values—that illumines our way through life, providing our steps with the cultural purchase necessary to move ahead comfortably and securely. This worldview as a source of illumination is Plato's sun, making life stable and predictable. When, with these cultural lights shining brightly, we attempt to look through a window into a very different culture, our lights render this window a mirror, and thus what we see is familiar—it is our own reflection. That is, we tend to foreground what is familiar in our own cultural experience while leaving behind precisely those resources that would recommend the comparative exercise as a source of growth and enrichment.

It is only in becoming alert to the uncommon assumptions sedimented into Chinese ways of living and thinking that we can resist the gravitational force of cultural reductionism. This is not to suggest that there is some objective reading of the *Analects* that is innocent. An underlying premise of the *Analects* itself is that the text must be personalized and internalized by each reader. While we believe our interpretative philosophical arguments are sound, we do not wish to impose and thereby claim a "final" reading of the text; the *Analects* is too rich for that. Moreover, while our historical introduction is fairly straightforward and not overly controversial—we have not endeavored to grind any scholarly axes while composing it—our philosophical materials are by no means equally straightforward and noncontroversial; a number of scholars whom we respect greatly will, in all probability, not concur with some of our interpretations of the ancient Chinese world, its people, their language, and consequently will disagree with at least parts of our own reading of the *Analects*.

Largely for these sinologists and other interested readers, we have, in defense of our interpretations, offered additional evidence and arguments for them in the appendices. We have also appended a discussion of the recently recovered archaeological manuscript—the oldest existing version of the *Analects*—which informs our translation.

This, then, is the structure of the book. The reader is invited to delve into the heart of it, the *Analects* itself; we hope to see you along the way.

In the past, each of us has participated in collaborative translations of the writings of major thinkers—i.e., Sun Bin, Leibniz—but this is the first time we have worked together on a text. It has been a richly rewarding experience for both of us, all the more so as it has validated a central theme of the text itself: we most efficaciously follow and re-create the way (dao) when we do so in the company of others.

For the most part, we have been in agreement from the outset on most issues, and it has been deeply satisfying to have one's reading, interpretation, linguistic, or philosophical argument endorsed by the other. In those areas in which we were in initial disagreement, we have each learned much from the detailed exploration of our differences, and have been able to jointly celebrate our eventual compromises because in the end neither of us has felt compromised by the result.

At the same time, both of us have felt a sense of, if not inadequacy, then at least humility, for having associated our names with a figure of the historical significance and stature of Confucius, who arguably ranks with Jesus of Nazareth, Buddha, and perhaps Plato in influencing the lives of the past and present human inhabitants of this fragile planet. Our feelings on this score are well captured in the poem from the *Book of Songs*, cited in the *Analects*: "Fearful, fearful; as if treading on thin ice, as if peering into an abyss."

For these reasons, we are deeply grateful to the many people who have assisted our work in producing this present translation of and commentary on the *Analects*; we feel at least minimally less fearful because of their efforts. In the first instance our thanks go to Daniel Cole, for working over, then reworking, then reworking again our several drafts of the translation, and then for putting the results into a scholarly, respectable, and aesthetically pleasing camera-ready copy for the publisher; a daunting task in itself, made all the more so by the necessity of accurately juxtaposing English and Chinese text.

In the same way, we are indebted to our Random House editor Owen Lock for his most careful reading and commentary on our drafts, and to the anonymous copy editor who not only (embarrassingly) caught our grammatical lapses, but also made us mind our '*p*'s and '*q*'s in referencing the text when our '*p*'s did not match up correctly with our '*q*'s.

Early drafts of the introduction, appendices, and notes thereto were most ably prepared by the mother-daughter manuscript preparation team of Ellen and Eva Corson, who did their work with warmth, wit, and grace, and an efficiency which lightened the work of Daniel Cole for these portions of the text.

We are also indebted to the students in our seminars on the *Analects* held at the University of Hawai'i and St. Mary's College of Maryland; they not only called our attention to—again, sometimes embarrassingly—positive mistakes and/or inconsistencies in our translation and commentaries, but aided us measurably by pointing up infelicities of expression, and in addition, generated an enthusiasm for the project which was sustaining for both of us.

Our many references, both in the text and in the notes, to the work of David Keightley, signals clearly, we hope, our deep indebtedness to his work. Although he might cavil at the association, we consider him a fellow comparative philosopher, his richly deserved stature as an archaeological historian notwithstanding.

In China, our collaborators have been Yang Jin and Cai Min of Wenwu Publishing House. The meticulous and sophisticated scholarship on the Dingzhou manuscript they made available to us has been invaluable in deciding where and/or when to alter the received texts of the *Analects* in preparing our own translation. We hope the present work is worthy of their considerable efforts.

Finally and filially, our work derives from the scholar/translators of the *Analects* who have preceded us, especially those three who first acquainted us with Confucius, from whom we have learned much, and with whom we have ventured to disagree only with trepidation: James Legge, Arthur Waley, and D. C. Lau.

All of the above deserve much of the credit for transmitting the wisdom of the past; for all failures to innovate well, the responsibility rests with the undersigned.

Roger T. Ames (Honolulu)
Henry Rosemont, Jr. (St. Mary's City)

Master Kong 孔子 (*Confucius*)

Confucius (551–479 BCE) is probably the most influential thinker in human history, if influence is determined by the sheer number of people who have lived their lives, and died, in accordance with the thinker's vision of how people ought to live, and die. Like many other epochal figures of the ancient world—Socrates, Buddha, Jesus— Confucius does not seem to have written anything that is clearly attributable to him; all that we know of his vision directly must be pieced together from the several accounts of his teachings, and his life, found in the present text, the *Analects*, and other collateral but perhaps less reliable sources such as the *Mencius* and the *Zuo Commentary to the Spring and Autumn Annals*.[1]

Recognized as China's first great teacher both chronologically and in importance, Confucius' ideas have been the fertile soil in which the Chinese cultural tradition has been cultivated and has flourished. In fact, whatever we might mean by "Chineseness" today, some two and a half millennia after his death, is inseparable from the example of personal character that Confucius provided for posterity. And his influence did not end with China. All of the sinitic cultures—especially Korea, Japan, and Vietnam—have evolved around ways of living and thinking derived in significant measure from his ideas as set down by his disciples and others after his death—ideas that are by no means irrelevant to contemporary social, political, moral, and religious concerns.

Confucius was born in the ancient state of Lu (in modern Shandong province) during one of the most formative periods of Chinese culture. Two centuries before his birth, scores of small city-states owing their allegiance to the imperial House of Zhou filled the Yellow River basin. This was the Zhou dynasty (traditionally, 1122–256 BCE) out of which the empire of China was later to emerge. By the time of Confucius' birth only fourteen independent states remained, with seven of the strongest contending with each other militarily for hegemony over the central plains. It was a period of escalating internecine violence, driven by the knowledge that no state was exempt, and that all comers were competing in a zero-sum game—to fail to win was to perish. The accelerating ferocity of battle was like the increasing frequency and severity of labor pains, anticipating the eventual birth of the imperial Chinese state.[2]

The landscape was diverse not only politically. Intellectually, Confucius set a pattern for the "Hundred Schools" that emerged during these centuries in their competition for doctrinal supremacy. He founded an academy in his own state of Lu and, later in his career, he began the practice of independent philosophers traveling from state to state to persuade political leaders that the particular teachings developed in their academies were a practicable formula for social and political success. In the decades that followed his death, intellectuals of every stripe—Confucians, Legalists, Mohists, Yinyang Theorists, Militarists—would take to the road, often attracted by court-sponsored academies which sprang up to host them. Within these seats of learning and at the courts themselves, the viability of their various strategies for political and social unity would be hotly debated.[3]

Confucius said of himself that "Following the proper way, I do not forge new paths" (7.1),[4] allowing that he was a transmitter rather than an innovator, a classicist rather than a philosopher. This autobiographical statement is not altogether accurate—Confucius was an original thinker by any standard—but the statement captures a basic characteristic of what came to be called Confucianism: a deep respect and affection for the rich cultural Chinese past, what in the *Analects* is called "the love of learning (*haoxue* 好學)." Confucius saw human flourishing as definitive of the reigns of the ancient sage kings, and he advocated a reauthorization of their ways of governing that had been passed on. According to Confucius—and the other two ancient texts he cites, the *Book of Documents* and the *Book of Songs*[5]—the ancient sage kings who governed by observing ritual propriety and custom (the *li* 禮) rather than by law and force, were themselves reverent toward their past, were more concerned to insure the material and the spiritual well-being of the people than to accumulate personal wealth, and saw as their main task the maintenance of harmony between their community and the rest of the natural order. Confucius wished to reanimate this tradition, and pass it on to succeeding generations.

As a teacher, Confucius expected a high degree of commitment to learning from his students. On the one hand, he was tolerant and inclusive. He made no distinction among the economic classes in selecting his students, and would take whatever they could afford in payment for his services (7.7). His favorite student, Yan Hui, was desperately poor, a fact that simply added to Confucius' admiration for him (6.11, 6.3). On the other hand, Confucius set high standards, and if students did not approach their lessons with seriousness and enthusiasm, Confucius would not suffer them (7.8).

Over his lifetime, Confucius attracted a fairly large group of such serious followers, and provided them not only with book learning, but with a curriculum that encouraged personal articulation and refinement on several fronts. His "six arts" included observing propriety and ceremony (*li*), performing music, and developing proficiency in archery, charioteering, writing, and calculation, all of which, in sum, were directed more at cultivating the moral character of his charges than at any set of practical skills. In the Chinese tradition broadly,

3

proficiency in the "arts" has been seen as the medium through which one reveals the quality of one's personhood.

Although Confucius enjoyed great popularity as a teacher and many of his students found their way into political office, his enduring frustration was that he personally achieved only marginal influence in the practical politics of the day. He was a *philosophe* rather than a theoretical philosopher; he wanted to be actively involved in intellectual and social trends, and to improve the quality of life that was dependent upon them. Although there were many occasions on which important political figures sought his advice and services during his years in the state of Lu, he held only minor offices at court. When finally Confucius was appointed as police commissioner late in his career, his advice was not heeded, and he was not treated by the Lu court with appropriate courtesy. Earlier, Confucius had made several brief trips to neighboring states, but, after being mistreated in the performance of court sacrifices at home, he determined to take his message on the road again, this time more broadly.

These were troubled times, and there was great adventure and much danger in offering counsel to the competing political centers of his day. In his early fifties, he traveled widely as an itinerant counselor, and several times came under the threat of death (9.5). He was not any more successful in securing preferment abroad than he had been at home, to which he eventually returned and lived out his last few years as a counselor of the lower rank and, according to later accounts, continued his compilation of the classics. He died in 479 BCE, almost surely believing his life had been, on the whole, politically and practically worthless.

The Disciples

Although, like his Western philosophical counterparts, Confucius had a "vision" of the way the world was, he did not, could not, attempt to convey that vision—unlike many of his Western counterparts—solely

4

in purely descriptive language (about which, more follows). His vision was not simply one to be *understood*, and then accepted, modified, or rejected on the basis of its congruence with the world "objectively" perceived by his students. On the contrary, his vision was one that had to be felt, experienced, practiced, and lived. He was interested in how to make one's way in life, not in discovering the "truth."[6]

If this is an accurate account of what Confucius was about as a teacher, and appreciating that his students differed in age, background, education, and temperament, then we can begin to understand why, in the *Analects*, Confucius occasionally speaks in generalizations, but much more often gives a specific answer to a specific question asked by one of the disciples. At times, the Master gives different answers to the same question, which may all too easily suggest that he was not a particularly consistent thinker. But when we read more closely, and see that it was different disciples who asked the same question, we might reasonably postulate that Confucius based his specific response to the question on the specific perspective—lived, learned, experienced— from which he thought the disciple asked it. (cf. 11.22).

In order, then, to read the *Analects* and get the most out of it, we must learn something about the questioners of the Master.[7]

Yan Hui is far and away Confucius' favorite. Living on a daily bowl of rice and a ladle of water (6.11), Yan Hui's eagerness to learn and his sincerity endear him to the Master (6.3). Of a somewhat mystical bent (9.11), Yan Hui is nevertheless seen by Confucius as highly intelligent and exceptional among his students, such that "learning one thing he will know ten" (5.9). Yan Hui is three decades younger than Confucius and heir apparent to his teachings—certainly one reason why the latter was so devastated by his young disciple's untimely death (11.7–11). In fact, as D. C. Lau speculates, classical Confucianism might have had a somewhat different style if it had been Yan Hui rather than the five disciples in the last five books who had been responsible for its earliest transmission.[8]

5

Zilu is another well-known disciple of the Master, and among his favorites, although not portrayed as uniformly exemplary as Yan Hui. Zilu is a courageous activist who is sometimes upbraided by Confucius for being too bold and impetuous (11.22). When he asks the Master whether courage is indeed the highest human excellence, Confucius replies that a bold person lacking a sense of appropriateness would be unruly, and a lesser person, a thief (17.23). At the same time, it is clear that Confucius respects Zilu's courage (5.7), and no less clear that Zilu in his own way is attempting to grasp the Confucian vision, especially when Confucius is speaking not only with him, but with Yan Hui as well (5.26).

Zigong excels as a statesman and as a merchant. Although Confucius twits him for being stingy (3.17), he does believe Zigong can be entrusted with an administrative position (6.8). Despite his occasional officiousness, Zigong asks the important questions (7.15, 17.19), and it is clear that Confucius is fond of him (1.15).

Zengzi, or "Master Zeng," is the foremost exponent of the filial virtues (*xiao* 孝) among the disciples (1.9, 8.3–7), and, as evidenced by the number of times in the *Analects* he is referred to as "Master Zeng" (8:3-7 19:16 -19), he clearly became leader of a Confucian school after the Master's death. He is not among the sharpest of the disciples (11.18), but can at least occasionally elaborate on an unusual remark by his teacher (14.26).

Zixia is a man of letters, and is remembered by tradition as having had an important role in establishing the early canonical texts. His name appears in the early strata of the *Analects* (6.13) as one who is capable of treading the way (*dao*), and Confucius weighs his shortcomings as no worse than another disciple, Zizhang, whom he is willing to instruct at length (2.18). The Master calls attention to Zixia's timidity (11.16), but also to his apprehending the richness of the cultural tradition (3.8).

Zizhang himself often asks detailed questions about the significance of past historical events (5.19), but clearly wishes to learn the answers to his questions so that he can attempt to realize the Confucian vision in practice (2.18, 2.23).

Ranyou has a rather curious profile in the *Analects*. On the one hand, he is a mediocre student lacking in initiative (11.22). On the other hand, Confucius has no question concerning his administrative abilities (5.8), nor qualms about recommending him for office (6.8). In many ways, Ranyou's failures are a fair demonstration of perhaps the main theme of the text: real education is the cultivation of one's character, not the accumulation of administrative skills. At the end of the day, Ranyou is not able to move the usurping Ji clan, which he serves, in the direction of appropriate conduct because, as a person, he is not worthy of deference (3.6 and 16.1).

Other disciples are either well described in the text and in our notes thereto, or their qualities made known by the kinds of questions they ask, and the answers given. At times Confucius can be seen as a harshly exacting mentor with his students (14.43), but on other occasions, depending on his audience and the circumstances, as a warm, modest, and entirely human partner on a quest. In fact, he evidences a wonderful sense of humor in his interactions with his young followers (for example, 5.7, 5.20, 11.19, 17.1, and 17.4). A generalization about his interaction with his students is found in 7.38: "The Master was always gracious yet serious, commanding yet not severe, deferential yet at ease."

The Text

Beginning shortly after he died, a few of the disciples of Confucius began setting down briefly what they remembered the Master saying to them. Some disciples of the first generation of his students continued this process, so that, as the story goes, within a century of the founder's demise there were at least ten such little "books" about his life and teachings. Another dozen or more were compiled by we know-not-whom during the following century, and it was to be yet another hundred years before a number of these "books" were gathered together to make up the volume we now know as the *Analects*—or "Sayings of Confucius."[9]

Thus the present work in twenty books was over three centuries in the making, and there were numerous difficulties in editing it into a coherent whole. In the first place, the savage civil wars plaguing China during Confucius' lifetime greatly intensified after his death: to this day, the Chinese refer to their historical times 403–221 BCE as "The Period of the Warring States." The disciples—and their disciples in turn—scattered; some were killed, some formed their own schools; undoubtedly much was written, but only a few copies of each text would be circulated, and of course, all were subject to loss or destruction.

Worse, in 213 BCE, less than a decade after the country had been unified by the First August Emperor of the Qin—he of the terra cotta army of tomb soldiers—the then Prime Minister Li Si ordered a general burning of all writings not dealing with the practical arts. Fair copies of each title destroyed were kept in an imperial library, but as the dynasty began to disintegrate after the death of the First Emperor, the imperial library was burned to the ground.[10]

From the ashes of the Qin dynasty the House of Han arose. It was one of China's longest reigning dynasties (202 BCE–220 CE), and within the first century of its rule, a syncretically fortified version of the philosophical and religious thought of what was then loosely called "Confucianism" came to dominate the intellectual life of the realm, beginning its ascendancy after Emperor Wu (140–87 BCE) took the throne. It was during this early Han period that the reconstitution of all surviving materials attributed to Confucius and his disciples took place, with one result being the text of the *Analects* as we have it today.

There are different stories told on the compilation of the *Analects*. D. C. Lau stands with traditional wisdom: this text was compiled shortly after the death of Confucius. He suggests that the first fifteen books were assembled relatively soon after the death of the Master, and the last five books came together sometime after the original disciples had attained maturity.

More recently, John Makeham has insisted upon the fluidity of the resources that would ultimately provide the content of our received text, dating its attainment of fixed status at about 150 BCE. Bruce and Taeko Brooks have surmised that the present books 4 through 8 are the oldest strata of the text, all composed by disciples who actually studied with Confucius. Books 9 through 11 may well have been composed by the disciples of the disciples, and the remaining books follow, variously ordered temporally and topically, except that book 20 is surely the most recent, written approximately two and a quarter centuries after Confucius' death.[11]

The question of "when" will probably be answered in due course by the accelerating number of texts being uncovered in the archaeological finds. At this juncture, two points might be made. First, over the last forty years, the archaeological finds have repeatedly overruled —in favor of traditional dating—many modern scholars and their speculations. And, second, the fragmentary Dingzhou text which informs the present translation was excavated from a 55 BCE Han dynasty tomb yet differs only incidentally from the many, much later texts which have come down to us. It thus provides us with an initial date before which the process of compilation must have been completed. However this mystery plays out, the enormous influence that the received *Analects* has had on defining "Chineseness" is never in question.

For all these reasons it is not surprising that, especially to the modern Western reader who is used to a linear, sequential text, the present *Analects* seems to be something less than a coherent whole. A great many hands, spanning some several centuries, have set down, sorted, re–sorted, edited, and collated these "sayings." Little wonder, then, that they can initially give the appearance of being fragmentary, disconnected, and occasionally, in conflict with each other.

In short, the present *Analects* is not easy to read through as a philosophical text even when it is appreciated fully that Confucius seldom speaks ex cathedra, never speaks at all on certain issues (7.21, 9.1, 9.4), and regularly leads his students on the way by giving varied answers to the same question, based upon his perception of the student's receptiveness to the "answer." But these difficulties in interpreting the *Analects* notwithstanding, it must be emphasized again that the text as we now have it was read very closely and carefully, and in fact, usually memorized, along with the names ot the dramatis personae mentioned in the text, by virtually every educated Chinese for two millennia. It was quite literally set in stone with the engraving of the Xiping stone classics over the period 175–183 CE, fragments of which have been recovered since the Song[12] dynasty. The last Chinese civil service examination based on the *Analects* was administered in the twentieth century, in 1905. It thus deserves to be read as carefully and as deliberately as it was read by seventy-odd generations of Chinese, in just the form in which it has been handed down to us. There is a greater degree of coherence to the *Analects* than a first reading would suggest; many sections cluster around specific themes and subjects, and thus the architecture of the text emerges as readers make it their own.

Several other texts of the Warring States period attribute sayings to Confucius which are not found in the present *Analects*, including importantly the *Mencius* 孟子, the *Zuo Commentary to the Spring and Autumn Annals (Zuozhuan* 左傳), and the *Xunzi* 荀子. We have used these three texts extensively as sources of early commentary on the *Analects*, citing them where they are consistent with and shed light upon the always laconic record. There were also a number of other "books" about Confucius in circulation that did not escape destruction during the civil wars.

Other Canonical Texts

In the *Analects*, Confucius regularly praises a number of the legendary sage kings of antiquity—Yao, Shun, Yu—who were traditionally assigned reigns in the third millennium BCE. Whether these legendary rulers were historical figures will probably never be known (apart from the legends, we have little direct evidence for their existence), but Confucius and the tradition that followed in his footsteps surely believed that they were. We know that Chinese civilization was already highly developed by the time Confucius was born, and had been so for at least a thousand years. And Confucius devoted his life to celebrating, renewing, and recommending that development. Thus, while it would not make much sense to speak of a Buddhism before the Buddha, or a Christianity before Christ, it actually does make good sense to speak of a "Confucianism" before Confucius: he articulated clearly and championed compellingly a great many of the artistic, social, ritual, religious, and other practices that had already defined the Chinese cultural tradition for a millennium.

Two of the books descriptive of that tradition predate Confucius, and are cited by him in the *Analects*. The first of these is the *Shujing* 書經—usually translated as the *Book of History* or the *Book of Documents*.[13] It is thought by some scholars that parts of the *Book of Documents* might well be China's oldest written work, predating even the oracle bones of the late Shang (traditionally 1766–1122 BCE), while other scholars would not allow that it is earlier than the Zhou dynasty (traditionally 1122–256 BCE). It is made up of a series of short essays, memorials, and documents which record parts of the reigns of several of the sage-kings and rulers of the early three dynasties (see *Analects* 2.23): the Xia (traditionally 2205–1766 BCE), the Shang or Yin, and the early Zhou. The book is by no means a complete account of antiquity, and even the oldest parts of it are generally thought to have been written long after the events they describe.[14]

Although parts of the *Book of Documents* are simply chronicles of events, other parts of it are the charges of rulers to their successors, and to their ministers. The themes repeated consistently in these exhortations had moral, political, and religious qualities that came to be definitive of the Confucian persuasion (which is probably why many

11

later commentators believed Confucius edited the text). Many of the practices described in the *Book of Documents* were surely informed by early beliefs in the supernatural, but these beliefs are not emphasized in the book as much as, for example, the exhortations to govern responsibly, and were largely ignored by the Master and his disciples when discussing the text.

In addition to Yao, Shun, and Yu, many personages are mentioned or quoted in the *Book of Documents*, and three deserve special mention here because of the esteem in which they were held by Confucius. They were the founders of the Zhou Dynasty: King Wen, his son King Wu, and the latter's younger brother, the Duke of Zhou. King Wen 文王—whose name means at once "culture," "refinement," "embellishment," and "literature"—is best known as the loyal vassal of the last Shang dynasty ruler, a tyrannical despot who oppressed the people. Wen constantly remonstrated with this ruler, attempting to get him to mend his evil ways, but was unsuccessful in this effort. When Wen died, his son Wu 武—which means "martial"—led a successful rebellion against the Shang, formally establishing the Zhou dynasty. As a filial son, the "Martial King" claimed his father as the posthumous first ruler of the House of Zhou.

By championing both of these early kings, Confucius bequeathed to two thousand years of Chinese officialdom a way of coming to terms with a great tension many of them had to confront directly: what is a moral minister to do in the service of an immoral ruler? Those who believed their ruler was reformable through remonstrance and example, could claim King Wen as their exemplar; those who believed otherwise could at least retire, or, more strongly, raise the flag of rebellion in the name of good King Wu.

It was toward the third member of this royal trio, however, that Confucius appears to have felt the closest personal bond (see especially 7.5). The Duke of Zhou was exemplary in at least two respects. First, in a very moving passage, the *Book of Documents* records the duke's offering sacrifice and prayers to the ancestors on behalf of his seriously ill elder brother, King Wu, in which he implores the ancestors to heal his brother, and take him (the duke) instead, if a royal death be necessary. These entreaties eventually proved fruitless; the king succumbed, leaving as his patrimony to the throne a three-year-old son. The duke of Zhou thereupon assumed the regency, but instead of usurping the throne himself, turned it over to his nephew as soon as the latter achieved his majority and was capable of assuming royal responsibility. Thereafter, like Cincinnatus, the duke retired to his own estate to live out his days; a worthy cultural hero indeed.

The second canonical work quoted more than any other source in the *Analects* is the *Shijing* 詩經, variously translated as the *Book of Poetry, Book of Odes*, or *Book of Songs*.[15] Although regularly cited in support of some weighty aesthetic, moral, or political point that Confucius wished to make, the original 305 poems that comprise the *Songs* are just that: poems to be intoned and chanted aloud. While some of them do indeed have a moral import that can be read out of them, the majority are simply reflective of life in earliest historical China. There are love poems, and poems lamenting a son or husband going off to war; poems dealing with nature, with hunting and fishing, with friendship, with festivals; and there are poems dealing with legends and ancient rituals. Collectively the poems of the *Songs* paint what must be the most accurate picture we have of the everyday life of the Chinese—aristocrats and commoners alike—living in approximately the ninth century BCE.

In the West, probably the best-known ancient Chinese work is, if not the *Analects*, then the *Yijing* 易經, or *Book of Changes*.[16] Although parts of it, like the *Book of Documents*, probably date from early Western Zhou (1122–771 BCE), the work as we have it today, with accretions spanning many centuries, only came together many generations after the death of Confucius. Originally a book of divination—and never ceasing to be such—the *Book of Changes* became the first among the canonical classics, and certainly influenced later Confucian thinking. It may well have been read in some form by the authors of the "books" that now make up the *Analects*. At the very least, Confucius is explicitly quoted as interpreting one of the hexagrams in this text (13.22). There is also one version of the *Analects* suggesting that Confucius late in his life was himself a student of the *Book of Changes* (7.17) that is gaining increased credibility from the Confucian commentaries recovered at Mawangdui in 1973. Although we still follow the Dingzhou text which does not reference the *Book of Changes*, the appearance of this variant speaks to the sustained importance that this text came to have in the intellectual life of China.[17]

Other texts now included in the Confucian canon—parts of which were probably extant while Confucius was alive—are three texts on ritual: the *Zhouli* 周禮 (*Rituals of Zhou*), *Yili* 義禮 (*Appropriateness and Rituals*), and the *Liji* 禮記 (*Records of Rituals*).[18] Another historical work, the *Chunqiu* 春秋 (*Spring and Autumn Annals*) is a chronicle of events at the court of Lu 722–481 BCE, an era which subsequently came to be known as the "Spring and Autumn" period after the chronicle's title. A series of commentaries written on this laconic record of court events were to become the focus of interpretative exegetical studies during the Han dynasty.[19] There also appears to have been a *Yuejing* 樂經 (*Book of Music*), but no copies or even significant fragments thereof have been extant for some two thousand years.

We see the beginning of the succession to Confucius in the last books of the *Analects* in which several of his now mature disciples pronounce on the meaning of Confucius' teachings. But the most famous successor to Confucius was the later "Master Meng" (Mengzi 孟子), Latinized as "Mencius," who flourished one hundred and fifty years after the Master (ca. 372–289 BCE). Mencius was himself supposed to have studied with a follower in the school of Zisi 子思 (491–431 BCE), a grandson of Confucius who is associated with the *Zhongyong* 中庸, the *Doctrine of the Mean*, and several of the newly recovered texts at the

1993 Guodian find in which he is named explicitly. In the book that bears his name, Mencius elaborated upon and embellished the views of Confucius, defending them against all comers with skill, passion, and grace.[20] He later was canonized as the "Second Sage" of Confucianism, in no small part because of his claim that human beings are naturally inclined toward good conduct. A number of passages in the *Mencius* are explicit commentary on the *Analects*, and have been included in the notes to this translation.

The next most famous successor to Confucius before the Han dynasty was "Master Xun" or Xunzi 荀子 (ca. 310–238 BCE), who, like Mencius, defended the Confucian vision against its rivals among the "Hundred Schools" of thought that were contending during the Warring States period. If perhaps less passionate in his thinking than Mencius, he was equally graceful, and far more rigorous (at least from a Western philosophical perspective). Given his role in co-opting much of the competing wisdom of his day for "Confucianism" and his unparalleled influence on the establishment of Confucianism as the state ideology a century after his death, Xunzi has, not inaccurately, been referred to as "the molder of ancient Confucianism."[21]

Although we cannot be sure that either of these famous successors to Confucius had available to them the *Analects* as we have it today, both of them regularly cite the Master as saying things that, while sometimes not found in the current text, are generally compatible with its philosophical spirit, at least as, *mutatis mutandis*, it would inform the intellectual world of the day. The recently recovered commentaries to the *Book of Changes* at Mawangdui (1973) that cite Confucius' reflections explicitly add to our store of Confucius-related materials. These references provide evidence for believing that there were several more "books" about Confucius in circulation during this period, and further, that Mencius and Xunzi deserve the interpretative successor status they achieved.

Shortly after the *Analects* as we have it today took form, a long and venerable commentarial tradition on the text began, a tradition probably rivaling that of biblical scholarship, both quantitatively and qualitatively.

After several centuries of competing intellectually and spiritually with the Buddhism imported from India, the *Analects* and other Confucian classical texts underwent a thorough reexamination in the light of changes in Chinese thought brought about by the sinicization of Buddhist doctrines and by the changes in political, economic, and cultural patterns that accompanied China's growth as an empire. This reexamination of the classical writings marked the beginning of what has come to be called neo-Confucianism, an intellectual and profoundly religious movement which reached its height during the Song dynasty (960–1279 CE), under the influence of the encyclopedic scholar-philosopher Zhu Xi (1130–1200 CE).[22]

Combining some themes from the *Analects,* the *Mencius,* the *Book of Changes,* and the books on ritual, the syncretic neo-Confucians constructed an explicit metaphysical system that is largely absent in the ancient writings, a system designed to counter the rich Buddhist metaphysics (and its Daoist variant) which had long held sway conceptually both among the literati and the common people. Continuing the pattern established early in its career—that is, a porous Confucianism absorbing whatever was necessary to sustain it against competing intellectual forces—neo-Confucianism, while overtly repudiating Buddhism and Daoism, expanded to embrace a much enhanced spiritual sensibility drawn from these other traditions. This is not to suggest that the neo-Confucians distorted fundamentally the views or writings of their classical predecessors. On the contrary, they used their metaphysics and enhanced sense of religious fellowship to justify and even fortify the Confucian way of life as described in the *Analects* and other early texts: aesthetic, moral, and spiritual advancement in one's life could only proceed by fulfilling one's many obligations to family and society.

Put another way, Zhu Xi and his colleagues did not—by their lights—break with the classical tradition; they saw themselves as returning to the tradition and providing metaphysical underpinnings for the views of Confucius and other ancient cultural heroes. One of the central threads which ties the early and late Confucians together is the importance of self-cultivation—the central theme of the *Analects*—not only for aesthetic development, but for moral strength, the social good, and spiritual insight as well. The neo-Confucian form of discipline involved in self-cultivation takes on a more contemplative aspect than is found in the early writings, but the emphasis on self-cultivation and personal discipline is persistent and pervasive.[23] The sacred is not transcendentally removed from the secular.

Zhu Xi's commentaries on the *Analects* (and on the *Mencius*) became definitive of the tradition from the early fourteenth through the twentieth centuries. Along with these two texts, Zhu Xi emphasized the importance of two chapters taken from the *Records of Rituals*, called the *Great Learning* (*Daxue* 大學) and the *Doctrine of the Mean* (*Zhongyong* 中庸). Taken together with the *Analects* and the *Mencius*, these texts came to be known as the "Four Books," and served as the core canon of China's civil service examinations for over six hundred years.

Moreover, Zhu Xi's legacy extended beyond the Middle Kingdom. When Western missionaries, merchants, and scholars came to China and began translating Confucian texts, they inherited Zhu's commentarial legacy from their own Chinese teachers, an inheritance that culminated in the monumental achievements of the Scottish Presbyterian missionary James Legge (1815–1897), whose *Chinese Classics* remains, in many respects, the benchmark for all translation work to this day.

One of the more recent ironies regarding the *Analects* occurred during the Cultural Revolution (1966–1976) in which China's political leadership tried to erase the country's cultural past. The "Anti-

Confucius Campaign" (*pikong* 批孔) orchestrated a nationwide critique of Confucius that had the entire literate Chinese population studying the *Analects* in order to call it into question—a strategy that did more to reauthorize this classic than to stem its influence.

In summary, it is essential for the reader of the *Analects*—and Confucian writings more generally—to appreciate the singular role played by the Master in shaping Chinese thought, government, culture, and daily life. The importance of Daoism and Buddhism notwithstanding, Confucianism has been the dominant cultural resource transmitted and elaborated upon by the literati for over two millennia, and because government officials were drawn from the ranks of the literati, it served as the official state ideology as well. Moreover, because it celebrated tradition, rituals, filial obligations, ancestor reverence, and other such popular institutions, Confucianism was exemplified in the lives of Chinese commoners, who were thereby followers of the Master in practice even though they had no firsthand knowledge of the *Analects* and related texts.

Confucius, then, was not simply one great thinker among many in China; his defense and enhancement of the early heritage established him as the enduring symbol of Chinese civilization. As a consequence, he has been honored even by those whose views were different (Daoists and Buddhists), and by those who could not read the writings which expressed those views. Thus the spirit of the *Analects* has been consistently reflected in the writings and actions of later Confucian philosophers, and continues to color the entire fabric of Chinese culture.

Finally, the contemporary Western reader of the *Analects* must bear in mind that the early emerging "Confucianism" was challenged at its inception by Daoists, Mohists, Legalists, and proponents of others of the "Hundred Schools" of classical Chinese thought. In the course of time, it was overshadowed by Buddhism for several centuries. And again later, it was challenged by Christianity, first by the Jesuits, Franciscans, and Dominicans of the late sixteenth and seventeenth centuries, and afterward by both Protestant and Catholic missionaries in the nineteenth and twentieth centuries. The earliest incursions of missionaries were buttressed by what they believed to be the unassailable rationality of classical Western learning, while the later reinforcements relied on the gunboat diplomacy of the imperialistic Western powers as they laid claim to China. And, of course, liberal democratic, capitalist, and Marxist ideas have contributed much to the Western onslaught against the resilient Confucian tradition. But in the face of all these challenges Confucianism has not only persisted, it has repeatedly risen and reasserted itself with renewed strength and substance derived from its appropriation of precisely those forces that would undermine it. Thus it would be presumptuous—and very probably false—to suggest that it cannot have any purchase on us today.

This endurance is not merely evidenced by the fact that the most successful—in strictly economic terms—of non-Western nations in modernizing their societies have been those heavily influenced by the Confucian tradition: Japan, South Korea, Taiwan, Singapore, Hong Kong, and more recently, China itself. The "Confucian Hypothesis"[24] which is regularly invoked to describe this success, often depicts an authoritarian Confucius who, in our opinion, is a very different one from the sagely teacher found in the *Analects*. Our Confucius is undogmatic (9.4), not concerned with personal profit (4.16, 7.7), dislikes competitiveness (3.7), sets little store by material possessions (1.15), and is more concerned about equitable distribution of wealth than wealth itself (16.1); it is neither an authoritarian nor a capitalist Confucius that is met in the pages of the present book.

For all these reasons, then, the *Analects* should not be read merely for antiquarian interest, or for modern economic insight either. Rather should the reader consider seriously the possibility that there might be much in this text that speaks not only to East Asians, but perhaps to everyone; not only to the scholars of the past, but perhaps to all those who wish to help shape a more decent and humane future today.

Metaphysics, With Reference to Language[25]

In order for the reader to appreciate fully the sophisticated depth of the Analects, we as translators must first attempt to describe the world as experienced by the ancient Chinese who walk through its pages. This is a daunting task, because underlying the grammar of the contemporary English language is a rather different "world." To say this is not to suggest Chinese exoticness: trees, birds, flowers, mountains, rivers, and most everything else in China do not differ radically from their counterparts closer to home. Nor is it to say that all ancient Chinese beliefs and attitudes differ radically from our own: many different Chinese held many different beliefs and attitudes, and a great many of them have Western counterparts.

Rather we are saying that there are *presuppositions* underlying all discourse about the world, about beliefs, and about attitudes, which are sedimented into the specific grammars of the languages in which these discourses take place. Proceeding from an awareness that the only thing more dangerous than making cultural generalizations is the reductionism that results from not doing so, we need to identify and elaborate some of these presuppositions. To establish some initial terms for comparison, we want to claim that English (and other Indo-European languages) is basically *substantive* and *essentialistic*, whereas classical Chinese should be seen more as an eventful language.

If this be so, then experiencing a world of *events*, seen as persistently episodic, will perhaps be different from experiencing a world of *things*, seen interactively.

To take an example, the tree seen in one's front yard is clearly the same tree all year long; its *substance*—underlying reality—remains the same, despite differing appearances throughout the year. But in the world of lived experience, it is not forced on us to focus on the tree's sameness, substance, or essence. Rather can we experience a tree with flowers and buds, a tree with green leaves, then with brown leaves, and finally, a tree with no leaves at all. The tree *appears* differently, and why can't the appearances be "real"? The tree can be perceived eventfully, relationally, with respect to the seasons, other natural phenomena, and with respect to ourselves as well: only during certain times will the tree shade us, and there are other times to rake its relentless crop of falling leaves, still another time to prune it.

This example will almost surely seem odd to anyone unfamiliar with the idea of being able to experience the world "nonsubstantially." A part of the reason for the oddness, however, lies not in any unreasonableness of the Chinese orientation—if we are right, their orientation is eminently reasonable—but rather lies at least partially in the grammatical rules of English which we cannot significantly violate in attempting to describe that orientation. The definite article in English signals "the one and only," and the use of the same pronoun in a sentence must refer to the same object. Thus when we say "*the* tree" it must be a "one and only" tree, and when we refer to "it," it must be the *same* tree, no matter what the season. Similarly, the boy who purportedly chopped down a cherry tree and confessed to the deed must be the *same* George Washington who served as the first president of the United States.

Thus it is important to note here—we will have more to say about the Chinese language in the next section—that classical Chinese has no definite articles (or any articles at all), and its pronouns do not function just as modern English pronouns do. Essentialism is virtually built into English—indeed, into all Indo-European languages—by the way things, essences, substances, (nouns) *do* something (they are verbed), or have something else attributed to them (*via* being auxiliary verbed). Consequently, moving from Chinese as our object language, which may properly be described as eventful, into an essentialistic target language, English, will require a stretching of the latter in order to better convey the former—as we have done in our translation of the *Analects* (and in the preceding sentence).

Aristotle's categories demand from us that experiences be factored into things, actions, attributes of things, and modalities of actions—nouns, verbs, adjectives, and adverbs. Hence, our first impulse in encountering the unfamiliar is to make such a determination. *Dao* 道 becomes reified and objectified as "the *dao*." Yet *dao* has as much to do with subject as it does with object, and as much to do with the subject's quality of understanding as it does with the various aspects of the felt experience. Said another way, *dao* defies Aristotle's categories, being all of them at once. And our experience of the tree is constitutive of *dao*, one experience among many which in sum make up one's day.

Some of the "eventful" properties of classical Chinese can be discerned in modern spoken Mandarin, or *Putonghua*. The very expression "thing," for example—*dongxi* 東西 , literally, "east-west,"—is a nonsubstantial relationship.[26] Again, noun phrases are, in linguistic terms, head-initial in English, and head-final in Mandarin. Thus the English sentence:

The young woman who just entered the room is very bright.

would have a very different word order in Chinese:

Just now room-inside enter that-young-woman very bright.
Gangcai wuzili laide xiaojie feichang congming.
剛才屋子裡來的小姐非常聰明。

For the two of us at least, the "English" young woman is considerably more substantial, but much less dynamic (more thingful/essential *vs.*

eventful/relational) than her "Chinese" counterpart, an impression strengthened by the lack of an auxiliary verb in the Chinese.

In our view, early Chinese thinkers, unlike their Western counterparts ancient and contemporary, were not concerned with seeking the essence of things—that which remained constant throughout the changes manifest to our senses. On the contrary, they seem to have presupposed that the only constant is change itself, as the *Book of Changes* makes explicit. The reality/appearance dualism that is so close to the heart of Western philosophizing is closely linked to the permanence/change and form/matter distinctions, and consequently we should not be surprised to find no discussions of underlying reality versus changing appearances in early Chinese texts: reality and appearance are one and the same, and the reality is that everything changes, in nature, in society, and at the personal level. Most of the changes are cyclic (the tree will flower and bud again next year) and harmoniously integrated (the birds and bees return when the flowers and buds do). Some changes are novel (an abundance of flowers one year), others unexpected (lightning may strike the tree). Within limits we may creatively affect the changes (pruning the tree this way rather than that), fully realizing that the cycle of changes is hierarchical, genealogical, and irreversible (one day the tree will wither and die—as will we—and our descendent grandchildren will nurture its descendent seedling). Significantly, the context and the persistence of the particular phenomenon is perceived as far more fluid in this Chinese worldview (much more of the fruit produces worm farms than apple trees).

If our interpretation on this score has merit, the reader should expect to find in classical Chinese texts a more relational focus; not a concern to describe how things are in themselves, but how they stand in relation to something else at particular times. Thus, if the world is ever-changing, then those relations, too, must be ever-changing and not only with respect to trees. We can see this clearly in the discussion of human relations which dominate a great deal of the *Analects*. Although children must be filial to their parents throughout life, the relation between them changes. When young, children stand in the relation of beneficiary to their parents, but change to benefactor when the children mature and their parents grow old. And the same holds cyclically for them after they have become parents and grandparents in turn. Stated more generally, no one, not just parents and children, is either benefactor or beneficiary in and of herself, but only in relation to specific others at specific times.

The nature of "relationality" needs to be clarified, for there is possible equivocation here. In a world of substances, people or things are related extrinsically, so that when the relationship between them is dissolved, they are remaindered intact. Such extrinsic relatedness can be represented as:

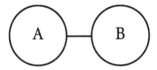

But relatedness defining of the Confucian worldview is intrinsic and constitutive. Perhaps "correlation" is a more felicitous term, so that it can be diagrammed as:

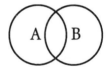

Under such circumstances, the dissolution of relationships is surgical, diminishing both parties in the degree that this particular relationship is important to them. In such a world, people literally rather than figuratively change each other's minds.

The point can be generalized still further perhaps: no-thing or nobody has an *essence*, but can be defined only "correlationally," at any given time, with differing relations holding at other times; we are both benefactors and beneficiaries of our friends, neighbors, lovers, colleagues, and so forth, dependent on specific circumstances. We see these patterns of thought not only in early Chinese philosophical writings, but in all other writings as well. The Chinese *materia medica* describes the chest as *yin* (receptive, soft, submissive) with respect to the back, which is *yang* (creative, hard, aggressive). But in relation to the abdomen, the chest is *yang*. But these relations, too, can be changed, depending on anatomical conditions (a broken leg, a pinched nerve, and so on). That is to say, nothing is altogether *yin* or *yang* in and of itself, but only in relation to one or more other "things," temporally contextualized.[27] (We can note here in passing that if there are no essences, there cannot be any peculiarly masculine or feminine essences, and consequently we must refrain from imposing Western concepts of gender on early Chinese thinkers despite the patriarchal structure of classical and imperial Chinese society.)[28]

It is significant, we believe, that although working with very different texts, the distinguished historian of Chinese science Nathan Sivin has made much the same point, not only about medicine, but all scientific pursuits as undertaken in China:

> Scientific thought began, in China as elsewhere, with attempts to comprehend how it is that although individual things are constantly changing, always coming to be and perishing, nature as a coherent order not only endures but remains conformable to itself. In the West the earliest such attempts identified the unchanging reality with some basic stuff out of which all the things around us, despite their apparent diversity, are formed.
>
> In China the earliest and in the long run the most influential scientific explanations were in terms of time. They made sense of the momentary event by fitting it into the cyclical rhythms of natural process.[29]

We would extend Sivin's observation to include not only scientific, but Chinese ethical discourse as well. The "basic stuff" of the scientific West resembles the enduring self, or soul ("strict self-identity") of the moral and religious West, whereas the Chinese made sense of personal identity "by fitting it into the cyclical rhythms of natural [and social] process." Many factors enter into the analysis of what we have referred to as benefactor-beneficiary roles, but time is fundamental. A common lament among the elderly in the West is that "I'm not the person I used to be." In the Chinese context, the statement is quite literally true. General Washington differed from President Washington, and neither bore a close resemblance to the boy who supposedly chopped down the cherry tree.

To elaborate these points in a Western philosophical context, first, the "basic stuff" of the scientific West came to be seen as *substances* (noun phrases), in which attributes inhere (auxiliary verbs) or which are active (transitive and intransitive verbs). Thus Heraclitus could ask how it was possible to step into the *same* river twice when all of its substance (water) was different. In attempting to get to the bottom of things, Descartes argued for two substances which share no predicates because they are absolutely distinct: body (that which is extended) and mind (that which thinks). But Cartesian efforts to account for how the two substances could interact were not persuasive to Descartes' successors. Like Spinoza, Leibniz believed that substances could not, in fact, interact, but while the former concluded there could therefore only be a single substance (with many modes and attributes), the latter instead argued for an indefinitely large number of them. These individual substances, "monads," could not causally affect each other, but could all dance to the same tune played in a preestablished harmony composed by God.

Metaphysically astigmatic, perhaps, the early Chinese thinkers never seem to have perceived any substances that remained the *same* through time; rather in our interpretation they saw "things" relationally, and related differently, at different periods of time. *Dao*, the totality of all things (*wanwu* 萬物), is a process that requires the language of both "change (*bian* 變)" and "persistence (*tong* 通)" to capture its dynamic disposition. This processional nature of experience is captured in the *Analects* 9.17:

26

> The Master was standing on the riverbank, and observed, "Isn't life's passing just like this, never ceasing day or night!"

Analogously, whereas for many if not most Western thinkers, each of us is clearly the *same* person throughout time—whether as the possessor of an immortal soul created by God or more agnostically, as a self with memory and moral responsibility—early Chinese thinkers, especially Confucians, seem to have seen persons *changing* and *growing* significantly from child to adult. For them, growing up through the cultivation and articulation of relationships makes us *different* persons, as does getting married, becoming a parent, and so forth. As the quality and quantity of our relationships proliferate, so, too, are we extended in the world. This idea should not be altogether foreign; if we may be said to "learn from experience"—especially our mistakes—is not the learning reflected in our changed attitudes, beliefs, and conduct? Do we "change our minds" only figuratively, or should we understand this in a much more literal sense?

There are, however, regularities and continuities underlying change; our lives are neither arbitrary nor solely subject to chance or whim. There are as many different ways to be a filial son or daughter as there are sons and daughters, but certain attitudes and conduct, such as hatred and disrespect, fall beyond the pale. New friends are nevertheless friends, and friendship makes demands on us because true friends must be relied upon to be such. We express our unique personhood—*not* individualism—by the creative ways we interact with others, as children, parents, lovers, friends, and so forth, within the constraints denoted by what is meant by "parent," "lover," "friend," and "neighbor." Although accordance with ritualized roles and behaviors requires personalization such that each daughter is uniquely "this one and only daughter," the disciplining effect of the formal aspect of ritual that makes growth and refinement possible cannot be overstated.

This point can be seen in another way by considering the passages in the *Analects* (6.25, 11.16, 12.11, and 13.3) which are usually described as

27

a concern of Confucius for "using names properly (*zhengming* 正名)." The passages are fairly straightforward: *junjun* 君君 (a ruler, to rule, "rulerly"), may be rendered as "the ruler should rule," without doing violence to English usage. And other English nouns can function similarly: we can easily interpret the meaning of *chenchen* 臣臣 as "ministers should minister." But shifts of meaning take place if we say *fufu* 父父 "fathers should father"—where the verbal function of "father" means "to sire"—and the Chinese becomes positively ungrammatical if we translate *zizi* 子子 as "sons should son."

What we wish to suggest is that we see a correlation between the dynamic—yet constrained—relational elements of Chinese characters (both in and of themselves, and with respect to other characters in a sentence) that mirror the dynamic yet constrained relational way the writers of those characters responded to the world they experienced. A "son son-ing" will neither allow the noun to be inactive, nor will it allow the verb to be random.

Further, it is well known that in classical Chinese the subject noun phrase is frequently omitted, strengthening a dynamic, eventful reading of the language, and, thereby to some extent, strengthening as well a dynamic, eventful sense of being in the world. In fact, the noun-verb distinction regularly gives way to a "gerundical" language. It is not "What do you mean by 'government'?" nor "What do you mean by 'to govern'?" nor "What do you mean by 'proper government'?" but "What do you mean by 'governing properly'?"

When we consult traditional Chinese dictionaries which themselves are endeavors to explain such a world—the second-century *Shuowen jiezi* 說文解字, for example—we discover that terms are not defined by appeal to essential, literal meanings, but rather are generally brought into focus paronomastically by semantic and phonetic associations. "Exemplary person (*jun* 君)," for example, is defined by its cognate and phonetically similar "gathering (群)," which must rest on the underlying assumption that "people gather round and defer to exemplary persons." As it insists in the *Analects* (4.25): "Excellent persons (*de* 德) do not dwell alone; they are sure to have neighbors." "Mirror (*jingzi* 鏡子)" is defined as "radiance (*jing* 景)": a mirror is a source of illumination. "Battle formation (*zhen* 陣)" is defined as "displaying (*chen* 陳)": a battle formation's most important service is to display strength as a means of deterring the enemy. A "ghost or spirit (*gui* 鬼)" is defined as "returning (*gui* 歸)": presumably it has found its way back to some more primordial state. "The way (*dao* 道)" is defined as "treading (*dao* 蹈)": as the *Zhuangzi* says, "The way is made in the walking of it 道行之而成 ."[30] Within the *Analects* itself, "authoritative person (*ren* 仁)" is defined as "being slow to speak (*ren* 訒)" (12.3), and "governing properly (*zheng* 政)" is regularly glossed as "acting properly (*zheng* 正)" (12.17).

What is remarkable about this way of generating meaning is that a term is defined nonreferentially by mining relevant and yet seemingly random associations implicated in the term itself. Further, erstwhile nominal expressions default to verbal expressions, "things" default to "events," underscoring the primacy of process over form as a grounding presupposition in this tradition.

When we extrapolate from the understanding of words to the understanding of persons, we find that instead of positing some intrinsically residing feature—some self-same identical characteristic that qualifies all human beings as members of a natural humankind—persons, like words, are to be understood by exploring relevant associations that constitute their specific patterns of meaningful relationships. Persons are not perceived as superordinated individuals—as agents who stand independent of their actions—but are rather ongoing "events" defined functionally by constitutive roles and relationships as they are performed within the context of their specific families and communities, that is, through the observance of ritual propriety (*li* 禮).

The dominant philosophical preoccupations of cultures are often a function of tacit assumptions made early in their narratives that are often reflected in their languages. Greek metaphysical presuppositions melded with Judeo-Christian beliefs to produce a "God–model," where an independent and superordinate principle determines order and value in the world while remaining aloof from it, making human freedom, autonomy, creativity, and individuality at once problematic and of key philosophical interest. On the Chinese side, the commitment to the processional, transformative, and always provisional nature of experience renders the "ten thousand things [or, perhaps better, 'events'] (*wanwu* 萬物)" which make up the world, including the human world, at once continuous one with another, and at the same time, unique. Thus the primary philosophical problem that emerges from these assumptions is *ars contextualis*: how do we correlate these unique particulars to achieve their most productive continuities? (This is the underlying general form of "questions" posed to the *Book of Changes* when casting the stalks.)

Ancestor reverence as the defining religious sensibility, family as the primary human unit, authoritative humanity (perhaps more literally, "co-humanity," *ren* 仁) and filiality (*xiao* 孝) as primary human values, ritualized roles, relationships, and practices (*li* 禮) as a communal discourse, are all strategies for achieving and sustaining communal harmony (*he* 和). As it states in the *Analects* 1.12:

> Achieving harmony (*he*) is the most valuable function of observing ritual propriety (*li*). In the ways of the Former Kings, this achievement of harmony made them elegant, and was a guiding standard in all things large and small. But when things are not going well, to realize harmony just for its own sake without regulating the situation through observing ritual propriety will not work.

The contrasts between things/essences, and events/relations, on the one hand, and words and grammar on the other, may be obscured by our having referred to "sentences" in the classical Chinese language. We all know what a (declarative) sentence is: it is that which expresses a complete thought, and is the kind of thing that is true or false. What is less clear, however, is that what "sentences" in classical Chinese express are the "complete thoughts" of the person(s) who wrote them.

Chad Hansen, for instance, has argued that ancient Chinese thinkers did not view language basically as a way of describing the world, or of communicating one's beliefs about it, but rather as a means of guiding actions in the world. "Speaking (*dao* 道)" is a "guiding discourse (*dao* 道)." Said a different way, language is both performative and prescriptive; it both does something to the world and recommends how it should be. While we would quarrel with a few of Hansen's specifics, for example his willingness to limit "discourse" to language while not taking into account the other dimensions of discourse, namely, physical body, ritual, music, and so on, we do endorse the overall thrust of this claim.[31]

To appreciate what Hansen is about, and to appreciate the way in which his arguments are congruent with our own, we must turn from metaphysics and grammar to religion. In the West, although there are many differences between the attributes of God in the three Abrahamic traditions, they affirm in unison, via Genesis and other writings, that He created the world for a purpose, and according to a plan, from which it must follow that the world must be explanatorily intelligible, no matter how difficult it might be to arrive at the true explanation. As the Koran records Allah saying, "Think ye I made the world in jest?" It follows in turn that the more we attempt to discern *what* the world He created is like, the more we may be enabled to know *why* He created it as He did, and thereby come to know why we, as parts of this world, are in it.

In this way, by grasping the One behind the many, we solve the riddle of the meaning of life, a riddle that has so thoroughly permeated the Western intellectual tradition. In discovering this "One," we discover "objectivity" itself: a privileged position outside of the world from which objective and hence universal statements about it, unconstrained by time or context, can be made. Further, it is by virtue of analogy with this "objective One" that we are able to disengage from our contexts, thereby resolving them into "objects" independent of ourselves.

Seen in this light, the Abrahamic religious traditions are not the competitors of science and philosophy in the West, but the parents of both. Until the Age of Enlightenment, the vast majority of thinkers we refer to as scientists or philosophers—Isaac Newton, for example—were deeply religious, and what we refer to as their scientific or philosophical interests may also be described as spiritual pursuits. Of the indefinitely large number of "facts" about the world that might be known, relatively few of them today seem to have any direct significance for our all-too-human lives, except instrumentally. But if any facts provide clues to God's purpose(s), then they can be significant indeed. The reasoning is straightforward: the better we come to understand deeply the world He created, the better we may be able to understand why He created it, and derivatively, why He created us to be a part of that world.

The pervasiveness of this originally religious orientation to the world—incorporating some less religiously inspired facets of early Greek thought into it—is evidenced, we believe, by the fact that the dominant mode of learning in the West, throughout its history, has been to acquire knowledge *about* the world, to learn the way the world *is*; and to describe that world in grammatical sentences, expressing complete thoughts, sentences which are true or false.

In contrast, there is no creation myth or legend in ancient China. There is no Genesis, nor New Testament or Koranic equivalents, nor a Chinese Cronos or Zeus, and there is no affirmation in any ancient text, explicit or implicit, that the world is explanatorily intelligible. In both cultures, of course, the world is discernible for what it is, through the testimony of the senses, that is, through appearances; but for the ancient Chinese at least, the appearances were not deceptive, and the *what* and the *why* of the world (the existence of some underlying ultimate reality) does not seem to have preoccupied them. They did not, in other words, have any good reason for thinking that there might be an explanation of why the world is as it is, and thereby had no reason for seeking a *transcendental* answer to the question of why we are in this world.

If our views on this issue are warranted, they will help to explain why Chinese philosophers in general, and Confucius in particular, were teachers in a very different way than their peers steeped in the Greek and Abrahamic traditions. For Chinese teachers do not seem to have been so much concerned with describing and thereby conveying knowledge about the world as they were to have their students learn *how to get on in the world*, which is clearly reflected in the written texts. To be sure, language in the Western educational tradition is at times employed to assist students in learning how to *be*, to get on in the world, but such recommendations are dependent upon complying with some true state of affairs. In early China, the reverse seems to have been more nearly the case: "the way (*dao*) is made in the walking of it."[32]

Reinforcing this point is the fact that classical Chinese has no close lexical equivalent for the English "true" and "truth," and even more significantly, the sense of "true to fact" does not have the importance invested in it that it does within the Western narrative. These English terms are, of course, properties of statements, sentences used to describe the world: if our descriptive statements are accurate, then what we stated is true; and if not, not. But if description is not taken to be the essential function of language, a concept of truth linked to declarative sentences need not arise, or at least, need not assume importance.

What we have presented above is a woefully inadequate account of the religious dimensions of both the Abrahamic and Chinese traditions, but may nevertheless serve to render more intelligible the ancient Chinese way of "looking at things." If their basic concern is to guide actions with effective discourse, thereby helping listeners and readers learn how to get on, to be in the world, as we would put it, then it might come to be appreciated that the Chinese *languages*—about which more will be said below and in Appendix II—can be as effective in this prescriptive way as English is for descriptive purposes. This distinction between descriptive and prescriptive also provides some further insight into what Confucius was about in giving different answers to the same question when asked by different disciples.

We are certainly not suggesting that the Chinese did not experience substantial things; in the Middle Kingdom no less than in the Middle East, kicking a rock must hurt one's foot more than kicking a pile of leaves. Nor were the ancients of Western civilization unaware of change through events: despite the logical acumen of his student Zeno, Parmenides did not gain many followers. And further, classical Chinese is just as capable of describing objects as Indo-European languages are of describing events. We are certainly not claiming that China knew nothing of "things," and Greece, nothing of "events."

Rather does it appear to be a matter of emphasis, here event-oriented, there thing-oriented. We are acutely aware of the difficulties involved in understanding what we are suggesting, namely that the ancient Chinese experienced "world," and the language that reports on it, are very different from our experienced "world," and our language. We hope that we are not merely returning China to the "inscrutable East" from which she has been emerging, thanks in large measure to the sinological scholarship of our predecessors in the West. But we want to insist that the "scruting" be done with great care. For example, the sinological linguist Peter Boodberg once lamented as follows:

> One must deplore the general tendency . . . (alas, too prominently figuring in sinological research on this continent) of insisting that the Chinese in the development of their writing, as in the evolution of many other of their cultural complexes, followed some mysterious esoteric principles that set them apart from the rest of the human race.[33]

For ourselves, we believe there is something profoundly right, and something profoundly wrong, in the sentiments Boodberg expressed. Right, in the sense that the Chinese are indeed equally members of the human community, and any "esoteric principles" invoked that suggest their being entirely "other" should be viewed with great suspicion. But this view is profoundly wrong when it suggests that the Chinese are "just like us" except for relatively inconsequential details, for the *Analects* could then only be read as the pronouncements of a man who was a well-meaning preacher at best, and at worst, an authoritarian dogmatist. But Confucius is arguably the most influential thinker in the history of the human race, and definitely so in China, and we are therefore extremely reluctant to ascribe preacherly, authoritarian, or dogmatic qualities to his pronouncements. We believe he has much to say to us today—otherwise we would not have essayed this translation—but before what he said can be heard twenty-four hundred years and half a world away from him, we must first give him, as other, his otherness. Perhaps, in allowing the Master his difference, we may appear to be relying on some "mysterious esoteric principles" of the kind Boodberg deplored. But in our view, only after we have understood deeply how different Confucius was from ourselves will we be able to appreciate with equal depth what he meant when he said that "Human beings are similar in their natural tendencies (*xing* 性), but vary greatly by virtue of their habits." (17.2)

Language, With Reference to Metaphysics

Our commitment to the belief that classical Chinese is an efficacious means of expression and communication, when combined with our belief that the language is nonessentialistic in its structural characteristics, commit us also to the view that essentialism—and derivatively, universalism or absolutism or both—are not the only ways of viewing, being in, or simply describing the world. On the other hand, we do not wish to provide either aid or comfort to those of a thoroughgoing relativistic bent.

One insight that emerges out of doing comparative philosophy is that the Chinese tradition is not, as often first assumed, a mirror opposite of the dominant Western one. The absence of transcendence is not

35

immanence, the absence of objectivity is not subjectivity, the absence of absolutism is not relativism, the absence of atomistic individuality is not some faceless collectivity. In trying to understand Chinese culture, we have to, with imagination, seek out a third position.

Suggesting that China, as the other, is *radically* other does not imply that the other is *wholly* other. If it did, we could not argue that Confucius could have anything of import to say to us today. Believing that he does have much to "say" today, we must examine more closely the language into which the "sayings" of Confucius were couched.

In 1890, a Christian missionary in China offered the following complaint:

> Is there any convenient method of stating the doctrine of the Trinity which does not imply the grossest materialism? . . . Use whatever language you please to express the resurrection, and the uninitiated will understand it to mean transmigration.[34]

Our own thesis is that the classical Chinese language—the language in which the books of the *Analects* were composed—is unique, being sharply distinct not only from all non-sinitic languages, but from spoken Chinese as well, both ancient and modern. In Appendix II we proffer a number of detailed arguments for this claim, but perhaps some more general reflections on the nature of the original language of the *Analects* will help orient the general reader more self-consciously to what it "says" in the language to which it has been translated.[35]

In the first place, a belief that classical Chinese writing is fundamentally a transcription of speech can not only obscure our perceptions of their dissimilarities, it may also lead us down barren research paths in Chinese philosophy. Too many writers have pointed to one or another particular linguistic constraint in classical Chinese and then gone on to argue that Chinese thinkers were thereby hindered in some conceptual endeavor such as thinking abstractly, logically, precisely, or what have you. Clearly these kinds of arguments need a very large number of supporting assumptions, necessary among them being that any semantic, syntactic, or phonetic feature found in the written language will also be found in the spoken. It must be assumed, in other words, that the same grammatical constraints apply to both languages. If they do not, there is no reason to believe that the written more than the spoken language reflects the intellectual capabilities of the Chinese peoples; indeed, all of the evidence shows—for all languages and peoples—that the opposite is the case. But then this assumption has no plausibility whatsoever, and consequently neither do any of these Chinese-think-concretely-not-abstractly arguments.[36] By focusing on the differences between the written and spoken languages, on the other hand, we can offer another hypothesis which suggests a different perspective: rather than being somehow constrained in thought and expression by their language, Chinese thinkers may have been twice blessed in having two distinctive linguistic media to choose from in transmitting their poetic, philosophical, and religious visions, concerns, and prescriptions.

Classical Chinese. How Does It Mean?

When we speak of "classical" or "literary" Chinese, we do not mean the language employed by everyone in China prior to the May Fourth Movement of 1919, nor do we mean the vernacular written language of today which is more or less a transcription of everyday speech. Rather, we mean the *wenyan* 文言 language of imperial China, the language in which the classics, the histories, poetry, literature, philosophy, and official documents have come down to us. Without peer in terms of continuity, the protoform of this language was in use in 1200 BCE, and the language is still used on occasion in China today—newspapers, for example, are written in a quasi-classical style, and it is also the medium in which Mao Zedong wrote his poems. The modern written and spoken languages are replete with short sayings (*chengyu* 成語) that are often direct allusions to the classical corpus, and often retain their classical form. Yet *wenyan* is not fundamentally spoken. Allowing that

37

many passages from the classics found expression in speech by being memorized and quoted, and that the more famous of them became proverbial, there is little direct evidence to show that basic verbal communication took place through this medium. Further, it is difficult to see how verbal communication ever could take place in classical Chinese because the extraordinarily large number of homophonous terms makes the language virtually uninterpretable by ear alone. Far too many semantically unrelated lexical items have exactly the same phonological realization to be understood aurally, even when important tonal differences are taken into account.

This homophony is unusual among languages, but has existed in Chinese almost since its inception. Phonetically, most consonantal endings of syllables have dropped off over the centuries, but even when they were present, the number of homonyms was very high, with anywhere from two to seven different characters pronounced identically. Today the situation is even worse. In a common five-thousand-word dictionary, for example, even when the tones are taken into account, forty semantically dissimilar graphs are pronounced identically /*yi*/; the sounds /*shi*/ and /*ji*/ each have thirty-two lexical entries; /*zhi*/ has thirty-one; and so on, with almost no phoneme having only one semantic correlate. It is the use of binomial expressions in the spoken language that significantly enhances oral communication.

Classical Chinese, however, is like the good little boy: it was primarily to be seen and not heard. A person who tried to deliver a speech in *wenyan* today would end up with a soliloquy. This is not to imply that sounds were and are totally irrelevant to the written language, for some puns and all rhymes, alliteration, and so forth are obviously phonetic in character. Further, such linguistic devices were undoubtedly of enormous value in facilitating the memorization of large tracts of text that could be recalled to fund discussion. What this does imply is the following, which is an important premise for our overall position: spoken Chinese is and was certainly understood aloud; classical Chinese is not now and may never have been understood aloud as a primarily spoken language; therefore spoken and literary Chinese are now and may always have been two distinct linguistic media, and if so, the latter should clearly not be seen as simply a transcription of speech.

The importance of this observation cannot be overstated. The distinguished philologist Bernhard Karlgren, reflecting on the possibility of rendering the classical Chinese language into an alphabetic script, concludes that the characters are indispensable. This is a language which can be read, but which cannot be understood when read aloud. What would be the not inconsequential cost to the culture of attempting to save the labor entailed by the memorization of the classical script? According to Karlgren,

> In the first place, by the introduction of alphabetic writing the Chinese would be compelled to discard his literature of some 4,000 years and with this the backbone of his entire civilization. And this for the reason that the Chinese literature transcribed in phonetic script would become absolutely unintelligible . . .[37]

It is well known that most of the grammatical features of Indo-European languages are absent in classical Chinese: there are no moods, voices, tenses; no declensions; no marking for pluralization. Perhaps most important, there are no formal "parts of speech" in classical Chinese; only in a context can a character be said to be a noun, adjective, verb, or adverb (and the reader should keep in mind that all of these grammatical categories stemmed from the study of Indo-European—essentialistic—languages).

The point deserves elaboration, because grammatical issues frequently demonstrate the impossibility of translation without interpretation. To render *junzi* as "Gentleman" is to impose a masculine reading of the term which is not marked in the term itself, and making it singular is also an extrapolation that is not indicated by the characters. One reason for doing so, of course, is because most translations wish to point up the patriarchal social hierarchy of ancient China, and "Gentleman" does this, as do "he" and "him" when a pronominal form refers back to *junzi*. But pronouns are not marked for gender or number either, and consequently the resultant sexist translation appears straightforward, even though altogether absent in the original. (And there is at least some evidence that women could be regarded as having some of the same qualities of the *junzi* at the time of, or shortly after, the composition of the *Analects*.)[38]

The absence of the singular in our translation underscores our relational and eventful interpretation of person in the Confucian world. Such persons, embedded in their respective fields of roles and relationships, act, for good or ill, on behalf of their communities.

In translating the *Analects* without the usual appeal to sexist language, we are not concealing and thus excusing a gender discrimination that has been an integral aspect of Chinese culture predating and certainly reinforced by the Confucian tradition. On the contrary, acknowledging the didactic and programmatic function of the Confucian text, which must be reinterpreted to serve the needs and enhance the possibilities of succeeding generations, our point is that Confucianism as a living tradition must be reconfigured to prompt a future free of gender prejudice. Confucianism is not a dogma, and there is nothing in the classical language that requires the gender distinction.

Unlike other linguistic scripts, the Chinese writing system has an unbroken history of more than three thousand years, and even today some of the characters are written pretty much as they were at the outset: those representing the sun 日 , moon 月 , a bow 弓 , human being 人 , door 門 , and so on. Called *pictograms*, these characters are stylized direct representations of objects. A second category of graphs—*ideograms*—combine pictograms to convey more abstract concepts, such as the sun and moon together (*ming* 明) to signify "bright," "intelligent," "illumined," or two trees together (*lin* 林) for "grove" and three (*sen* 森) for "forest."

In modern Chinese, only about ten percent of the characters are either pictographic or ideographic in nature, the remaining ninety percent being called *phonograms*, characters with one component supposedly indicative of meaning (semantic), the other component(s) indicating sound (phonetic). A further discussion of these categories of characters is proffered in Appendix II, but for now it merely needs to be noted that of the 2200-odd characters found in the *Analects*, the great majority of the philosophically significant among them are either pictograms or ideograms; that is to say, they are basically semantic in nature, and are to be interpreted more visually than aurally, and are to be read in relation to each other.

It must also be realized that at the time of the writing of the books comprising the *Analects*, both pictograms and ideograms, while conventional in one sense, nevertheless resembled fairly closely what they represented. The Chinese did not, of course, *have* to represent the concept bright/illumined/intelligent by concatenating the graphs for sun and moon; they might have used the graph for "fire," or "white." In this sense the graphs are conventional. But the sun and the moon *are* bright, and one can see the meaning of the compound graph *ming*—especially in its earliest forms—from its components in a way that is unavailable to those English readers who simply confront visually the symbol *bright*, a sign conveying no semantic information directly despite its curious spelling.

In addition to carrying its own linguistic weight, then, the semantic component of classical Chinese had to perform functions which are more commonly served by the phonetic and syntactic components of the grammars of other languages, which is an additional reason for thinking that classical Chinese is a unique linguistic medium. Additional material can be adduced in support of the uniqueness thesis and more detailed arguments will be given in Appendix II, but enough should have been presented thus far to at least establish the importance of distinguishing the grammatical structures of spoken and written classical Chinese in much greater detail than has heretofore been the case, and concomitantly, to generate skepticism for the too easily accepted assumption that classical Chinese is simply the transcribed version of the early spoken language, but badly done. With these minimum linguistic warrants for the thesis in hand, let us turn briefly to a few of its more philosophical implications.

In the first place, the heavy grammatical burden placed on the semantic component of classical Chinese contributes to what may appropriately be called "semantic overload" in the literary language. The average lexical item found in the literature (especially the basic 2500+ characters) is so rich in semantic content that meaning differentiation is difficult, with the consequence that virtually every passage is ambiguous, being subject to a multiplicity of readings until and unless a specific interpretation is given to it (which is then handed down orally or in the form of commentary). This ambiguity is compounded by the use of "loan" characters which as homophones or abbreviated graphs, would substitute for more abstract or complex ideas. Even as late as the Dingzhou strips dating from almost the middle Han, this practice is still apparent: *zheng* 正 is used for *zheng* 政 ; *bi* 辟 for *pi* 譬 ; *er* 耳 for *chi* 恥 , and so on.

Many Western scholars have of course called attention—often loudly—to this ambiguity and lack of precision in classical Chinese, seeing it as a distinctive linguistic liability. But perhaps their perceptions are biased. The lack of precision could be a decided communicative asset, a kind of "productive vagueness" that requires the reader to participate in establishing an interpretation, and to internalize the given passage in the process of doing so.

In those instances where detail or exactness of expression was necessary, we might assume Chinese thinkers availed themselves of their spoken language, wherein there is every reason to believe as much precision was and is possible as can be achieved in any other natural language. On the other hand, if what was to be expressed involved a broad vision, or a manifold attitudinal stance, or a complex of relations, then precision might be counterproductive because it could, for example, make the elements of the expression too discrete, and their interrelations too obscure. In such cases, the written language might be employed instead to effect the communication concisely, competently, and elegantly. In large measure the semantic content of a message is determined not only by the specific lexical items utilized, but also by their structure and organization. The reader of classical Chinese knows well that there is a subtlety and a richness to the characters and their arrangements that allow a communicative style that can be as effective as it is terse, and unattainable verbally. Without disparaging the significance or worth of exact expression, it should nevertheless not be alarming to note that our general philosophical views and perspectives are often transmitted best by very general terms (no matter what the language), nor should it be perplexing to realize that ordinary language is not always adequate for communicating extraordinary experiences and insights.

In classical Chinese this extraordinary kind of communication is made possible semantically by the fact that each lexical item carries all of its meanings with it on every occasion of its use, and the concatenation of two or more characters therefore associates all of the meanings of each one with the others. It is unlikely that many associations would be lost in reading, because even though word order was important, it was not *firmly* fixed in the literary language, so the reader would have to examine almost every passage several times, attending to multiple possible orderings of the characters before settling on an interpretation. This type of communication was further enhanced by the pictorial, imagistic, and æsthetic quality of the characters. One way to relate two or more characters in a passage would be to see that they all contained a certain element; the characters for "virtue (*de* 德)" and "thought (*si* 思)", for example, could be associated together at least visually because they both contain the character for "heart-and-mind (*xin* 心)." The majority of the basic 2500+ characters which formed the lexicon of classical Chinese are constituted in the same graphic way; hence, what might be overlooked completely or passed off lightly as mere punning or ungrammatical in an alphabetic language could be employed seriously for expressive and communicative purposes in an ideographic one.

This point can be seen in another way by attending to a (technically) nonlinguistic feature of classical Chinese: style preference. Parallel sentence construction was prized, a sign of education, intelligence, and æsthetic sensibility on the part of the writer. There were undoubtedly cultural factors that influenced this style preference, but we must note here its significance for interpreting and translating texts: when faced with, say, four parallel sentences, some will be less syntactically (or semantically) ambiguous than others, and it is therefore a splendid heuristic device to interpret the syntactic (and/or semantic) structures of the more ambiguous sentences on the basis of the reading given to those that are much less so, where they are at all times construed relationally. Earlier we employed this system of parallel construction ourselves in the discussion of using names properly. If we translate the relevant *Analects* passages as "Let rulers rule, let ministers minister," then we may proceed—without obfuscation, we hope—to "let fathers father, let sons son."

There is a further implication of the nature of the classical written language that complicates, but certainly does not vitiate, the claim we are making for maintaining a separation between the written and the spoken language. The parallel structure, rhythm, repetition, rhyme, and other features of the written language facilitate memorization, and memorization was a major discipline in the appropriation of a tradition that had limited material resources available to it for its transmission. This factor would mean that there would be important overlaps between the expressive and more precise spoken language and the terse, poetic written language committed to memory and repeated orally as an enhancement for the spoken language. Then and now, the Chinese language is freighted with classical allusions made available by dressing the spoken (and now written) vernacular language with a shared range of phrases that have become proverbial.

Against this background, we may turn now to a brief account of a number of key philosophical terms frequently occurring in the *Analects*.

The Chinese Lexicon[39]

道 *Dao* occurs some eighty times in the *Analects*, and is of central importance for interpreting the thinking not only of Confucius, but all other early Chinese thinkers as well; it is very probably the single most important term in the philosophical lexicon, and in significant measure, to understand what and how a thinker means when he uses *dao* is to understand that thinker's philosophy.

The character has two elements: *chuo* 辶 "to pass over," "to go over," "to lead through" (on foot), and *shou* 首, itself a compound literally meaning "head"—hair and eye together—and therefore "foremost." *Dao* is used often as a loan character for its cognate, *dao* 導, "to lead." Thus the character is significantly verbal, processional, and dynamic. The earliest appearance of *dao* in the *Book of Documents* is in the context of cutting a channel and "leading" a river to prevent the overflowing of its banks.[40] Even the *shou* "head" component has the suggestion of "to lead," or "to give a heading."

Taking the verbal *dao* as primary, its several derived meanings emerge rather naturally: to lead through, and hence, road, path, way, method, art, teachings; to explain, to tell, doctrines. At its most fundamental level, *dao* seems to denote the active project of "road building," and by extension, to connote a road that has been made, and hence can be traveled. It is by this connotation that *dao* is so often nominalized in translation ("the Way"), but we must distinguish between simply traveling on a road, and making the journey one's own. In our interpretation, to realize the *dao* is to experience, to interpret, and to influence the world in such a way as to reinforce and extend the way of life inherited from one's cultural predecessors. This way of living in the world then provides a road map and direction for one's cultural successors.

45

For Confucius, *dao* is primarily *rendao* 人道, that is, "a way of becoming consummately and authoritatively human." As 15.29 tells us: "It is the person who is able to broaden the way, not the way that broadens the person."

Above we have made the argument that *dao* defies Aristotle's categories, and that it has as much to do with subject as object, as much to do with the quality of understanding as the conditions of the world understood. This point might be reinforced by citing a passage in John Dewey which makes a similar point:

> If ideas, meanings, conceptions, notions, theories, systems are instrumental to an active reorganization of the given environment, to a removal of some specific trouble and perplexity, then the test of their validity and value lies in accomplishing this work. . . . That which guides us truly is true—demonstrated capacity for such guidance is precisely what is meant by truth. The adverb "truly" is more fundamental than either the adjective true, or the noun, truth. An adverb expresses a way, a mode of acting.[41]

In pursuing our translation of this text, we have tried wherever possible to respect the extent to which the "path" metaphor pervades the text. A sustained image that the Chinese text presents is Confucius finding his way. That is, in reading the *Analects* in the original language, a term such as *guo* 過 that is often nominalized as "faults," or if its verbal aspect is acknowledged, translated as "to err," has the specific sense of "going astray" or "going too far": not just erring, but straying from the path.

天   *Tian* is a term that we have chosen not to translate, largely because we believe its normal English rendering as "Heaven" cannot but conjure up images derived from the Judeo-Christian tradition that are not to be found in China; and "Nature" will not work either. In the first place, *tian* is often used alone to render *tiandi* 天地 —"the heavens and the earth"—suggesting that *tian* is not independent of this world. The God of the Bible, often referred to as metonymically "Heaven," *created* the world, but *tian* in classical Chinese *is* the world.

Tian is both *what* our world is and *how* it is. The "ten thousand things (*wanwu* 萬物)," an expression for "everything," are not the creatures of a *tian* which is independent of what is ordered; rather, they are constitutive of it. *Tian* is both the creator and the field of creatures. There is no apparent distinction between the order itself, and what orders it. This absence of superordination is a condition made familiar in related notions of the Daoist *dao* and the Buddhist *dharma* which at once reference concrete phenomena and the order that obtains among them.

On this basis, *tian* can be described as an inhering, emergent order negotiated out of the dispositioning of the particulars that are constitutive of it. But *tian* is not just "things"; it is a living culture—crafted, transmitted, and now resident in a human community. *Tian* is anthropomorphic, suggesting its intimate relationship with the process of euhemerization—historical human beings becoming gods—that grounds Chinese ancestor reverence. It is probably this common foundation in ancestor reverence that allowed for the conflation of the culturally sophisticated Shang dynasty's *di* 帝 (ancestral spirits) with the notion of *tian* associated with the Zhou tribes, militant and Romanesque, who conquered the Yellow River valley. There seems to be sufficient reason to assume that *tian* is consistent with the claim of Sarah Allan and Emily Ahern that Chinese gods are, by and large, dead people.[42] In the absence of some transcendent creator deity as the repository of truth, beauty and goodness, *tian* would seem to stand for a cumulative and continuing cultural legacy focused in the spirits of those who have come before. It is not surprising, then, that the relationship between *mythos, logos,* and *historia* is radically different from the Western tradition. Culturally significant human beings—persons such as the Duke of Zhou and Confucius—are "theomorphized" to become *tian,* and *tian* is itself made anthropomorphic and determinate in their persons.

47

Finally, *tian* does not speak, but communicates effectively although not always clearly through oracles, through perturbations in the climate, and through alterations in the natural conditions of the human world. *Tian* participates in a discourse shared by the human community—at least by the most worthy among them. Given the interrelatedness and interdependency of the orders defining the Confucian world, what affects one, affects all. A failure of order in the human world will symbiotically be reflected in the natural environment. Although *tian* is not the "personal" deity responsive to individual needs as found in the Judeo-Christian worldview, as aggregate ancestor it would seem that *tian* functions impartially on behalf of its progeny to maximize the possibilities of emergent harmony at all levels. That *tian* is not transcendental, but indeed functions on behalf of its progeny, is seen clearly in the *Book of Documents*: "*Tian* hears and sees as the people hear and see."[43]

仁   *Ren*, translated herein as "authoritative conduct," "to act authoritatively," or "authoritative person," is the foremost project taken up by Confucius, and occurs over one hundred times in the text. It is a fairly simple graph, and according to the *Shuowen* lexicon, is made up of the elements *ren* 人 "person", and *er* 二 , the number "two." This etymological analysis underscores the Confucian assumption that one cannot become a person by oneself—we are, from our inchoate beginnings, irreducibly social. Herbert Fingarette has stated the matter concisely: "For Confucius, unless there are at least two human beings, there can be no human beings."[44]

An alternative explanation of the character *ren* 仁 we might derive from oracle bone inscriptions is that what appears to be the number "two 二 " is in fact an early form of "above, to ascend *shang* 上," which was also written as 二 .[45] Such a reading would highlight the growing distinction one accrues in becoming *ren*, thereby setting a bearing for one's community and the world to come: "those authoritative in their

48

conduct enjoy mountains . . . are still . . . [and] are long-enduring (6.23; see also 2.1 and 17.3).

Ren is most commonly translated as "benevolence," "goodness," and "humanity," occasionally as "humanheartedness," and less occasionally by the clumsy and sexist "manhood-at-its-best."

While "benevolence" and "humanity" might be more comfortable choices for translating *ren* into English, our decision to use the less elegant "authoritative person" is a considered one. First, *ren* is one's entire person: one's cultivated cognitive, æsthetic, moral, and religious sensibilities as they are expressed in one's ritualized roles and relationships. It is one's "field of selves," the sum of significant relationships, that constitute one as a resolutely social person. *Ren* is not only mental, but physical as well: one's posture and comportment, gestures and bodily communication. Hence, translating *ren* as "benevolence" is to "psychologize" it in a tradition that does not rely upon the notion of *psyche* as a way of defining the human experience. It is to impoverish *ren* by isolating one out of many moral dispositions at the expense of so much more that comes together in the complexity of becoming human.

Again, "humanity" suggests a shared, essential condition of being human owned by all members of the species. Yet *ren* does not come so easy. It is an æsthetic project, an accomplishment, something done (12.1). The human *being* is not something we are; it is something that we do, and become. Perhaps "human *becoming*" might thus be a more appropriate term to capture the processional and emergent nature of what it means to become human. It is not an essential endowed potential, but what one is able to make of oneself given the interface between one's initial conditions and one's natural, social, and cultural environments.

Certainly the human being as a focus of constitutive relationships has an initial disposition (17.2). But *ren* is foremost the process of "growing (*sheng* 生)" these relationships into vital, robust, and healthy participation in the human community.

The fact that Confucius is asked so often what he means by the expression *ren* would suggest that he is reinventing this term for his own purposes, and that those in conversation with him are not comfortable in their understanding of it. Confucius' creative investment of new meaning in *ren* is borne out by a survey of its infrequent, and relatively unimportant usage in the earlier corpus. *Ren* does not occur in the earliest portions of the ancient classics, and only three times in the later parts. This unexceptional usage compares with 105 occurrences in the *Analects* in 58 of the 499 sections.[46]

Given that *ren* denotes the qualitative transformation of a *particular* person, it is further ambiguous because it must be understood relative to the specific concrete conditions of that person. There is no formula, no ideal. Like a work of art, it is a process of disclosure rather than closure, resisting fixed definition and replication.

Our term "authoritative person" as a translation of *ren* then, is a somewhat novel expression, as was, *ren* itself, and will probably prompt a similar desire for clarification. "Authoritative" entails the "authority" that a person comes to represent in community by becoming *ren*, embodying in oneself the values and customs of one's tradition through the observance of ritual propriety (*li*). The prominence and visibility of the authoritative person is captured in the metaphor of the mountain (6.23): still, stately, spiritual, enduring, a landmark of the local culture and community.

At the same time, the way of becoming human (*dao*) is not a given; the authoritative person must be a "road builder," a participant in "authoring" the culture for one's own place and time (15.29). Observing ritual propriety (*li*) is, by definition, a process of internalization— "making the tradition one's own"—requiring personalization of the roles and relationships that locate one within community. It is this creative aspect of *ren* that is implicit in the process of becoming authoritative for one's own community.

The contrast between top-down and impositional "authoritarian" order, and the bottom-up, deferential sense of "authoritative" order is also salutary. The authoritative person is a model that others, recognizing the achievement, gladly and without coercion, defer to and appropriate in the construction of their own personhood. Confucius is as explicit in expressing the same reservations about authoritative relations becoming authoritarian as he is about a deference-driven ritualized community surrendering this noncoercive structure for the rule of law (2.3).

禮 *Li* has been translated as "ritual," "rites," "customs," "etiquette," "propriety," "morals," "rules of proper behavior," and "worship." The compound character is an ideograph connoting the presentation of sacrifices to the spirits at an altar (*li* 豊). It is defined in the *Shuowen* paronomasticahy as *lü* M, meaning "to tread a path; hence, conduct, behavior"—that is, "how to serve the spirits to bring about good fortune." Properly contextualized, each of these English terms can render *li* on occasion, but in classical Chinese the character carries *all* of these meanings on every occasion of its use.

We have chosen to translate *li* as "observing ritual propriety." Again, this rendering is a considered choice.

Li are those meaning-invested roles, relationships, and institutions which facilitate communication, and which foster a sense of community. The compass is broad: all formal conduct, from table manners to patterns of greeting and leave-taking, to graduations, weddings, funerals, from gestures of deference to ancestral sacrifices—all of these, and more, are *li*. They are a social grammar that provides each member with a defined place and status within the family, community, and polity. *Li* are life forms transmitted from generation to generation as repositories of meaning, enabling the youth to appropriate persisting values and to make them appropriate to their own situations.

Full participation in a ritually-constituted community requires the personalization of prevailing customs, institutions, and values. What makes ritual profoundly different from law or rule is this process of making the tradition one's own. The Latin *proprius*, "making something one's own" as in "property," gives us a series of cognate expressions that are useful in translating key philosophical terms to capture this sense of participation: *yi* 義 is not "righteousness" but "appropriateness"; *zheng* 正 is not "rectification" or "correct conduct," but "proper conduct"; *zheng* 政 is not "government" but "governing properly" in our translation.

For Westerners, there is ostensibly a distinction to be made between being boorish and being immoral. For Confucius, however, there are simply varying degrees of inappropriate, demeaning, and hurtful behavior along a continuum on which a failure in personal responsiveness is not just bad manners, but fully a lapse in moral responsibility.

In defining filial piety (*xiao* 孝), for example, Confucius is not concerned about providing parents with food and shelter—we do as much for our domestic animals. The substance of filial piety lies in the "face (*se* 色)" one brings to filial responsibility—the bounce in the step, the cheerful heart, the goodwill with which one conducts the otherwise rather ordinary business of caring for aging parents (2.8).

Perhaps the greatest obstacle to understanding what *li* means in the world of Confucius is thinking that "ritual" is a familiar dimension of our own world, and like "benevolence," we fully understand what it entails. "Ritual" in English is almost always pejorative, suggesting as it often does compliance with hollow and hence meaningless social conventions. A careful reading of the *Analects*, however, uncovers a way of life carefully choreographed down to appropriate facial expressions and physical gestures, a world in which a life is a performance requiring enormous attention to detail. Importantly, this *li*-constituted performance begins from the insight that personal refinement is only possible through the discipline provided by formalized roles and behaviors. Form without creative personalization is coercive and dehumanizing law; creative personal expression without form is randomness at best, and license at worst. It is only with the appropriate combination of form and personalization that community can be self-regulating and refined.

信 *Xin*, which we have translated as "making good on one's word," has been described by Ezra Pound, following his teacher Ernest Fenollosa, as a picture of "a man standing by his word."[47] No small number of scholars have excoriated Pound for his philological flights of fancy, but every sinologist must analyze this particular character in the same way: the character for "person" 人 stands to the left of the character for "speaking" or "words" 言. When it is now remembered just how many characters in the classical Confucian lexicon were pictographic or ideographic in nature, we should be willing to allow Pound and Fenollosa their rendering. Modern research has shown that the *Shuowen* is mistaken in classifying *xin* under the *huiyi* 會意 "ideographic compound" category of Chinese graphs; *ren* 人 is almost surely the phonetic in *xin*. But the excellence of the philological detective work on this graph in no way invalidates the importance of the fact that every reader of the *Analects* confronts visually "person" standing by "words" or "speech." *Xin* is often translated as "trustworthy." However, being simply well intended in what one says and does is not good enough; one must have the resources to follow through and make good on what one proposes to do. Interestingly, as with most classical Chinese terms, in understanding *xin* we must appreciate the priority of situation over agency. That is, *xin* in describing the situation of persons making good on their word goes in both directions, meaning both the commitment of the benefactor and the confidence of the beneficiary. *Xin*, then, is the consummation of fiduciary relationships.

義 *Yi*. In his translation of the *Analects*, the distinguished scholar D. C. Lau translates *yi* sometimes as "right," other times as "duty," and on occasion as "moral" or "morality" more generally. If one is committed, as Lau is, to portraying Confucius as a "moral philosopher" in more or less the Western sense, then *yi* is probably the best candidate as a Chinese lexical equivalent for "morals" or "morality." But the term "morality" in contemporary English, and particularly in post-Kantian ethics, is linked intimately with a number of other terms: "freedom," "liberty," "choice," "ought," "individual," "reason," "autonomy," "dilemma," "objective," "subjective." *None* of these English terms has a close analogue in classical Chinese, and hence in the absence of these associations, we are skeptical of using "morality" for *yi*, which is linked intimately with a very different cluster of terms: "observing ritual propriety (*li* 禮)," "authoritative conduct (*ren* 仁)," "making good on one's word (*xin* 信)" (1.13), and so on.

Several variants of the original Shang dynasty characters for *yi* suggest another interpretation. *Yi*, etymologically, is an adumbrated picture of a sheep (*yang* 羊) over a first-person pronoun (*wo* 我) "I," "we," "me," "us," the origins of which are unknown. As an aside, it is revealing that in a tradition in which person is irreducibly social, the distinction between the singular "I" and the plural "we" is not indicated in the language. The "I" and the social context are reflexive and mutually entailing.

This pronoun *wo* is itself, in many of its early representations and attested in the *Shuowen* lexicon, a picture of a human hand holding a dagger-axe (*ge* 戈). When it is remembered that sheep were periodically sacrificed at large communal gatherings (3.17), we may gloss *yi* as the attitude one has, the stance one takes, when literally preparing the lamb for the ritual slaughter.

This attitude, this stance, is making oneself a sacred representative of the community, and thereby purifying and making appropriately sacred the sacrificial animal. If this be so, then *yi* should not be rendered as "moral" or "morality." "Appropriate" or "fitting" are perhaps closer English equivalents for *yi*, and that is how the term is translated herein. *Yi*, then, is one's sense of appropriateness that enables one to act in a proper and fitting manner, given the specific situation (4.10, 9.4, 18.8). By extension, it is also the meaning invested by a cumulative tradition in the forms of ritual propriety that define it—import that can be appropriated by a person in the performance of these roles and rituals. It is because *yi* is the sense of appropriateness that makes relationships truly meaningful in a community of mutual trust, that Confucius says "making good on one's word (*xin* 信) gets one close to appropriateness."

The reader should keep in mind that "appropriate," as we use it for translating *yi*, should be understood in terms of not only its æsthetic and moral connotations, but also with its social and religious implications in mind as well.

/ 智   *Zhi*, with or without the sun radical 日 beneath it, is usually translated as "knowledge," "wisdom," and "to know." Donald Munro has rendered *zhi* "moral knowledge," but this introduces "moral" again—with its attendant unwarranted associations as discussed above.[48] Also, while bringing attention to the important axiological dimension of *zhi*, it sets a limit on a more holistic sense of wisdom that might not be altogether desirable. We translate it, whenever possible, as "to realize." "To realize" has the same strong epistemic connotations as "to know" or "knowledge" in English. You may say you believe whatever you like, but you can only *know*, or *realize* something, if that something is indeed the case. In addition, it underscores the performative, perlocutionary meaning of *zhi*: the need to author a situation and "make it real." Furthermore, by translating *zhi* as *to realize*, we believe we are paying proper attention to the Confucian precept generally described as "the continuity between knowledge and action (*zhixing heyi* 知行合一)"—that is, "to know is to authenticate in action." This practical entailment of the classical Chinese *zhi* precludes the familiar distinction between knowledge and wisdom that we find in English. If to finalize is to make final and to personalize is to make personal, then "to realize" must mean "to make real," again, an expression which exploits the richness of English without having to invoke all the philosophical associations that come immediately to mind upon coming across the terms "moral" and "knowledge."

心   *Xin* was originally a picture of the aorta, but the character has been rendered as "mind" as often as "heart." There is much justification for this, for there are many passages in the classical texts which do not make much sense in English unless the *xin* thinks. But to divorce the mind from the heart—the cognitive from the affective—is to reenter the Western metaphysical realm again, most especially via the mind-body dichotomy, and embrace the notion of an ahistorical, acultural seat of pure rationality. To avoid this reference, we render *xin* as "heart-and-mind," which is inelegant perhaps, but serves to remind the reader that there are no altogether disembodied thoughts for Confucius, nor any raw feelings altogether lacking (what in English would be called) "cognitive content."

In the classical Chinese worldview, in which process and change have priority over form and stasis, it is frequently observed that, with respect to the human body, physiology has priority over anatomy, and function takes precedence over site. This being the case, it might well be argued that *xin* means "thoughts and feeling," and then derivatively and metaphorically, the organ with which these experiences are to be associated.

和   *He* is conventionally translated "harmony," and we follow that rendering. The etymology of the term is culinary: harmony is the art of combining and blending two or more foodstuffs so that they come together with mutual benefit and enhancement without losing their separate and particular identities.[49] Throughout the early corpus, the preparation of food is appealed to as a gloss on this sense of elegant harmony. Harmony so considered entails both the integrity of the particular ingredient and its ease of integration into some larger whole. Signatory of this harmony is the endurance of the particular ingredients and the cosmetic nature of the harmony in an order that emerges out of the collaboration of intrinsically related details to embellish the contribution of each one.

In the *Analects*, this sense of harmony is celebrated as the highest cultural achievement. Here, harmony is distinguished from mere agreement by invoking the central role of particularity. The family metaphor pervades this text, encouraged by the intuition that this is the institution in which the members give themselves most fully and unreservedly to the group nexus, in interactions that are governed by the customs (*li*) appropriate (*yi*) to the occasion. Importantly, such a commitment to family, far from entailing self-sacrifice or self-abnegation, requires the full expression of personal integrity, and thus becomes the context in which one can most effectively pursue personal realization.

德 *De* is conventionally translated as "virtue," or "power," but the Chinese term more nearly approximates *dharma* in signifying what we can do and be, if we "realize (*zhi*)" the most from our personal qualities and careers as contextualized members of a specific community. We translate *de* as "excellence" in the sense of excelling at becoming one's own person. The late justice Thurgood Marshall asked for his tombstone to read: "He did the best he could with what he had." What he "had" was his *de*, and he surely developed it to the fullest.

De has a range of meaning which again reflects the priority of situation over agency, characterizing both giving and getting. *De* is both the "beneficence" and the "gratitude" expressed in response to such largesse (cf. 14.34).

善 *Shan* is most frequently translated as "good," but such a rendering has the disadvantage of "essentializing" what is fundamentally relational. A popular anecdote about John Dewey is perhaps useful in making this point.

One afternoon Dewey and a colleague attended a lecture. Having taken their seats, the colleague leaned over and said to Dewey, "Look at those two gentlemen on the end of the row—don't they look alike!" And Dewey, taking a long look at the two gentlemen, replied with a smile, "You know, you are right, they do look alike. Especially the gentleman on the left."

Appreciating Dewey's point, we need to understand that *shan* is first and foremost "good to" or "good for" or "good with" or "good in" or "good at," and only derivatively and abstractly, "good." We have struggled to retain this relational sense of *shan*, translating it variously as "truly adept," "ability," and so on. This understanding of *shan*, like "appropriateness (*yi* 義)," highlights the fundamentally æsthetic nature of Confucianism, where the common good is achieved in the productive relationships of a flourishing community. The character or "ethos" of person and community is an ongoing æsthetic achievement.

文　*Wen* means "to inscribe," "to embellish," and by extension, "culture." What is interesting about *wen* is that, given the absence of a severe *phusis/nomos*, nature/nurture distinction in the classical Chinese world, this term like *dao* is used to characterized the patterned regularity that defines both nature and human culture. For example, *tianwen* 天文 is the pattern of the heavens, while in the modern language, *wenzi* 文字 are written characters, *wenxue* 文學 is literature, *wenming* 文明 is civilization, and *wenhua* 文化 is culture. In the classical language, the single character *wen* does much of the work of these various binomial expressions. This continuity between nature and the human world is another indication of priority of situation over agency and the radical situatedness of the human experience in this tradition.

孝　*Xiao* is, straightforwardly, "filial piety" or "filial responsibility." Given the central place of the family for the Confucian way, appropriate family feelings are that resource from which a pathway through life emerges (1.2). It is important to note that in promoting the family as the pervasive model of order, the Confucian worldview does not accept that hierarchical social institutions are necessarily pernicious, or that simple egalitarianism should be an uncritical value. Having said this, an obstacle to understanding *xiao* can arise from a simplistic equation between filial responsibility and obedience. At times being truly filial within the family, like being a loyal minister within the court, requires remonstrance rather than automatic compliance, yet such a responsibility to question authority has its limits, and is not a warrant to pit one's own opinions against one's elders. (2.5, 4.18).

There are other important terms in the *Analects.* The two elements of Confucius' "one strand" that give coherence to his philosophy are described in 4.15 as *zhong* 忠 and *shu* 恕, which we have rendered as "doing one's utmost" and "putting oneself in the other's place." This, then, is Confucius' prescription for how best to determine appropriate conduct. Perhaps it seems odd that the "one" strand is in fact "two," *zhong* and *shu,* but in addition to being two aspects of one method, what ties them together is the presence of the shared "heart-and-mind (*xin* 心)."

In the absence of appeal to principles or rules which exist independent of a situation, Confucius allows that "Correlating one's conduct with those near at hand can be said to be the method of becoming an authoritative person" (6.30).

Two terms best understood in relation to each other are *xue* 學 "learning" or "studying," and *si* 思 "reflecting." Just as observing ritual propriety (*li*) entails a process of making the culture one's own by appropriating meaning from the communal memory and conducting oneself appropriately (*yi*) in one's roles and behaviors, learning similarly requires personalization through reflecting on what we have learned and the application of this learning in an appropriate way to the business of the day.

It is important that *xue* be construed as an unmediated process of becoming aware (*xue* is actually cognate with and defined paronomastically as *jue* 覺 "to become aware") rather than as conceptually mediated knowledge of an objective world described in sentences that are "true," as discussed earlier. At the time of Confucius, this "becoming aware" denoted the heightening awareness of the scholar engaged in both studying and teaching as one pursues the goal of becoming a learned person. It was only later in the tradition that the focus of *xue* came to rest on studying. Learning, in the *xue* sense, also involved inheriting, reauthorizing, and transmitting one's cultural legacy; it is not passive acquisition of "the facts."

As for *si*, "reflecting," it has several defining characteristics. It is generic in covering various modes of thinking: pondering, entertaining, imagining, deliberating, and so on. Not unexpectedly, it is often associated with tolerance. The term also connotes a directed concern. It must also be borne in mind that the seat of *si* is the *xin*, heart-and-mind; hence such reflection is not solely a cognitive process, but an affective one as well. The Master sums up this complementarity between *xue* and *si* in 2.15:

> Learning without due reflection leads to perplexity; reflection without learning leads to perilous circumstances.

Finally, in the *Analects,* Confucius and at times his disciples, make approbationary remarks about several categories of persons: *daren* 大人 "persons in high station," *shanren* 善人 "truly adept persons," *chengren* 成人 "consummate persons," *renzhe* 仁者 or *renren* 仁人 "authoritative persons," and so on. We wish, however, to focus on three other categories of persons: the *shi* 士 or "scholar-apprentice," *junzi* 君子 "exemplary person," and *sheng* 聖, or *shengren* 聖人, "sage," contrasting these three with the *xiaoren* 小人, "petty person."

All three of these expressions were in use before the time of Confucius. In the *Book of Songs,* for example, the term *shi* is used for a man of middle social status, at other times for a retainer, and yet again to designate a servant. It also appeared to be the term for a lower level functionary of a lord, perhaps a man of arms, somewhat akin to the old English knight (and Waley so translates the term). A *junzi* was a lord's son, or perhaps, as Boodberg has argued, the bastard son of a lord.[50] The character *sheng* in the *Book of Songs* and *Book of Documents* would appear to have the meaning of "very wise person."

Confucius appropriated all of these terms for his own use, giving them connotations and denotations that shifted their sense and reference away from position, rank, birth, or function toward what we (not he) would term æsthetic, moral, and spiritual characteristics. Owing to Kierkegaard and others, these three cultural interests are distinct realms in the West; their interrelatedness would, we would maintain, be self-evident to Confucius. Again, the sacred is not *transcendentally* distinct from the secular in China.

Twelve passages in the *Analects* make reference to the *shi*, most of which suggest that he is an apprentice of some kind. The *shi* is to be precise and formal, punctilious perhaps. He has already extended himself beyond the family, for in no passage in the *Analects* is *xiao*—filial piety—associated with the *shi*. Moreover, while the structure of the twelve passages has suggested to most translators that what is being described are the *shi*'s qualities, what he *is*, we believe those passages are better construed as instructions for what the *shi* should *do*. He has set out on a path, a road, but he still has a long way to go, and there is much yet to be done. As Master Zeng says (8.7):

> Scholar-apprentices (*shi* 士) cannot but be strong and resolved, for they bear a heavy charge and their way (*dao*) is long. Where they take authoritative conduct (*ren*) as their charge, is it not a heavy one? And where their way ends only in death, is it not indeed long?

By describing the *shi* as one who has assumed the burden of *ren*, we get a strong hint that it is a moral and spiritual apprenticeship the *shi* is serving, for *ren* is, again, the highest excellence for Confucius. Further evidence that the *shi* is one who has set out on a spiritual path is found elsewhere (4.9 and 14.2) in which negative instructions are given, the thrust of which is to eschew material well-being.

There are, of course, numerous positive instructions the Master proffers, not only for the *shi*, but for others as well: become steeped in poetry, and in history; study and practice the *li*; listen to, play, become absorbed in music; perform public service when it is appropriate to do so; and above all—and by so engaging in these efforts—learn to extend one's human sympathies beyond the family, clan, and village, and learn to become benefactor and beneficiary within a much larger circle. Again, the *shi* are never instructed in the proper behavior and demeanor due one's parents, children, or other relatives.

If our reading of these passages is warranted, it will follow that the major goal toward which the *shi* is striving is to become an exemplary person, or *junzi*. The *shi does*, while the *junzi* more nearly *is*. In the text, the *junzi* is almost always described (for the benefit of the disciples), not instructed (because presumably he doesn't need it). He has traveled a goodly distance along the way, and lives a goodly number of roles. A benefactor to many, he is still a beneficiary of others like himself. While he is still capable of anger in the presence of inappropriateness and concomitant injustice, he is in his person tranquil. He knows many rituals and much music, and performs all of his functions not only with skill, but with grace, dignity, and beauty, and he takes delight in the performances. He is still filial toward his parents and elders, but now takes "all under *tian*" as his dwelling. While real enough to be still capable of the occasional lapse in his otherwise exemplary conduct (14.6), he is resolutely proper in the conduct of his roles—conduct which is not forced, but rather effortless, spontaneous, creative. There is, in sum, a very strong æsthetic and ethical dimension to his life; he has reauthorized the *li*, and is therefore a respected author of the *dao* of humankind.

For most of us, the goal of *junzi* is the highest to which we can aspire. There is, however, an even loftier human goal, to become a "sage" or *shengren*; but in the *Analects* it is a distant goal indeed. What the *shengren* shares in common with the *junzi* is that both categories emerge out of effective communication. Etymologically, the *junzi* 君子 is one who "oversees (*yin* 尹)" community through effective "communication (*kou* 口)." The *shengren* (聖人) is a virtuoso of communication, "listening (*er* 耳)" and "presenting ideas (*cheng* 呈)" that not only come to define the human experience, but which further have cosmic implications. As we recall from Confucius' notion of "the proper use of names (*zhengming* 正名)" in 13.3, to name (*ming* 名) a world properly commands (*ming* 命) a proper world into being.

There are eight references to *shengren* in the text. In one passage Confucius dares not rank himself a *shengren* (7.34), in another he laments that he never has, and probably never will, meet one (7.26), and in still another he gently chastises Zigong when the latter likens him to a *shengren* (9.6). And later, even though Mencius allows that the man in the street who acts like a Yao or a Shun (that is, a *shengren*) is a sage, he, too, suggests strongly that this goal is beyond the reach of most mortals.[51]

Yet it is there. There are *shengren*. They have risen beyond the level of *junzi*, because 16.8 describes *junzi* as those who stand in awe of the words of the *shengren*. From 6.30 we learn that one who confers benefits on, and assists everyone, is a *shengren*.

And finally, Zixia allows that it is not even the *junzi*, but the *shengren* alone "who walks this path every step from start to finish" (19.12). There is a slight hint of the mystical here that is not common in the *Analects*. But if mysticism it is, it is a mysticism of an unusual sort, coming as it does as the culmination of an active and engaged social and political life, beginning with what was near, and getting to what was distant (14.35). If the career of Confucius is one example of sagehood, perhaps walking the path from start to finish reports on Confucius who, at the end of his life, could give his "heart-and-mind free rein without overstepping the boundaries" (2.4).

To summarize this brief reading of the qualities of, and relations between, the *shi*, the *junzi*, and the *shengren*: all *shengren* are *junzi*, and all *junzi* were formerly *shi*, but the converse does not hold. These are, in other words, ranked types of persons, and the ranking is based on a progression from scholarly apprenticeship to sagehood. *Shi* are, relatively speaking, fairly numerous, *junzi* are more scarce, and *sheng* are very few and far between, owing to the heaviness of the burden, and the distance of the journey (8.7).

The *shi* are resolute in following the *dao* as it is embodied in ritual propriety (*li*) that governs the interpersonal relations definitive of the *shi*'s several roles. Much farther along this journey of learning and doing we have the *junzi*, who know the *li* thoroughly enough to express their spirit even in the absence of precedent; they perform their roles masterfully, and derive a deep satisfaction from the grace, dignity, effortlessness, and creativity with which they have come to conduct themselves with others, strangers no less than kin. And it is the *junzi* who ascend in the midst of many to provide a bearing for exemplary conduct through effective service in roles of social and political responsibility.

At the upper end of this continuum, then, are the *shengren*. In addition to possessing all of the qualities of the *junzi*, the *shengren* appear to see and feel custom, rituals, and traditions holistically, as defining and integrating the human community broadly, and as defining and integrating as well the communities of the past, and of the future. This seeing and feeling of the *shengren* can be described as an awareness which gives one the capacity to go beyond the particular time and place in which we live, effecting a continuity not only with our contemporaries, but with those who have preceded us, and with those who will follow behind.

The metaphors used to describe the *shengren* are cosmic and celestial: "Confucius is the sun and moon which no one can climb beyond" (19.24). The culture that finds its focus in this rare person elevates the human experience to heights of profound æsthetic and religious refinement, making the human being a worthy partner with the heavens and the earth. The model of the *shengren* shines across generations and across geographical boundaries as a light that not only stabilizes and secures the human world, but that also serves humankind as a source of cultural nourishment and inspiration. It is the *shengren* who leads the way of the human being (*rendao* 人道) into its more certain future.

In reading the relationship between the *shi, junzi,* and *shengren* hierarchically, we must emphasize that the hierarchy should not just be imagined vertically, concluding in a transcendent we-know-not-what. Rather do we want to maintain the rich path imagery of *dao*: the *shengren* have traveled, appropriated, and enlarged a longer stretch of the road than the *shi* and *junzi,* and they are providing signposts and a bearing for the latter as well. The later Confucian Xunzi has succinctly described this relationship at the close of his masterful essay on ritual, the *li*:

> Only the *shengren* is able to understand the observance of ritual propriety. The *shengren* understands this observance with clarity; the *shi* and *junzi* perform it with ease; the officials maintain it, and the common people use it to create their own customs. In the hands of the *junzi*, it becomes the way of humanity; in the hands of the common people, it becomes the business of ghosts and spirits.[52]

This, then, in all too brief a compass is our interpretation of the eventful world of the *Analects*, the relational people who experience it, and the language which per-, in-, and re-forms that world and those people. We hope it will enable the Western reader of this text to appreciate how a Chinese Hamlet may have spoken somewhat differently had he read it. Rather than "There are *more things* in heaven and earth than are dreamed of in your philosophy," he may well have said, "There are *more ways of experiencing the heavens and the earth* than are dreamed of in your philosophy."

1. Later in this Introduction we mention James Legge, whose translations and commentaries on classical Chinese texts every serious student will wish to consult eventually. See especially *The Chinese Classics*, in five volumes, originally published in Shanghai during the nineteenth century, reprinted by the University of Hong Kong Press in 1960. The first volume contains a biography of Confucius, pp. 56–90. Other biographies in English include Raymond Dawson's *Confucius*, Richard Wilhelm's *Confucius and Confucianism*, and perhaps the most readable, *Confucius and the Chinese Way* by H. G. Creel.

2. Thus we should not be surprised to find that writings devoted explicitly to military strategy and tactics were a major genre in ancient China. See for example, *Sun-tzu: The Art of Warfare*, and the newly recovered *Sun Pin: The Art of Warfare*, the first translated by Roger T. Ames, and the second by D. C. Lau and Roger T. Ames, both published in this same Classics of Ancient China series.

3. The *locus classicus* for surveying Chinese philosophy has been Fung Yu-lan (1953). It has been superseded in most respects by more recent, and more interpretative—but well done—works including A. C. Graham (1989), Benjamin Schwartz (1985), and Chad Hansen (1992).

4. This notation refers to book 7 (of 20 books), passage 1 of the *Analects*.

5. Volume III in James Legge, under the title *The Shoo King*, and volume IV, *The She King*, respectively. The former has also been translated by Bernhard Karlgren as *The Book of Documents*. Karlgren produced an equally literal translation of *The Book of Odes*. A more flowing rendition of *The Book*

of Songs is Arthur Waley's, and a more creatively interpretative version is Ezra Pound's *The Confucian Odes.*

6. See Hall and Ames (1998):Part II that distinguishes "truth-seekers" from "way-seekers."

7. See D. C. Lau (1992) Appendix 2, "The Disciples as They Appear in the *Analects.*" Legge (1960) Volume I, pp. 112-28 also provides an account of the disciples.

8. D. C. Lau (1992):262.

9. Other translations of the *Analects* include James Legge, Volume I; Arthur Waley, *The Analects of Confucius*; D. C. Lau, *Confucius: The Analects*; Raymond Dawson, *Confucius: The Analects*; Simon Leys, *The Analects of Confucius.* We have also profited from reading the manuscript translation and commentary of the *Analects* by E. Bruce and A. Taeko Brooks published by Columbia University Press under the title *The Original Analects.* Most of these earlier translations have something particular to recommend them: the Lau translation is unmatched in its philological sensibilities; the principle driving the Brooks translation is that historical detail is essential for a full understanding of the text. We hope that their translations and our philosophical presentation of the text will be seen to complement each other.

10. For more on these events, see Derk Bodde's *China's First Unifier*, and the first volume of *The Cambridge History of China.*

11. The Brooks interpretation is consistent in important degree with the detailed textual work on the *Analects* by John Makeham (1996).

12. Makeham (1997):263 n9 states:

> The redaction of LY included in the so-called Xiping stone classics (but actually cut over the period 175–183) is said to have been based on the Lu Lun.

13. See note 5.

14. See Shaughnessy (1993):378.

15. See note 5.

16. Far and away the most influential translation of the *Book of Changes* has been by Richard Wilhelm (1961). Two recent additions are Lynn (1994) and Shaughnessy (1996), the latter published in this Classics of Ancient China series.

17. The associations between Confucius and the commentaries on the *Book of Changes* is an old story that has fresh corroboration in the new commentaries on this text found at Mawangdui. See Shaughnessy (1996).

18. There is no full English translation of the *Zhouli*. The *Yili* was translated by John Steele as the *I-Li* (Probsthain, 1917), and Legge did the *Liji* as *Li Chi*.

19. Legge (1960) V.

20. Legge (1960) has translated the *Mencius* (vol II), as has D. C. Lau (1984).

21. The full text of the *Xunzi* has been translated by John Knoblock (1988– 1994). Partial translations have been published earlier by Burton Watson (1963), and H. H. Dubs (1928). Dubs also wrote *Hsun-tzu: The Moulder of Ancient Confucianism* (1929a). See Hall and Ames (1995): 205–11 for a discussion of the unrecognized importance of Xunzi.

22. A useful reference for Zhu Xi is *Chu Hsi and Neo-Confucianism*, Wing-tsit Chan (1986).

23. See P. J. Ivanhoe (1993), and Tu Wei-ming (1979) and (1985).

24. Consult Tu Wei-ming (1996). A brief, skeptical account of the "Confucian Hypotheses" is found in Rosemont (1995), "Why the Chinese Economic Miracle Isn't One."

25. Much of the material in this and the following sections reflects positions we have elaborated on in other writings. See Hall and Ames (1987), (1995), and (1998), and Rosemont (1974) and (1991).

26. Suggested to us by Wang Qingjie.

27. See Veith (1972).

28. Hall and Ames (1998):chapter 4.

29. Sivin (1965):110.

30. *Zhuangzi* 4/2/33.

31. Hansen (1992):passim, especially 33–52.

32. *Zhuangzi* 4/2/33.

33. Cited in John DeFrancis (1984):69. While we disagree with DeFrancis about the phonetic significance of classical Chinese, we do so with diffidence

because of our respect for his contribution to scholarship. Further, while we have greater reservations than he does about the alphabetic reforms for written Chinese, we are entirely sympathetic to the pedagogical reasons which motivate his pressing for them: literacy would become more widespread.

34. Cited in Wright (1953):291. His entire essay—"The Chinese Language and Foreign Ideas"—is well worth the reader's attention.

35. These few pages are a summary of a portion of Rosemont (1974) which contains relevant references.

36. A persistent theme of both "old China hands" and many scholars. See Dubs (1929b), especially 26–29, and Ullman (1969), 18–20. Plato, Wittgenstein, and most recently, Borges in his "Funes the Memorius" all present a relatively persuasive argument that human beings cannot think "concretely."

37. Karlgren (1923):40.

38. See Lisa Raphals, "A Woman Who Understood the Rites: Confucius on Ji of Lu" in Bryan Van Norden (ed.), *Essays on the* Analects of Confucius (forthcoming). See also Raphals (1998).

39. This lexical section is informed by Hall and Ames (1987), *Thinking Through Confucius*. Throughout, we describe the Chinese terms dynamically and relationally as much as the grammar of English will allow rather than as fundamentally referential, denoting things, substances, essences. Although Noam Chomsky (1996):52 is arguing in a different context, he is formulating an understanding of language that would seem to provide corroboration for our approach to classical Chinese in particular, and to languages more generally:

> . . .[T]here need be no objects in the world that correspond to what we are talking about, even in the simplest cases, nor does anyone believe that there are. *People* use words to refer to things in complex ways, reflecting interests and circumstances, but the *words* do not refer; there is no word-thing relation . . . nor a more complex word-thing-person relation . . . [Italics in the original]

40. Legge III:92ff. "The Tribute of Yu."

41. Dewey (1950):128.

42. See Allan (1979) and Ahern (1981).

43. Legge III:292.

44. Fingarette (1983):217.

45. Karlgren (1950c):191.

46. Takeuchi (1965) and Wing-tsit Chan (1969).

47. Pound (1951):22.

48. Munro (1969):75–76.

49. See the endnotes to 13.23 for an extensive discussion of the culinary associations that have been used to gloss this term.

50. Boodberg (1953):320–22.

51. *Mencius* 4B32 and 6B2.

52. *Xunzi* 75/19/121. A fuller account of this path of spiritual progress is in Rosemont (1999) and Ames (1999).

1.1　子曰：「學而時習之，不亦說乎？有朋自遠方來，不
亦樂乎？人不知而不慍，不亦君子乎？」

The Master said: "Having studied,[1] to then repeatedly apply what you have learned—is this not a source of pleasure? To have friends come from distant quarters[2]—is this not a source of enjoyment? To go unacknowledged by others without harboring frustration—is this not the mark of an exemplary person (*junzi* 君子)?

1.2　有子曰：「其爲人也孝弟，而好犯上者，鮮矣；不好
犯上，而好作亂者，未之有也。君子務本，本立而道
生。孝弟也者，其爲人（仁）之本與！」

Master You[3] said: "It is a rare thing for someone who has a sense of filial and fraternal responsibility (*xiaodi* 孝弟) to have a taste for defying authority. And it is unheard of for those who have no taste for defying authority to be keen on initiating rebellion. Exemplary persons (*junzi* 君子) concentrate their efforts on the root, for the root having taken hold, the way (*dao* 道) will grow therefrom. As for filial and fraternal responsibility, it is, I suspect, the root of authoritative conduct (*ren* 仁)."[4]

1.3　子曰：「巧言令色，鮮矣仁！」

The Master said: "It is a rare thing for glib speech and an insinuating appearance to accompany authoritative conduct (*ren* 仁)."[5]

1.4 曾子曰：「吾日三省吾身：爲人謀而不忠乎？與朋友交而不信乎？傳不習乎？」

Master Zeng said: "Daily I examine my person on three counts. In my undertakings on behalf of other people, have I failed to do my utmost (*zhong* 忠)? In my interactions with colleagues and friends, have I failed to make good on my word (*xin* 信)? In what has been passed on to me, have I failed to carry it into practice?"

1.5 子曰：「道千乘之國，敬事而信，節用而愛人，使民以時。」

The Master said: "The way (*dao* 道) to lead a thousand-chariot state effectively is to carry out your official duties respectfully and make good on your word (*xin* 信); be frugal in your expenditures and love your peers; and put the common people to work only at the proper time of year."[6]

1.6 子曰：「弟子入則孝，出則悌，謹而信，汎愛眾，而親人（仁）。行有餘力，則以學文。」

The Master said: "As a younger brother and son, be filial (*xiao* 孝) at home and deferential (*di* 弟) in the community; be cautious in what you say and then make good on your word (*xin* 信); love the multitude broadly and be intimate with those who are authoritative in their conduct (*ren* 仁).[7] If in so behaving you still have energy left, use it to improve yourself through study."

1.7 子夏曰：「賢賢易色；事父母，能竭其力；事君，能致其身；與朋友交，言而有信。雖曰未學，吾必謂之學矣。」

Zixia[8] said: "As for persons who care for character much more than beauty, who in serving their parents are able to exert themselves utterly, who give their whole person in the service of their ruler, and who, in interactions with colleagues and friends, make good on their word (*xin* 信)—even if it were said of such persons that they are unschooled, I would insist that they are well educated indeed."

1.8 子曰：「君子不重則不威；學則不固。主忠信。無友不如己者。過則勿憚改。」

The Master said: "Exemplary persons (*junzi* 君子) lacking in gravity would have no dignity. Yet in their studies they are not inflexible.[9] Take doing your utmost and making good on your word (*xin* 信) as your mainstay. Do not have as a friend anyone who is not as good as you are.[10] And where you have erred, do not hesitate to mend your ways."

1.9 曾子曰：「慎終追遠，民德歸厚矣。」

Master Zeng said: "Be circumspect in funerary services and continue sacrifices to the distant ancestors, and the virtue (*de* 德) of the common people will thrive."[11]

1.10 子禽問於子貢曰：「夫子至於是邦也，必聞其政，求之與？抑與之與？」子貢曰：「夫子溫、良、恭、儉、讓以得之。夫子之求之也，其諸異乎人之求之與？」

Ziqin asked Zigong:[12] "When the Master arrives in a particular state and needs to learn how it is being governed, does he seek out this information or is it offered to him?" Zigong replied: "The Master gets all he needs by being cordial, proper, deferential, frugal, and unassuming. Perhaps this way of seeking information is somewhat different from how others go about it."

1.11 子曰：「父在，觀其志；父沒，觀其行；三年無改於父之道，可謂孝矣。」

The Master said: "While a person's father is still alive, observe what he intends; when his father dies, observe what he does.[13] A person who for three years refrains from reforming[14] the ways (*dao* 道) of his late father can be called a filial son (*xiao* 孝)."[15]

1.12 　有子曰：「禮之用，和爲貴。先王之道，斯爲美；小
　　　大由之。有所不行，知和而和，不以禮節之，亦不可
　　　行也。」

Master You said: "Achieving harmony (*he* 和) is the most valuable function of observing ritual propriety (*li* 禮). In the ways of the Former Kings, this achievement of harmony made them elegant, and was a guiding standard in all things large and small. But when things are not going well, to realize harmony just for its own sake without regulating the situation through observing ritual propriety will not work."[16]

1.13 　有子曰：「信近於義，言可復也。恭近於禮，遠恥辱
　　　也。因不失其親，亦可宗也。」

Master You said: "That making good on one's word (*xin* 信) gets one close to being appropriate (*yi* 義) is because then what one says will bear repeating. That being deferential gets one close to observing ritual propriety (*li* 禮) is because it keeps disgrace and insult at a distance. Those who are accommodating and do not lose those with whom they are close are deserving of esteem."

1.14 　子曰：「君子食無求飽，居無求安，敏於事而慎於
　　　言，就有道而正焉，可謂好學也已。」

The Master said: "In eating, exemplary persons (*junzi* 君子) do not look for a full stomach, nor in their lodgings for comfort and contentment. They are persons of action yet cautious in what they say. They repair to those who know the way (*dao* 道), and find improvement in their company. Such persons can indeed be said to have a love of learning (*haoxue* 好學)."[17]

1.15 　子貢曰：「貧而無諂，富而無驕，何如？」子曰：「可也；未若貧而樂道，富而好禮者也。」

　　　子貢曰：「《詩》云：『如切如磋，如琢如磨。』其斯之謂與？」子曰：「賜也，始可與言《詩》已矣，告諸往而知來者。」

Zigong said: "What do you think of the saying: 'Poor but not inferior; rich but not superior'?" The Master replied: "Not bad, but not as good as: 'Poor but enjoying the way (*dao* 道);[18] rich but loving ritual propriety (*li* 禮).'"

Zigong said: "The *Book of Songs* states:

Like bone carved and polished,
Like jade cut and ground.[19]

Is this not what you have in mind?"

The Master said: "Zigong, it is only with the likes of you then that I can discuss the *Songs*! On the basis of what has been said, you know what is yet to come."

1.16 　子曰：「不患人之不己知，患不知人也。」

The Master said: "Don't worry about not being acknowledged by others; worry about failing to acknowledge them."

2.1　子曰：「爲政以德，譬如北辰，居其所而衆星共之。」

The Master said: "Governing[20] with excellence (de 德) can be compared to being the North Star: the North Star dwells in its place, and the multitude of stars pay it tribute."[21]

2.2　子曰：「《詩》三百，一言以蔽之，曰：『思無邪。』」

The Master said: "Although the *Songs* are three hundred in number, they can be covered in one expression: 'Go vigorously without swerving.'"[22]

2.3　子曰：「道之以政，齊之以刑，民免而無恥；道之以德，齊之以禮，有恥且格。」

The Master said: "Lead the people with administrative injunctions (*zheng* 政) and keep them orderly with penal law (*xing* 刑), and they will avoid punishments but will be without a sense of shame. Lead them with excellence (*de* 德) and keep them orderly through observing ritual propriety (*li* 禮) and they will develop a sense of shame, and moreover, will order themselves."[23]

2.4　子曰：「吾十有五而志于學，三十而立，四十而不惑，五十而知天命，六十而耳順，七十而從心所欲，不踰矩。」

The Master said: "From fifteen, my heart-and-mind was set upon learning; from thirty I took my stance; from forty I was no longer doubtful; from fifty I realized the propensities of *tian* (*tianming* 天命); from sixty my ear was attuned; from seventy I could give my heart-and-mind free rein without overstepping the boundaries."[24]

2.5　孟懿子問孝。子曰：「無違。」
　　　樊遲御，子告之曰：「孟孫問孝於我，我對曰，『無違。」」樊遲曰：「何謂也？」子曰：「生，事之以禮；死，葬之以禮，祭之以禮。」

Meng Yizi[25] asked about filial conduct (*xiao* 孝). The Master replied: "Do not act contrary." Fan Chi[26] was driving the Master's chariot, and the Master informed him further: "Meng Yizi asked me about filial conduct, and I replied: 'Do not act contrary.'" Fan Chi asked, "What did you mean by that?" The Master replied: "While they are living, serve them according to the observances of ritual propriety (*li* 禮); when they are dead, bury them and sacrifice to them according to the observances of ritual propriety."

2.6　孟武伯問孝。子曰：「父母唯其疾之憂。」

Meng Wubo[27] asked about filial conduct (*xiao* 孝). The Master replied: "Give your mother and father nothing to worry about beyond your physical well-being."[28]

2.7　子游問孝。子曰：「今之孝者，是謂能養。至於犬馬，皆能有養；不敬，何以別乎？」

Ziyou[29] asked about filial conduct (*xiao* 孝). The Master replied: "Those today who are filial are considered so because they are able to provide for their parents. But even dogs and horses are given that much care. If you do not respect your parents, what is the difference?"

2.8　子夏問孝。子曰：「色難。有事，弟子服其勞；有酒食，先生饌，曾是以爲孝乎？」

Zixia asked about filial conduct (*xiao* 孝). The Master replied: "It all lies in showing the proper countenance. As for the young contributing their energies when there is work to be done, and deferring to their elders when there is wine and food to be had—how can merely doing this be considered being filial?"

2.9　子曰：「吾與回言終日，不違，如愚。退而省其私，亦足以發，回也不愚。」

The Master said: "I can speak with Yan Hui for an entire day without his raising an objection, as though he were slow. But when he has withdrawn and I examine what he says and does on his own, it illustrates perfectly what I have been saying. Indeed, there is nothing slow about Yan Hui!"

2.10　子曰：「視其所以，觀其所由，察其所安。人焉廋哉？人焉廋哉？」

The Master said: "Watch their actions, observe their motives, examine wherein they dwell content; won't you know what kind of person they are? Won't you know what kind of person they are?"

2.11　子曰：「溫故而知新，可以爲師矣。」

The Master said: "Reviewing the old as a means of realizing the new—such a person can be considered a teacher."[30]

2.12　子曰：「君子不器。」

The Master said: "Exemplary persons (*junzi* 君子) are not mere vessels."[31]

2.13　子貢問君子。子曰：「先行其言而後從之。」

Zigong asked about exemplary persons (*junzi* 君子). The Master replied: "They first accomplish what they are going to say, and only then say it."[32]

2.14 子曰：「君子周而不比，小人比而不周。」

The Master said: "Exemplary persons (*junzi* 君子) associating openly with others are not partisan; petty persons being partisan do not associate openly with others."

2.15 子曰：「學而不思則罔，思而不學則殆。」

The Master said: "Learning without due reflection leads to perplexity; reflection without learning leads to perilous circumstances."[33]

2.16 子曰：「攻乎異端，斯害也已。」

The Master said: "To become accomplished in some heterodox doctrine will bring nothing but harm."[34]

2.17 子曰：「由！誨女知之乎！知之爲知之，不知爲不知，是知也。」

The Master said: "Zilu,[35] shall I teach you what wisdom (*zhi* 知) means?" To know (*zhi* 知) what you know and know what you do not know—this then is wisdom."[36]

2.18 子張學干祿。子曰：「多聞闕疑，慎言其餘，則寡尤；多見闕殆，慎行其餘，則寡悔。言寡尤，行寡悔，祿在其中矣。」

Zizhang[37] was studying in order to take office. The Master said: "If you listen broadly, set aside what you are unsure of, and speak cautiously on the rest, you will make few errors; if you look broadly, set aside what is perilous, and act cautiously on the rest, you will have few regrets. To speak with few errors and to act with few regrets is the substance of taking office."

2.19 哀公問曰：「何爲則民服？」孔子對曰：「舉直錯諸枉，則民服；舉枉錯諸直，則民不服。」

Duke Ai of Lu inquired of Confucius, asking: "What does one do to gain the allegiance of the people?" Confucius replied: "Raise up the true and place them over the crooked, and the allegiance of the people will be yours; raise up the crooked and place them over the true, and the people will not be yours."

2.20 季康子問：「使民敬、忠以勤，如之何？」子曰：「臨之以莊，則敬；孝慈，則忠；舉善而教不能，則勤。」

Ji Kangzi[38] asked: "How do you get the people to be respectful, to do their utmost for you (*zhong* 忠), and to be eager?" The Master replied: "Oversee them with dignity and the people will be respectful; be filial to your elders (*xiao* 孝) and kind to your juniors, and the people will do their utmost for you; raise up those who are adept (*shan* 善) and instruct those who are not and the people will be eager."[39]

2.21 或謂孔子曰：「子奚不爲政？」子曰：「《書》云：『孝乎惟孝，友于兄弟，施於有政。』是亦爲政，奚其爲爲政？」

Someone asked Confucius, "Why are you not employed in governing?" The Master replied, "The *Book of Documents* says:

It is all in filial conduct (*xiao* 孝)! Just being filial to your parents and befriending your brothers is carrying out the work of government.

80

In doing this I am employed in governing. Why must I be 'employed in governing'?"

2.22　子曰：「人而無信，不知其可也。大車無輗，小車無軏，其何以行之哉？」

The Master said, "I am not sure that anyone who does not make good on their word (*xin* 信) is viable as a person. If a large carriage does not have the pin for its yoke, or a small carriage does not have the pin for its crossbar, how can you drive them anywhere?"[40]

2.23　子張問：「十世可知也？」子曰：「殷因於夏禮，所損益，可知也；周因於殷禮，所損益，可知也。其或繼周者，雖百世可知也。」

Zizhang asked, "Can we know what ten generations hence will be like?"

The Master replied, "The Yin dynasty adapted the observances of ritual propriety (*li* 禮) of the Xia dynasty, and how they altered them can be known. The Zhou adapted the observances of ritual propriety of the Yin, and how they altered them can be known. If there is a dynasty that succeeds the Zhou, even if it happens a hundred generations from now, the continuities and changes can be known."[41]

2.24　子曰：「非其鬼而祭之，諂也。見義不爲，無勇也。」

The Master said, "Sacrificing to ancestral spirits other than one's own is being unctuous. Failing to act on what is seen as appropriate (*yi* 義) is a want of courage."

3.1　孔子謂季氏，「八佾舞於庭，是可忍也，孰不可忍
也？」

Confucius remarked on the Ji clan: "If the Ji clan's use of the imperial eight rows of eight dancers in the courtyard of their estate can be condoned, what cannot be?"[42]

3.2　三家者以《雍》徹。子曰：「『相維辟公，天子穆
穆』，奚取於三家之堂？」

The Three Families of Lu—Meng-sun, Shu-sun, and Ji-sun—had the *yong* ode[43] performed at the conclusion of their sacrifices as the implements were being gathered. The Master said:

> "Assisting were the various nobles,
> And the Emperor stood regal and majestic.

What relevance does this ode have to the ancestral halls of the Three Families?"

3.3　子曰：「人而不仁，如禮何？人而不仁，如樂何？」

The Master said: "What has a person who is not authoritative (*ren* 仁) got to do with observing ritual propriety (*li* 禮)? What has a person who is not authoritative got to do with the playing of music (*yue* 樂)?"[44]

3.4　林放問禮之本。子曰：「大哉問！禮，與其奢也，寧
儉；喪，與其易也，寧戚。」

Lin Fang[45] asked about the roots of observing ritual propriety
(*li* 禮). The Master replied: "What an important question! In
observing ritual propriety, it is better to be modest than extravagant; in mourning, it is better to express real grief than
to worry over formal details."

3.5　子曰：「夷狄之有君，不如諸夏之亡也。」

The Master said: "The Yi and Di barbarian tribes[46] with rulers are not as viable as the various Chinese states without
them."

3.6　季氏旅於泰山。子謂冉有曰：「女弗能救與？」對
曰：「不能。」子曰：「嗚呼！曾謂泰山不如林放
乎？」

The Ji clan was going to perform the *lü* sacrifice on Mount
Tai. Confucius spoke to Ranyou,[47] "Are you not able to save
them from this impropriety?" He replied, "I cannot." The
Master said: "Oh, my! Can it really be that Lin Fang knows
more about observing ritual propriety than Mount Tai!"

3.7　子曰：「君子無所爭。必也射乎！揖讓而升，下而
飲。其爭也君子。」

The Master said: "Exemplary persons (*junzi* 君子) are not
competitive, except where they have to be in the archery ceremony. Greeting and making way for each other, the archers
ascend the hall, and returning they drink a salute. Even in
contesting, they are exemplary persons."

3.8　子夏問曰：「『巧笑倩兮，美目盼兮，素以爲絢兮。』
何謂也？」子曰：「繪事後素。」
　　　曰：「禮後乎？」子曰：「起予者商也！始可與
言《詩》已矣。」

Zixia[48] inquired: "What does the song[49] mean when its says:

Her smiling cheeks—so radiant,
Her dazzling eyes—so sharp and clear,
It is the unadorned that enhances color?"

The Master replied: "The application of color is to the unadorned."

"Does this mean that observing ritual propriety (li 禮) itself comes after?" asked Zixia.

The Master replied: "Zixia, you have stimulated my thoughts. It is only with the likes of you that one can discuss the *Songs*."

3.9　子曰：「夏禮，吾能言之，杞不足徵也；殷禮，吾能言之，宋不足徵也。文獻不足故也。足，則吾能徵之矣。」

The Master said: "I am able to speak on ritual propriety (li 禮) during the Xia dynasty, but its descendent state, Qi, does not provide adequate evidence. I am able to speak on ritual propriety during the Yin dynasty, but its descendent state, Song, does not provide adequate evidence. It is because these states have inadequate documentation and few men of letters. If they were adequate in these respects, I would be able to give evidence for what I say."

3.10　子曰：「禘自既灌而往者，吾不欲觀之矣。」

The Master said: "As for what follows in the *di* imperial ancestral sacrifice once the libation has been made, I do not desire to watch it."[50]

3.11　或問禘之說。子曰：「不知也；知其說者之於天下也，其如示諸斯乎！」指其掌。

Someone asked the Master for an explanation of the *di* imperial ancestral sacrifice, and he replied: "I don't have one. Anyone who did know how to explain it could rule the empire as easily as having it here." And he pointed to the palm of his hand.

3.12 祭如在，祭神如神在。子曰：「吾不與祭，如不祭。」

The expression "sacrifice as though present" is taken to mean "sacrifice to the spirits as though the spirits are present." But the Master said: "If I myself do not participate in the sacrifice, it is as though I have not sacrificed at all."

3.13 王孫賈問曰：「『與其媚於奧，寧媚於竈』，何謂也？」子曰：「不然；獲罪於天，無所禱也。」

Wang-sun Jia inquired of Confucius, quoting the saying:

> "It is better to pay homage to the spirit of the stove
> Than to the spirits of the household shrine.

What does this mean?"

The Master replied: "It is not so. A person who offends against *tian* 天 has nowhere else to pray."

3.14 子曰：「周監於二代，郁郁乎文哉！吾從周。」

The Master said: "The Zhou dynasty looked back to the Xia and Shang dynasties. Such a wealth of culture! I follow the Zhou."

3.15 子入太廟，每事問。或曰：「孰謂鄹人之子知禮乎？入太廟，每事問。」子聞之，曰：「是禮也。」

The Master on entering the Grand Ancestral Hall asked questions about everything. Someone remarked: "Who said this son of a man from the Zou village[51] knows about observing ritual propriety (*li* 禮)? On entering the Grand Ancestral Hall he asks questions about everything."

When Confucius heard of this, he said: "To do so is itself observing ritual propriety."

3.16　子曰：「射不主皮，爲力不同科，古之道也。」

The Master said: "Marksmanship does not lie in piercing the leather target, because the strength of the archers varies. This is the way of the ancients."

3.17　子貢欲去告朔之餼羊。子曰：「賜也！爾愛其羊，我愛其禮。」

Zigong wanted to dispense[52] with the sacrifice of a live sheep at the Declaration of the New Moon ceremony. The Master said: "Zigong! You grudge the sheep —I, ritual propriety (*li* 禮)."[53]

3.18　子曰：「事君盡禮，人以爲諂也。」

The Master said: "If in serving your lord you are scrupulous about what is ritual (*li* 禮), other people will think you unctuous."

3.19　定公問：「君使臣，臣事君，如之何？」孔子對曰：「君使臣以禮，臣事君以忠。」

Duke Ding of Lu inquired: "How should rulers employ their ministers, and how should ministers serve their lord?"

Confucius replied, "Rulers should employ their ministers by observing ritual propriety (*li* 禮), and ministers should serve their lord by doing their utmost (*zhong* 忠)."

3.20　子曰：「《關雎》、樂而不淫，哀而不傷。」

The Master said: "'The Cry of the Osprey'[54] is pleasing without being excessive, is mournful without being injurious."

3.21　哀公問社於宰我。宰我對曰：「夏后氏以松，殷人以柏，周人以栗，曰，使民戰栗。」子聞之，曰：「成事不說，遂事不諫，既往不咎。」

Duke Ai asked Zaiwo[55] about the altar pole to the god of the soil.[56] Zaiwo replied: "The Xia clans used wood of the pine, the Yin peoples used the cypress, and the Zhou peoples used the chestnut (*li* 栗). It is said that they wanted to make the people fearful (*zhanli* 戰栗)."[57]

When the Master heard of this, he said: "You don't discuss what is finished and done with; you don't remonstrate over what happens as a matter of course; you don't level blame against what is long gone."

3.22　子曰：「管仲之器小哉。」

或曰：「管仲儉乎？」曰：「管氏有三歸，官事不攝，焉得儉？」

「然則管仲知禮乎？」曰：「邦君樹塞門，管氏亦樹塞門。邦君為兩君之好，有反坫，管氏亦有反坫。管氏而知禮，孰不知禮？」

The Master said: "Guanzhong was lacking in capacity."
Someone asked: "Do you mean that Guanzhong was frugal?" The Master replied: "Guanzhong had three residences and each member of his staff had only one responsibility. Where's the frugality?"

"This being so, did Guanzhong understand the observance of ritual propriety (*li* 禮)?" he was asked.

The Master replied: "The ruler of the state set up ornamental stone blinds before his gates, and Guanzhong did the same; for entertaining other rulers the ruler of the state[58] had a stand for inverting drinking vessels, and Guanzhong had the same. If we say that Guanzhong understood the observance of ritual propriety, then who doesn't?"

3.23 子語魯大師樂，曰：「樂其可知也：始作，翕如也；從之，純如也，皦如也，繹如也，以成。」

The Master talked to the Grand Music Master of Lu about music, and said: "Much can be realized with music if one begins by playing in unison, and then goes on to improvise with purity of tone and distinctness and flow,[59] thereby bringing all to completion."

3.24 儀封人請見，曰：「君子之至於斯也，吾未嘗不得見也。」從者見之。出曰：「二三子何患於喪乎？天下之無道也久矣，天將以夫子爲木鐸。」

A border official at Yi asked for an interview with the Master, saying: "I have always been accorded an interview with those distinguished persons who have made their way here." Confucius' followers presented him. On taking his leave, he said:[60] "Why worry over the loss of office, my friends? All under *tian* 天 have long since lost their way (*dao* 道), and *tian* is going to use your Master as a wooden bell-clapper."

3.25 子謂《韶》，「盡美矣，又盡善也。」謂《武》，「盡美矣，未盡善也。」

The Master said of the *shao* music that it is both superbly beautiful (*mei* 美) and superbly felicitous (*shan* 善).[61] Of the *wu* music he said that it is superbly beautiful but not superbly felicitous.

3.26 子曰：「居上不寬，爲禮不敬，臨喪不哀，吾何以觀之哉？」

The Master said, "What could I see in a person who in holding a position of influence is not tolerant, who in observing ritual propriety (*li* 禮) is not respectful, and who in overseeing the mourning rites does not grieve?"

4.1 子曰：「里仁爲美。擇不處仁，焉得知？」

The Master said, "In taking up one's residence, it is the presence of authoritative persons (*ren* 仁) that is the greatest attraction. How can anyone be called wise who, in having the choice, does not seek to dwell among authoritative people?"[62]

4.2 子曰：「不仁者不可以久處約，不可以長處樂。仁者安仁，知者利仁。」

The Master said, "Those persons who are not authoritative (*ren* 仁) are neither able to endure hardship for long, nor to enjoy happy circumstances for any period of time. Authoritative persons are content in being authoritative; wise persons (*zhi* 知) flourish in it."

4.3 子曰：「唯仁者能好人，能惡人。」

The Master said, "The authoritative person (*ren* 仁) alone has the wherewithal to properly discriminate the good person from the bad."[63]

4.4 子曰：「苟志於仁矣，無惡也。」

The Master said, "If indeed one's purposes are set on authoritative conduct (*ren* 仁), one could do no wrong."

4.5 子曰：「富與貴，是人之所欲也；不以其道得之，不處也。貧與賤，是人之所惡也；不以其道得之，不去也。君子去仁，惡乎成名？君子無終食之間違仁，造次必於是，顛沛必於是。」

The Master said, "Wealth and honor are what people want, but if they are the consequence of deviating from the way (*dao* 道), I would have no part in them. Poverty and disgrace are what people deplore, but if they are the consequence of staying on the way, I would not avoid them. Wherein do the exemplary persons (*junzi* 君子) who would abandon their authoritative conduct (*ren* 仁) warrant that name? Exemplary persons do not take leave of their authoritative conduct even for the space of a meal. When they are troubled, they certainly turn to it, as they do in facing difficulties."

4.6　子曰：「我未見好仁者、惡不仁者。好仁者，無以尙之；惡不仁者，其爲仁矣，不使不仁者加乎其身。有能一日用其力於仁矣乎？我未見力不足者。蓋有之矣，我未之見也。」

The Master said, "I have yet to meet people who are truly fond of authoritative conduct (*ren* 仁) and who truly abhor behavior contrary to it. There are none superior to those who are fond of authoritative conduct. And those who abhor behavior contrary to it, in becoming authoritative themselves, will not allow such conduct to attach itself to them. Are there people who, for the space of a single day, have given their full strength to authoritative conduct? I have yet to meet them. As for lacking the strength to do so, I doubt there are such people—at least I have yet to meet them."[64]

4.7　子曰：「人之過也，各於其黨。觀過，斯知人（仁）矣。」

The Master said, "In going astray, people fall into groups. In observing these divergencies, the degree to which they are authoritative (*ren* 仁) can be known."[65]

4.8 子曰：「朝聞道，夕死可矣。」

The Master said, "If at dawn you learn of and tread the way (*dao* 道), you can face death at dusk."[66]

4.9 子曰：「士志於道，而恥惡衣惡食者，未足與議也。」

The Master said, "Those scholar-apprentices (*shi* 士) who, having set their purposes on walking the way (*dao* 道), are ashamed of rude clothing and coarse food, are not worth engaging in discussion."

4.10 子曰：「君子之於天下也，無適也，無莫也，義之與比。」

The Master said, "Exemplary persons (*junzi* 君子) in making their way in the world are neither bent on nor against anything; rather, they go with what is appropriate (*yi* 義)."

4.11 子曰：「君子懷德，小人懷土；君子懷刑，小人懷惠。」

The Master said, "Exemplary persons (*junzi* 君子) cherish their excellence; petty persons cherish their land. Exemplary persons cherish fairness; petty persons cherish the thought of gain."[67]

4.12 子曰：「放於利而行，多怨。」

The Master said, "To act with an eye to personal profit will incur a lot of resentment."

4.13 子曰：「能以禮讓爲國，於從政乎何有？ 不能以禮讓爲國，如禮何？ 」

The Master said, "If rulers are able to effect order in the state through the combination of observing ritual propriety (*li* 禮) and deferring to others (*rang* 讓), what more is needed? But if they are unable to accomplish this, what have they to do with observing ritual propriety?"

4.14　子曰：「不患無位，患所以立。不患莫己知，求爲可知也。」

The Master said, "Do not worry over not having an official position; worry about what it takes to have one. Do not worry that no one acknowledges you; seek to do what will earn you acknowledgment."

4.15　子曰：「參乎！吾道一以貫之。」曾子曰：「唯。」
　　子出，門人問曰：「何謂也？」曾子曰：「夫子之道，忠恕而已矣。」

The Master said, "Zeng, my friend! My way (*dao* 道) is bound together with one continuous strand."

Master Zeng replied, "Indeed."

When the Master had left, the disciples asked, "What was he referring to?"

Master Zeng said, "The way of the Master is doing one's utmost (*zhong* 忠) and putting oneself in the other's place (*shu* 恕), nothing more."

4.16　子曰：「君子喻於義，小人喻於利。」

The Master said, "Exemplary persons (*junzi* 君子) understand what is appropriate (*yi* 義); petty persons understand what is of personal advantage (*li* 利)."

4.17　子曰：「見賢思齊焉，見不賢而內自省也。」

The Master said, "When you meet persons of exceptional character think to stand shoulder to shoulder with them;

meeting persons of little character, look inward and examine yourself."

4.18 子曰：「事父母幾諫，見志不從，又敬不違，勞而不怨。」

The Master said, "In serving your father and mother, remonstrate with them gently. On seeing that they do not heed your suggestions, remain respectful and do not act contrary. Although concerned, voice no resentment."

4.19 子曰：「父母在，不遠游，游必有方。」

The Master said, "When your father and mother are alive, do not journey far, and when you do travel, be sure to have a specific destination."

4.20 子曰：「三年無改於父之道，可謂孝矣。」

The Master said, "A person who for three years refrains from reforming the ways (*dao* 道) of his late father can be called a filial son (*xiao* 孝)."[68]

4.21 子曰：「父母之年，不可不知也。一則以喜，一則以懼。」

The Master said, "Children must know the age of their father and mother. On one hand, it is a source of joy; on the other, of trepidation."

4.22 子曰：「古者言之不出，恥躬之不逮也。」

The Master said, "The ancients were loath to speak because they would be ashamed if they personally did not live up to what they said."

4.23 子曰：「以約失之者鮮矣。」

The Master said, "It is rare indeed for someone to go wrong due to personal restraint."

4.24 子曰：「君子欲訥於言而敏於行。」

The Master said, "The exemplary person (*junzi* 君子) wants to be slow to speak yet quick to act."

4.25 子曰：「德不孤，必有鄰。」

The Master said, "Excellent persons (*de* 德) do not dwell alone; they are sure to have neighbors."

4.26 子游曰：「事君數，斯辱矣；朋友數，斯疏矣。」

Ziyou[69] said, "If in serving your lord you are unrelenting, you will bring on disgrace; if in your friendships you are unrelenting, you will find yourself ostracized."[70]

5.1 子謂公冶長，「可妻也。雖在縲絏之中，非其罪也。」
以其子妻之。

The Master remarked, "Gongye Chang will be a good husband. Even though he has spent time in prison, it was
through no fault of his own." He then gave him his daughter
in marriage.

5.2 子謂南容，「邦有道，不廢；邦無道，免於刑戮。」
以其兄之子妻之。

The Master remarked, "As for Nanrong, when the way (*dao*
道) prevails in the land, he does not go unemployed, but
when it does not prevail, he avoids punishment and execution." He then gave him his niece in marriage.

5.3 子謂子賤，「君子哉若人！魯無君子者，斯焉取斯？」

The Master remarked about Zijian, "He is truly an exemplary
person (*junzi* 君子). If Lu had no other exemplary persons,
where could he have gotten his character from?"

5.4 子貢問曰：「賜也何如？」子曰：「女、器也。」
曰：「何器也？」曰：「瑚璉也。」

Zigong[71] inquired, "And what do you think of me?" The Master replied, "You are a vessel."[72] Zigong asked, "What kind of
a vessel?" The Master replied, "You are a most precious and
sacred kind of vessel."[73]

5.5 　或曰：「雍也仁而不佞。」子曰：「焉用佞？禦人以口給，屢憎於人。不知其仁，焉用佞？」

Someone said, "As for Yong, he is an authoritative person (*ren* 仁) but is not eloquent." The Master said, "What is the use of eloquence? A person who disputes with a ready wit often earns the enmity of others. I cannot say whether or not he is an authoritative person, but what need is there for eloquence?"

5.6 　子使漆彫開仕。對曰：「吾斯之未能信。」子說。

The Master recommended that Qidiao Kai seek office. He replied, "I am not sure that I am adequate to it." The Master was pleased.

5.7 　子曰：「道不行，乘桴浮于海。從我者，其由與？」子路聞之喜。子曰：「由也好勇過我，無所取材。」

The Master said, "If the way (*dao* 道) did not prevail in the land, and I had to take to the high seas on a raft, the person who would follow me I expect would be Zilu."[74] Zilu on hearing of this was delighted. The Master said, "With Zilu, his boldness certainly exceeds mine, but he brings nothing with him from which to build the raft."

5.8 　孟武伯問：「子路仁乎？」子曰：「不知也。」又問。子曰：「由也，千乘之國，可使治其賦也，不知其仁也。」
　　　　「求也何如？」子曰：「求也，千室之邑，百乘之家，可使爲之宰也，不知其仁也。」
　　　　「赤也何如？」子曰：「赤也，束帶立於朝，可使與賓客言也，不知其仁也。」

Meng Wubo[75] asked Confucius, "Is Zilu an authoritative person (*ren* 仁)?" The Master said, "I am not sure that he is."

He asked again. The Master replied, "With Zilu, you could put him in charge of the military taxes in a large state of a thousand chariots, but I am not sure that he is an authoritative person."

"What about Ranyou?"[76] he asked. "With Ranyou, you could make him chief of staff in a city of a thousand households or on the estate of a family with a hundred chariots, but I am not sure that he is an authoritative person."

"What about Zihua,"[77] he asked? The Master replied, "With Zihua, wearing his sash and taking his place in the court, he can be sent to converse with the guests and visitors, but I am not sure that he is an authoritative person."

5.9　子謂子貢曰：「女與回也孰愈？」對曰：「賜也何敢望回？回也聞一以知十，賜也聞一以知二。」子曰：「弗如也；吾與女弗如也。」

The Master remarked to Zigong,[78] "Comparing yourself with Yan Hui, who is the better person?" He replied, "How dare I have such expectations. With Yan Hui, learning one thing he will know ten; with me, learning one thing I will know two." The Master said, "You are not his match; neither you nor I are a match for him."

5.10　宰予晝寢。子曰：「朽木不可雕也，糞土之牆不可杇也；於予與何誅？」子曰：「始吾於人也，聽其言而信其行；今吾於人也，聽其言而觀其行。於予與改是。」

Zaiwo[79] was still sleeping during the daytime. The Master said, "You cannot carve rotten wood, and cannot trowel over a wall of manure. As for Zaiwo, what is the point in upbraiding him?"[80]

The Master said further, "There was a time when, in my dealings with others, on hearing what they had to say, I believed they would live up to it. Nowadays in my dealings with others, on hearing what they have to say, I then watch what they do. It is Zaiwo that has taught me as much."

5.11 子曰：「吾未見剛者。」或對曰：「申棖。」子曰：「棖也慾，焉得剛？」

The Master said, "I have yet to meet the person who is truly steadfast." "What about Shen Cheng?" someone replied. "Shen Cheng is too acquisitive; how can he be steadfast?"

5.12 子貢曰：「我不欲人之加諸我也，吾亦欲無加諸人。」子曰：「賜也，非爾所及也。」

Zigong said, "I do not want others to impose on me, nor do I want to impose on others." Confucius replied, "Zigong, this is quite beyond your reach."

5.13 子貢曰：「夫子之文章，可得而聞也；夫子之言性與天道，不可得而聞也。」

Zigong said, "We can learn from the Master's cultural refinements, but do not hear him discourse on subjects such as our 'natural disposition (*xing* 性)' and 'the way of *tian* (*tiandao* 天道)'"[81]

5.14 子路有聞，未之能行，唯恐有聞。

When Zilu had learned something but had not yet been able to act upon it, his only fear was that he would learn something more.[82]

5.15 子貢問曰：「孔文子何以謂之『文』也？」子曰：「敏而好學，不恥下問，是以謂之『文』也。」

Zigong inquired, "Why has Kong Wenzi been given the posthumous title of 'refined (*wen* 文)'?" The Master replied, "He was diligent and fond of learning, and was not ashamed to ask those of a lower status—this is why he has been called 'refined.'"[83]

5.16　子謂子產，「有君子之道四焉：其行己也恭，其事上也敬，其養民也惠，其使民也義。」

The Master remarked that Zichan accorded with the way (*dao* 道) of the exemplary person (*junzi* 君子) in four respects: he was gracious in deporting himself, he was deferential in serving his superiors, he was generous in attending to needs of the common people, and he was appropriate (*yi* 義) in employing their services.

5.17　子曰：「晏平仲善與人交，久而敬之。」

The Master said, "Yen Pingzhong is very good (*shan* 善) in his relations with others: even with old friends he treats them with respect."

5.18　子曰：「臧文仲居蔡，山節藻梲，何如其知也？」

The Master said, "Zang Wenzhong, in preparing a chamber in which to keep his giant ceremonial tortoise, had mountains carved on the column dividers and aquatic grasses painted on the rafters. What was he thinking?"[84]

5.19　子張問曰：「令尹子文三仕爲令尹，無喜色；三已之，無慍色。舊令尹之政，必以告新令尹。何如？」子曰：「忠矣。」曰：「仁矣乎？」曰：「未知；焉得仁？」

「崔子弒齊君，陳文子有馬十乘，棄而違之。至於他邦，則曰，『猶吾大夫崔子也。』違之。之一邦，則又曰：『猶吾大夫崔子也。』違之。何如？」子曰：「清矣。」曰：「仁矣乎？」曰：「未知；焉得仁？」

99

Zizhang inquired, "On the three occasions the Prime Minister Ziwen was made prime minister, there was no happiness in his face; on the three occasions when he was dismissed from office, there was no sense of loss in his face. As the outgoing prime minister, he made every effort to bring the incoming prime minister up to date on the affairs of state. What do you think of him?"

The Master replied, "He certainly did his utmost (*zhong* 忠)."

"But did he exemplify authoritative conduct (*ren* 仁)?" asked Zizhang.

"I am not sure," said the Master. "What did he do that he should be regarded as authoritative?"

Zizhang asked, "When Cuizi assassinated the Lord of Qi, Chen Wenzi, who had an estate of ten chariots, abandoned it all and took his leave. On arriving in another state,[85] Chen Wenzi said, 'They are all just like our minister Cuizi,' and took his leave. Reaching another state, he again said, 'They are all just like our minister Cuizi,' and took his leave. What do you think of him?"

The Master replied, "He certainly was incorruptible."

"But did he exemplify authoritative conduct?" asked Zizhang.

"I am not sure," said the Master. "What did he do that he should be regarded as authoritative?"

5.20 　季文子三思而後行。子聞之，曰：「再，斯可矣。」

Ji Wenzi only took action after thinking about it three times. On hearing of this, the Master said, "Twice would suffice."

5.21 　子曰：「甯武子，邦有道，則知；邦無道，則愚。其知可及也，其愚不可及也。」

The Master said, "As for Ning Wuzi, when the way (*dao* 道) prevailed in the land, he was wise; when it was without the way, he was stupid. Others might attain his level of wisdom, but none could match his stupidity."

5.22 子在陳，曰：「歸與！歸與！吾黨之小子狂簡，斐然成章，不知所以裁之。」

The Master was in the state of Chen, and said, "Homeward! Homeward! My young friends at home are rash and ambitious, while perhaps careless in the details. With the lofty elegance of the literatus, they put on a full display of culture, but they don't know how to cut and tailor it."[86]

5.23 子曰：「伯夷、叔齊不念舊惡，怨是用希。」

The Master said, "Bo Yi and Shu Qi did not nurse old grudges, so others bore them little ill will."[87]

5.24 子曰：「孰謂微生高直？或乞醯焉，乞諸其鄰而與之。」

The Master said, "Who said that Weisheng Gao is true? When someone begged vinegar from him, he in turn begged it from his neighbors and then presented it to the person who had asked him for it."

5.25 子曰：「巧言、令色、足恭，左丘明恥之，丘亦恥之。匿怨而友其人，左丘明恥之，丘亦恥之。」

The Master said, "Glib speech, an obsequious countenance, and excessive solicitude—Zuoqiu Ming thought this kind of conduct shameless, and so do I. To seek out someone's friendship while harboring ill will towards them—Zuoqiu Ming thought this kind of conduct shameless, and so do I."

5.26 顏淵季路侍。子曰：「盍各言爾志？」子路曰：「願車馬衣裘與朋友共，敝之而無憾。」顏淵曰：「願無伐善，無施勞。」子路曰：「願聞子之志。」子曰：「老者安之，朋友信之，少者懷之。」

Yan Hui and Zilu were in attendance on Confucius when the Master said to them, "Why don't each of you tell me what it is you would most like to do."

Zilu said, "I would like to share my horses and carriages, my clothing and furs, with my friends, and if they damage them, to bear them no ill will."

Yan Hui said, "I would like to refrain from bragging about my own abilities, and to not exaggerate my own accomplishments."

Zilu said, "We would like to hear what it is that you, Master, would most like to do."

The Master said, "I would like to bring peace and contentment to the aged, to share relationships of trust and confidence with my friends, and to love and protect the young."

5.27 子曰：「已矣乎！吾未見能見其過而自訟者也。」

The Master said, "My, my! I have yet to meet anyone who, on seeing their own excesses, is ready to accuse themselves."

5.28 子曰：「十室之邑，必有忠信如丘者焉，不如丘之好學也。」

The Master said, "There are, in a town of ten households, bound to be people who are better than I am in doing their utmost (*zhong* 忠) and in making good on their word (*xin* 信), but there will be no one who can compare with me in the love of learning (*haoxue* 好學)."

6.1 子曰：「雍也可使南面。」

The Master said, "This Zhonggong[88]—he could as ruler take his place facing south."

6.2 仲弓問子桑伯子。子曰：「可也簡。」

仲弓曰：「居敬而行簡，以臨其民，不亦可乎？
居簡而行簡，無乃大簡乎？」子曰：「雍之言然。」

Zhonggong asked about Zisang Bozi. The Master said, "It is his candor that recommends him."

Zhonggong responded, "In overseeing the people, wouldn't acting with candor while maintaining an attitude of respect for them recommend him more? In fact, wouldn't acting with candor while being candid in his attitude amount to an excess of candor?"

The Master replied, "It is as you say."

6.3 哀公問：「弟子孰為好學？」孔子對曰：「有顏回者
好學，不遷怒，不貳過。不幸短命死矣，今也則亡，
未聞好學者也。」

Duke Ai inquired, "Which of your disciples truly loves learning (haoxue 好學)?"

Confucius replied, "There was one Yan Hui who truly loved learning. He did not take his anger out on others; he did not make the same mistake twice. Unfortunately, he was to die young. Nowadays, there is no one—at least, I haven't come across anyone—who truly loves learning."

6.4　子華使於齊，冉子爲其母請粟。子曰：「與之釜。」
　　　請益。曰：「與之庾。」
　　　冉子與之粟五秉。
　　　子曰：「赤之適齊也，乘肥馬，衣輕裘。吾聞之也：君子周急不繼富。」

When Zihua[89] was recommended by Confucius to serve in the state of Qi, Master Ranyou asked to supply Zihua's mother with some grain. The Master said, "Give her a full measure of grain." Master Ranyou asked to give her more. The Master said, "Then give her a double measure." Master Ranyou gave her ten measures of grain.

The Master said, "In traveling to Qi, Zihua was driving choice horses and was wearing fine furs. I have heard it said, 'Exemplary persons help out the needy; they do not make the rich richer.'"

6.5　原思爲之宰，與之粟九百，辭。子曰：「毋以與爾鄰里鄉黨乎。」

When Yuansi served as the Master's household steward, he was given nine hundred measures of grain. Yuansi would not accept so much. "You must not refuse it," the Master said. "It is to give to your family, friends, and neighbors."

6.6　子謂仲弓曰：「犁牛之子騂且角，雖欲勿用，山川其舍諸？」

The Master, remarking on the humble origins of Zhonggong, said, "If the calf of a plow ox has the red coat and the nicely shaped horns of a sacrificial ox, even though some might not want to use it in the sacrifice, do you think the spirits of the mountains and rivers would turn it down?"

6.7 子曰：「回也，其心三月不違仁，其餘則日月至焉而已矣。」

The Master said, "With my disciple, Yan Hui, he could go for several months without departing from authoritative (*ren* 仁) thoughts and feelings (*xin* 心);[90] as for the others, only every once in a long while, might authoritative thoughts and feelings make an appearance."

6.8 季康子問：「仲由可使從政也與？」子曰：「由也果，於從政乎何有？」

曰：「賜也可使從政也與？」曰：「賜也達，於從政乎何有？」

曰：「求也可使從政也與？」曰：「求也藝，於從政乎何有？」

Ji Kangzi[91] inquired, "Do you think Zilu could serve in political office?"

The Master replied, "Zilu is decisive. What problem would he have serving in office?"

Ji Kangzi asked, "What about Zigong?"

The Master replied, "Zigong knows what is going on. What problem would he have serving in office?"

He asked, "What about Ranyou?"

The Master replied, "Ranyou is cultivated and refined. What problem would he have serving in office?"

6.9 季氏使閔子騫為費宰。閔子騫曰：「善為我辭焉！如有復我者，則吾必在汶上矣。」

The Ji house wanted to make Min Ziqian the steward on their Bi estate. Min Ziqian replied, "Please do your best (*shan* 善) to decline their offer for me. If they come to ask for me again, I will already be on the other side of the Wen River in the state of Qi."

6.10 伯牛有疾，子問之，自牖執其手，曰：「亡之，命矣夫！斯人也有斯疾也！斯人也而有斯疾也！」

Boniu was very ill, and the Master went to visit him. Grasping his hand through the portal, he said, "We are losing him,[92] and there is nothing we can do. But that this man should have this illness, and there is nothing we can do![93] That this man should have this illness!"

6.11 子曰：「賢哉回也！一簞食，一瓢飲，在陋巷，人不堪其憂，回也不改其樂。賢哉回也！」

The Master said, "A person of character (*xian* 賢) is this Yan Hui! He has a bamboo bowl of rice to eat, a gourd of water to drink, and a dirty little hovel in which to live. Other people would not be able to endure his hardships, yet for Hui it has no effect on his enjoyment. A person of character is this Yan Hui!"

6.12 冉求曰：「非不說子之道，力不足也。」子曰：「力不足者，中道而廢。今女畫。」

Ranyou said, "It is not that I do not rejoice in the way (*dao* 道) of the Master, but that I do not have the strength to walk it."

The Master said, "Those who do not have the strength for it collapse somewhere along the way. But with you, you have drawn your own line before you start."

6.13 子謂子夏曰：「女爲君子儒！無爲小人儒！」

The Master remarked to Zixia, "You want to become the kind of counselor (*ru* 儒) who is an exemplary person (*junzi* 君子), not the kind that is a petty person."

6.14 子游爲武城宰。子曰：「女得人焉耳乎？」曰：「有澹臺滅明者，行不由徑，非公事，未嘗至於偃之室也。」

Ziyou served in the walled town of Wu as prefect. The Master asked him, "Have you been able to find any good people there?"

Ziyou replied, "There is one person named Tantai Mieming who is not given to byways, and who has never come to my quarters except on public matters."

6.15 子曰：「孟之反不伐，奔而殿，將入門，策其馬，曰：『非敢後也，馬不進也。』」

The Master said, "Meng Zhifan was not given to bragging of his accomplishments. Once on being routed he stayed with the rear guard, and it was only as he was about to enter the gates that he took the whip to his horse. In explanation, he said, 'It was not that I dared to take up the rear; only that my horse could not be roused.'"

6.16 子曰：「不有祝鮀之佞，而有宋朝之美，難乎免於今之世矣。」

The Master said, "If you have only the pleasing countenance (*mei* 美) of Song Chao without the authoritative conduct (*ren* 仁)[94] of Priest Tuo, it is difficult to go unscathed in the world of today."

6.17 子曰：「誰能出不由戶？何莫由斯道也？」

The Master said, "Since none can go out except through a gateway, how is it that none go out from this way (*dao* 道)?"[95]

6.18 子曰：「質勝文則野，文勝質則史。文質彬彬，然後君子。」

The Master said, "When one's basic disposition (*zhi* 質) overwhelms refinement (*wen* 文), the person is boorish; when refinement overwhelms one's basic disposition, the person is an officious scribe. It is only when one's basic disposition and refinement are in appropriate balance that you have the exemplary person (*junzi* 君子)."

6.19　子曰：「人之生也直，罔之生也幸而免。」

The Master said, "The life of a person lies in being true; as for the life of someone who is crooked, they will need good fortune to avoid losing it."

6.20　子曰：「知之者不如好之者，好之者不如樂之者。」

The Master said, "To truly love it is better than just to understand it, and to enjoy it is better than simply to love it."[96]

6.21　子曰：「中人以上，可以語上也；中人以下，不可以語上也。」

The Master said, "You can acquaint those above the common lot with higher things, but you cannot acquaint those below the common lot with them."

6.22　樊遲問知。子曰：「務民之義，敬鬼神而遠之，可謂知矣。」
　　　　問仁。曰：「仁者先難而後獲，可謂仁矣。」

Fan Chi[97] inquired about wisdom (*zhi* 知). The Master replied, "To devote yourself to what is appropriate (*yi* 義) for the people, and to show respect for the ghosts and spirits while keeping them at a distance can be called wisdom."

He then inquired about authoritative conduct (*ren* 仁).

The Master responded, "As for authoritative conduct—to reap one's successes only after having dealt with difficulties can be called being authoritative."

6.23　子曰：「知者樂水，仁者樂山。知者動，仁者靜。知者樂，仁者壽。」

The Master said, "The wise (*zhi* 知) enjoy water; those authoritative in their conduct (*ren* 仁) enjoy mountains. The wise are active; the authoritative are still. The wise find enjoyment; the authoritative are long-enduring."

6.24 子曰：「齊一變，至於魯；魯一變，至於道。」

The Master said, "With one turn the state of Qi could become a Lu; with one turn the state of Lu could attain the way (*dao* 道)."

6.25 子曰：「觚不觚，觚哉！觚哉！」

The Master said, "A *gu* ritual drinking vessel that is not a *gu* ritual drinking vessel—a *gu* indeed! A *gu* indeed!"

6.26 宰我問曰：「仁者，雖告之曰，『井有仁焉。』其從之也？子曰：「何為其然也。君子可逝也，不可陷也；可欺也，不可罔也。」

Zaiwo[98] inquired, "If an authoritative person (*ren* 仁) were informed that there is another authoritative person down in the well, would he go in after him?"

The Master replied, "How could this be? The exemplary person (*junzi* 君子) can be sent to save him, but not to jump in after him; he can be deceived, but not duped."[99]

6.27 子曰：「君子博學於文，約之以禮，亦可以弗畔矣夫！」

The Master said, "Exemplary persons (*junzi* 君子) learn broadly of culture (*wen* 文), discipline this learning through observing ritual propriety (*li* 禮), and moreover, in so doing, can remain on course without straying from it."[100]

6.28 子見南子，子路不說。夫子矢之曰：「予所否者，天厭之！天厭之！」

The Master went to see Nanzi,[101] and Zilu was not at all happy about it. The Master swore an oath to him, "For whatever I have done to offend, may *tian* 天 abandon me! May *tian* abandon me!"

6.29　子曰：「中庸之爲德也，其至矣乎！民鮮久矣。」

The Master said, "The excellence (*de* 德) required to hit the mark in the everyday is of the highest order. That it is rare among the people is an old story."

6.30　子貢曰：「如有博施於民而能濟衆，何如？可謂仁乎？」子曰：「何事於仁！必也聖乎！堯、舜其猶病諸！夫仁者，己欲立而立人，己欲達而達人。能近取譬，可謂仁之方也已。」

Zigong said, "What about the person who is broadly generous with the people and is able to help the multitude—is this what we could call authoritative conduct (*ren* 仁)?"

The Master replied, "Why stop at authoritative conduct? This is certainly a sage (*sheng* 聖). Even a Yao or a Shun would find such a task daunting. Authoritative persons establish others in seeking to establish themselves and promote others in seeking to get there themselves. Correlating one's conduct with those near at hand can be said to be the method of becoming an authoritative person."[102]

7.1 子曰：「述而不作，信而好古，竊比於我老彭。」

The Master said, "Following the proper way,[103] I do not forge new paths;[104] with confidence I cherish the ancients—in these respects I am comparable to our venerable Old Peng."[105]

7.2 子曰：「默而識之，學而不厭，誨人不倦，何有於我哉？」

The Master said, "To quietly persevere in storing up what is learned, to continue studying without respite, to instruct others without growing weary—is this not me?"

7.3 子曰：「德之不脩，學之不講，聞義不能徒，不善不能改，是吾憂也。」

The Master said, "To fail to cultivate excellence (*de* 德), to fail to practice what I learn, on coming to understand what is appropriate (*yi* 義) in the circumstances to fail to attend to it, and to be unable to reform conduct that is not productive—these things I worry over."

7.4 子之燕居，申申如也，夭夭如也。

When relaxing at home, the Master remained dignified, and was good-natured and agreeable.

7.5 子曰：「甚矣吾衰也！久矣吾不復夢見周公！」

The Master said, "My how I have regressed! It has been a long time now since I dreamed again of meeting with the Duke of Zhou."

7.6　子曰：「志於道，據於德，依於仁，游於藝。」

The Master said, "Set your sights on the way (*dao* 道), sustain yourself with excellence (*de* 德), lean upon authoritative conduct (*ren* 仁), and sojourn in the arts."

7.7　子曰：「自行束脩以上，吾未嘗無誨焉。」

The Master said, "I have never failed to instruct students who, using their own resources, could only afford a gift of dried meat."

7.8　子曰：「不憤不啓，不悱不發。舉一隅不以三隅反，則不復也。」

The Master said, "I do not open the way for students who are not driven with eagerness; I do not supply a vocabulary for students who are not trying desperately to find the language for their ideas. If on showing students one corner they do not come back to me with the other three, I will not repeat myself."

7.9　子食於有喪者之側，未嘗飽也。

When dining in the presence of someone in mourning, the Master would not eat his usual portions.

7.10　子於是日哭，則不歌。

On a day when the Master had wailed in grief, he would not sing.

7.11　子謂顏淵曰：「用之則行，舍之則藏，唯我與爾有是夫！」

子路曰：「子行三軍，則誰與？」

　子曰：「暴虎馮河，死而無悔者，吾不與也。必也臨事而懼，好謀而成者也。」

The Master remarked to Yan Hui,

　"'Advance when given office;

　Hold yourself in reserve when removed from office.'

Is it only you and I who can do this?"

　Zilu said, "If you, Master, were given command of the combined armies, who would you want to go along?"

　The Master replied, "The person who would wrestle a tiger bare-handed or march across the Yellow River,[106] and who would go to his death without regret—this person I would not take along. It would have to be someone who would approach any situation with trepidation, and who would be fond of planning with an eye to success."

7.12　子曰：「富而可求也，雖執鞭之士，吾亦爲之。如不可求，從吾所好。」

The Master said, "If wealth were an acceptable goal, even though I would have to serve as a groom holding a whip in the marketplace, I would gladly do it. But if it is not an acceptable goal, I will follow my own devices."

7.13　子之所慎：齊、戰、疾。

There were three matters the Master approached with special care: fasting, warfare, and illness.

7.14　子在齊聞《韶》，三月不知肉味，曰：「不圖爲樂之至於斯也。」

When the Master was in the state of Qi he heard the *shao* music, and for several months he did not know the taste of meat. He said, "I had no idea that music could achieve such heights!"

7.15 冉有曰：「夫子為衛君乎？」子貢曰：「諾；吾將問之。」

入，曰：「伯夷、叔齊何人也？」曰：「古之賢人也。」曰：「怨乎？」曰：「求仁而得仁，又何怨？」

出，曰：「夫子不為也。」

Ranyou said, "Does the Master take the part of the Lord of Wey?" Zigong said, "Indeed, I shall have to ask him about that."

He went in to see the Master, and asked him, "What kind of persons were Bo Yi and Shu Qi?"[107]

The Master replied, "They were persons of character (*xian* 賢) from bygone days."

"Did they harbor any ill will?"

"Seeking to be authoritative in their conduct (*ren* 仁) they achieved their ends—why should they harbor ill will?"

Zigong came out from the interview, and said, "The Master does not take the part of the Lord of Wey."

7.16 子曰：「飯疏食飲水，曲肱而枕之，樂亦在其中矣。不義而富且貴，於我如浮雲。」

The Master said, "To eat coarse food, drink plain water, and pillow oneself on a bent arm—there is pleasure to be found in these things. But wealth and position gained through inappropriate (*buyi* 不義) means—these are to me like floating clouds."

7.17 子曰：「加我數年，五十以學，亦可以無大過矣。」

The Master said, "Let me live a few more years so that I will have had fifty years of study in which after all[108] I will have remained free of any serious oversight."

7.18 子所雅言，《詩》、《書》、執禮，皆雅言也。

Instances on which the Master would insist upon proper pronunciation were in reciting the *Songs* and the *Documents*, and in observing ritual propriety (*li* 禮). On all such occasions, the Master would use proper pronunciation.

7.19 葉公問孔子於子路，子路不對。子曰：「女奚不曰，其為人也，發憤忘食，樂以忘憂，不知老之將至云爾。」

The Duke of She[109] asked Zilu about Confucius, but Zilu did not reply. The Master said, "Why didn't you just say to him: As a person, Confucius is driven by such eagerness to teach and learn that he forgets to eat, he enjoys himself so much that he forgets to worry, and does not even realize that old age is on its way."[110]

7.20 子曰：「我非生而知之者，好古，敏以求之者也。」

The Master said, "I am not the kind of person who has gained knowledge (*zhi* 知) through some natural propensity for it.[111] Rather, loving antiquity, I am earnest in seeking it out."

7.21 子不語：怪、力、亂、神。

The Master had nothing to say about strange happenings, the use of force, disorder, or the spirits.

7.22 子曰：「三人行，必有我師焉，擇其善者而從之，其不善者而改之。」

The Master said, "In strolling in the company of just two other persons, I am bound to find a teacher. Identifying their strengths, I follow them, and identifying their weaknesses, I reform myself accordingly."

7.23　子曰：「天生德於予，桓魋其如予何？」

The Master said, "*Tian* 天 has given life to and nourished excellence (*de* 德) in me—what can Huan Tui do to me!"

7.24　子曰：「二三子以我爲隱乎？吾無隱乎爾。吾無行而不與二三子者，是丘也。」

The Master said, "My young friends, you think that I have something hidden away, but I do not. There is nothing I do that I do not share with you—this is the person I am."

7.25　子以四教：文、行、忠、信。

The Master taught under four categories: culture (*wen* 文), proper conduct (*xing* 行), doing one's utmost (*zhong* 忠), and making good on one's word (*xin* 信).

7.26　子曰：「聖人，吾不得而見之矣；得見君子者，斯可矣。」

　　　子曰：「善人，吾不得而見之矣；得見有恆者，斯可矣。亡而爲有，虛而爲盈，約而爲泰，難乎有恆矣。」

The Master said, "I will never get to meet a sage (*sheng ren* 聖人)—I would be content to meet an exemplary person (*junzi* 君子)."

　　　The Master said, "I will never get to meet a truly efficacious person (*shanren* 善人)[112]—I would be content to meet someone who is constant. It is difficult indeed for persons to be constant in a world where nothing is taken to be something, emptiness is taken to be fullness, and poverty is taken to be comfort."

7.27 子釣而不綱，弋不射宿。

The Master fished with a line, but did not use a net; he used an arrow and line, but did not shoot at roosting birds.[113]

7.28 子曰：「蓋有不知而作之者，我無是也。多聞，擇其善者而從之；多見而識之；知之次也。」

The Master said, "There are probably those who can initiate new paths while still not understanding them, but I am not one of them.[114] I learn much, select out of it what works well, and then follow it. I observe much, and remember it. This is a lower level of wisdom."

7.29 互鄉難與言，童子見，門人惑。子曰：「與其進也，不與其退也，唯何甚？人絜己以進，與其絜也，不保其往也。」

The people of Huxiang are difficult to talk with, so when a youth from there had an audience with Confucius, his disciples were of two minds. The Master responded, "To approve of his interview is not to approve of what he does once he retires. Why be so judgmental? A person purifies himself to gain entry, so we approve of his purity. We are not endorsing where he comes from or where he is going."

7.30 子曰：「仁遠乎哉？我欲仁，斯仁至矣。」

The Master said, "How could authoritative conduct (ren 仁) be at all remote? No sooner do I seek it than it has arrived."

7.31 陳司敗問昭公知禮乎？孔子曰：「知禮。」
孔子退，揖巫馬期而進之，曰：「吾聞君子不黨，君子亦黨乎？君取於吳，為同姓，謂之吳孟子。

君而知禮，孰不知禮？」

　　巫馬期以告。子曰：「丘也幸，苟有過，人必知之。」

The Minister of Justice of the state of Chen inquired, "Did your late Duke Zhao of Lu know how to observe ritual propriety (*li* 禮)?" and Confucius replied, "He knew how to observe ritual propriety." Confucius then withdrew.

The Minister then bowed to Wuma Qi, and summoned him to come closer. "I have heard your Master say that the exemplary person (*junzi* 君子) is not partisan,"[115] and yet isn't Confucius himself acting partisan in this?" he said. "The Lord of Lu took a wife from the state of Wu who had his same surname, 'Ji,' and then called her 'Wu' Mengzi. If he knew how to observe ritual propriety, who doesn't!"

Wuma Qi told the Master of this exchange, and the Master said, "I am so fortunate. If I go astray, others are certain to notice it."[116]

7.32　子與人歌而善，必使反之，而後和之。

When the Master was with others who were singing and they sang well (*shan* 善), he would invariably ask them to sing the piece again before joining in the harmony (*he* 和).

7.33　子曰：「文莫吾猶人也。躬行君子，則吾未之有得。」

The Master said, "In the niceties of culture (*wen* 文), I am perhaps like other people. But as far as personally succeeding in living the life of the exemplary person (*junzi* 君子), I have accomplished little."

7.34　子曰：「若聖與仁，則吾豈敢？抑爲之不厭，誨人不倦，則可謂云爾已矣。」公西華曰：「正唯弟子不能學也。」

The Master said, "How would I dare to consider myself a sage (*sheng* 聖) or an authoritative person (*ren* 仁)? What can be said about me is simply that I continue my studies without respite and instruct others without growing weary."[117]

Gongxi Hua remarked, "It is precisely[118] this commitment that we students are unable to learn."[119]

7.35 子疾病，子路請禱。子曰：「有諸？」子路對曰：「有之。《誄》曰：『禱爾于上下神祇。』」子曰：「丘之禱久矣。」

The Master was gravely ill, and Zilu asked to pray on his behalf. The Master said, "Is this done?"

Zilu replied, "Yes, indeed. There is a eulogy which states: 'We pray for you to the gods of the heavens above and the earth below.'"

The Master said, "Then I have already been praying for myself for a long time now."

7.36 子曰：「奢則不孫，儉則固。與其不孫也，寧固。」

The Master said, "Extravagance leads to immodesty; frugality leads to miserliness. But it is better to be miserly than immodest."

7.37 子曰：「君子坦蕩蕩，小人長戚戚。」

The Master said, "The exemplary person (*junzi* 君子) is calm and unperturbed; the petty person is always agitated and anxious."

7.38 子溫而厲，威而不猛，恭而安。

The Master was always gracious yet serious, commanding yet not severe, deferential yet at ease.

8.1 子曰：「泰伯，其可謂至德也已矣。三以天下讓，民無得而稱焉。」

The Master said, "As for Taibo,[120] he can certainly be said to be a person of unsurpassed excellence (*de* 德). He repeatedly renounced his claim to the empire, and the people could not find words adequate to praise him."

8.2 子曰：「恭而無禮則勞，慎而無禮則葸，勇而無禮則亂，直而無禮則絞。君子篤於親，則民興於仁；故舊不遺，則民不偷。」

The Master said, "Deference unmediated by observing ritual propriety (*li* 禮) is lethargy; caution unmediated by observing ritual propriety is timidity; boldness unmediated by observing ritual propriety is rowdiness; candor unmediated by observing ritual propriety is rudeness. Where exemplary persons (*junzi* 君子) are earnestly committed to their parents, the people will aspire to authoritative conduct (*ren* 仁); where they do not neglect their old friends, the people will not be indifferent to each other."

8.3 曾子有疾，召門弟子曰：「啓予足！啓予手！《詩》云：『戰戰兢兢，如臨深淵，如履薄冰。』而今而後吾知免夫！小子！」

Master Zeng[121] was ill, and summoned his students to him, saying, "Look at my feet! Look at my hands! The *Book of Songs* says:

> Fearful! Trembling!
> As if peering over a deep abyss,
> As if walking across thin ice.[122]

It is only from this moment hence that I can be sure I have avoided desecration of my body, my young friends."

8.4 曾子有疾，孟敬子問之。曾子言曰：「鳥之將死，其鳴也哀；人之將死，其言也善。君子所貴乎道者三：動容貌，斯遠暴慢矣；正顏色，斯近信矣；出辭氣，斯遠鄙倍矣。籩豆之事，則有司存。」

Master Zeng was ill, and when Meng Jingzi questioned him, Master Zeng said to him, "Baleful is the cry of a dying bird; felicitous (*shan* 善) are the words of a dying person. There are three things that exemplary persons (*junzi* 君子) consider of utmost importance in making their way (*dao* 道): by maintaining a dignified demeanor, they keep violent and rancorous conduct at a distance; by maintaining a proper countenance, they keep trust and confidence near at hand; by taking care in choice of language and mode of expression, they keep vulgarity and impropriety at a distance. As for the details in the arrangement of ritual vessels, there are minor officers to take care of such things."

8.5 曾子曰：「以能問於不能，以多問於寡；有若無，實若虛，犯而不校。昔者吾友嘗從事於斯矣。」

Master Zeng said, "Able himself yet asking those who are not so, informed himself yet asking those who are less so, having much to offer himself yet seeming to have nothing, substantial himself yet seeming to be empty, transgressed against himself yet paying it no notice—in the old days I had a friend[123] who proceeded in just such a way."

8.6　曾子曰：「可以託六尺之孤，可以寄百里之命，臨大節而不可奪也。君子人與？君子人也。」

Master Zeng said, "A person to whom you can entrust an orphaned youth or commission the command of a sovereign state, who in approaching great matters of life and death remains unperturbed—is this an exemplary person (*junzi* 君子)? Such is an exemplary person indeed!"

8.7　曾子曰：「士不可以不弘毅，任重而道遠。仁以爲己任，不亦重乎？死而後已，不亦遠乎？」

Master Zeng said, "Scholar-apprentices (*shi* 士) cannot but be strong and resolved, for they bear a heavy charge and their way (*dao* 道) is long. Where they take authoritative conduct (*ren* 仁) as their charge, is it not a heavy one? And where their way ends only in death, is it not indeed long?"

8.8　子曰：「興於《詩》，立於禮，成於樂。」

The Master said, "I find inspiration by intoning the songs, I learn where to stand from observing ritual propriety (*li* 禮), and I find fulfillment in playing music."[124]

8.9　子曰：「民可使由之，不可使知之。」

The Master said, "The common people can be induced to travel along the way, but they cannot be induced to realize (*zhi* 知) it."[125]

8.10　子曰：「好勇疾貧，亂也。人而不仁，疾之已甚，亂也。」

The Master said, "A person fond of boldness who despises poverty will be a source of trouble; a person lacking in character who is overly despised by others will be a source of trouble."

8.11 子曰：「如有周公之才之美，使驕且吝，其餘不足觀也已。」

The Master said, "If a person with talents more admirable than those of the Duke of Zhou is arrogant and niggardly, the rest is not worthy of notice."[126]

8.12 子曰：「三年學，不至於穀，不易得也。」

The Master said, "It is not easy to find students who will study for three years without their thoughts turning to an official salary."

8.13 子曰：「篤信好學，守死善道。危邦不入，亂邦不居，天下有道則見，無道則隱。邦有道，貧且賤焉，恥也；邦無道，富且貴焉，恥也。」

The Master said, "Make an earnest commitment to the love of learning (*haoxue* 好學) and be steadfast to the death in service to the efficacious way (*shandao* 善道). Do not enter a state in crisis, and do not tarry in one that is in revolt. Be known when the way prevails in the world, but remain hidden away when it does not. It is a disgrace to remain poor and without rank when the way prevails in the state; it is a disgrace to be wealthy and of noble rank when it does not."

8.14 子曰：「不在其位，不謀其政。」

The Master said, "Do not plan the policies of an office you do not hold."[127]

8.15 子曰：「師摯之始，《關雎》之亂，洋洋乎盈耳哉！」

123

The Master said, "In the Grand Musician Zhi's overture and in his crescendo to 'The Cry of the Osprey,'[128] what a flood of music fills the ear!"

8.16 子曰：「狂而不直，侗而不愿，悾悾而不信，吾不知之矣。」

The Master said, "I cannot understand people who are impetuous yet lacking in discipline, who are slow yet lacking in caution, and who are simple yet lacking in honesty."[129]

8.17 子曰：「學如不及，猶恐失之。」

The Master said, "Study as though you cannot catch up to it, and as though you fear you are going to lose it."[130]

8.18 子曰：「巍巍乎，舜、禹之有天下也而不與焉！」

The Master said, "How majestic they were—Yao and Shun reigned over the world but did not rule it."

8.19 子曰：「大哉！堯之為君也！巍巍乎！唯天為大，唯堯則之。蕩蕩乎！民無能名焉。巍巍乎！其有成功也，煥乎！其有文章也！」

The Master said, "How great indeed was Yao as ruler! How majestic! Only *tian* 天 is truly great, and only Yao took it as his model. How expansive was he—the people could not find the words adequate to praise him. How majestic was he in his accomplishments, and how brilliant was he in his cultural achievements."

8.20 舜有臣五人而天下治。武王曰：「予有亂臣十人。」孔子曰：「才難，不其然乎？唐、虞之際，於斯為盛。有婦人焉，九人而已。三分天下有其二，以服事殷。周之德，其可謂至德也已矣。」

Shun had only five ministers and the world was properly governed. King Wu also said, "I have ten ministers who bring proper order to the world."[131] Confucius said, "As the saying has it: 'Human talent is hard to come by.' Isn't it indeed the case. And it was at the transition from Yao's Tang dynasty to Shun's Yu dynasty that talented ministers were in greatest abundance. In King Wu's case with a woman, perhaps his wife, among them, there were really only nine ministers. The Zhou, with two thirds of the world in its possession, continued to submit to and serve the House of Yin. The excellence (de 德) of Zhou can be said to be the highest excellence of all."

8.21 子曰：「禹，吾無間然矣。菲飲食而致孝乎鬼神，惡衣服而致美乎黻冕，卑宮室而盡力乎溝洫。禹，吾無間然矣。」

The Master said, "As for the sage-king Yu, I can find no fault with him at all. He was simple in his food and drink yet was generous in his devotion to the gods and the spirits of his ancestors; he wore coarse clothing yet was lavish in his ceremonial robes and cap; he lived in the humblest circumstances yet gave all of his strength to the construction of drain canals and irrigation ditches. As for Yu, I can find no fault with him at all."

9.1　子罕言利與命與仁。

The Master only rarely spoke about personal advantage (*li* 利), the propensity of circumstances (*ming* 命), or authoritative conduct (*ren* 仁).[132]

9.2　達巷黨人曰：「大哉孔子！博學而無所成名。」子聞之，謂門弟子曰：「吾何執？執御乎？執射乎？吾執御矣。」

A villager[133] from Daxiang said, "How grand is Confucius! He is broad in his learning, and yet he is not renowned in any particular area." The Master on hearing of this, said to his disciples, "What should I specialize in? Perhaps charioteering? Or maybe archery? No, I think I'll take charioteering."

9.3　子曰：「麻冕，禮也；今也純，儉，吾從眾。拜下，禮也；今拜乎上，泰也。雖違眾，吾從下。」

The Master said, "The use of a hemp cap is prescribed in the observance of ritual propriety (*li* 禮). Nowadays, that a silk cap is used instead is a matter of frugality. I would follow accepted practice on this. A subject kowtowing on entering the hall is prescribed in the observance of ritual propriety (*li* 禮). Nowadays that one kowtows only after ascending the hall is a matter of hubris. Although it goes contrary to accepted practice, I still kowtow on entering the hall."

9.4 子絕四：毋意，毋必，毋固，毋我。

There were four things the Master abstained from entirely: he did not speculate, he did not claim or demand certainty, he was not inflexible, and he was not self-absorbed.[134]

9.5 子畏於匡，曰：「文王既沒，文不在茲乎？天之將喪斯文也，後死者不得與於斯文也；天之未喪斯文也，匡人其如予何？」

When the Master was surrounded in Kuang, he said, "With King Wen (文) long dead, does not our cultural heritage (wen 文) reside here in us?[135] If tian 天 were going to destroy this legacy, we latecomers would not have had access to it. If tian is not going to destroy this culture, what can the people of Kuang do to me!"[136]

9.6 大宰問於子貢曰：「夫子聖者與？何其多能也？」子貢曰：「固天縱之將聖，又多能也。」

子聞之，曰：「大宰知我乎！吾少也賤，故多能鄙事。君子多乎哉？不多也。」

The Grand Minister asked Zigong, "Your Master is a sage, is he not? Then how is it he is skilled in so many things?"

Zigong replied, "Tian 天 definitely set him on course to become a sage (sheng 聖), but he also has many skills."

On hearing of this, the Master said, "The Grand Minister certainly knows me! We were poor when I was young, so I learned many a menial skill. Does an exemplary person (junzi 君子) have these skills? I think not."

9.7 牢曰：「子云：『吾不試，故藝。』」

Lao said, "The Master says of himself, 'It is because I have never been appointed to office that I have learned these many arts.'"

9.8 子曰：「吾有知乎哉？無知也。有鄙夫問於我，空空如也。我叩其兩端而竭焉。」

The Master said, "Do I possess wisdom (*zhi* 知)? No, I do not. But if a simple peasant puts a question to me, and I come up empty, I attack the question from both ends until I have gotten to the bottom of it."

9.9 子曰：「鳳鳥不至，河不出圖，吾已矣乎！」

The Master said, "The auspicious phoenix does not appear; the Yellow River does not yield up its magical chart. All is lost with me!"

9.10 子見齊衰者、冕衣裳者與瞽者，見之，雖少，必作；過之，必趨。

On encountering those attired in mourning dress, in ceremonial cap and robes, or those who are blind, even where such people might be his juniors, the Master would, on first catching sight of them, invariably rise to his feet, and on passing them, would invariably hasten his step.

9.11 顏淵喟然歎曰：「仰之彌高，鑽之彌堅。瞻之在前，忽焉在後。夫子循循然善誘人，博我以文，約我以禮，欲罷不能。既竭吾才，如有所立卓爾。雖欲從之，末由也已。」

Yan Hui, with a deep sigh, said, "The more I look up at it, the higher it soars; the more I penetrate into it, the harder it becomes. I am looking at it in front of me, and suddenly it is behind me. The Master is good at drawing me forward a step at a time; he broadens me with culture (*wen* 文) and disciplines my behavior through the observance of ritual propriety (*li* 禮). Even if I wanted to quit, I could not. And when I have exhausted my abilities, it is as though something rises up right in front of me, and even though I want to follow it, there is no road to take."

9.12 子疾病，子路使門人爲臣。病間，曰：「久矣哉，由之行詐也！無臣而爲有臣。吾誰欺？欺天乎！且予與其死於臣之手也，無寧死於二三子之手乎！且予縱不得大葬，予死於道路乎！」

The Master was gravely ill, and so Zilu sent some of his disciples to serve as retainers. On improving slightly, Confucius said, "It has been a long time indeed that Zilu has been up to such pretenses. If I have no retainers and yet pretend to have them, who am I going to fool? Am I going to fool *tian* 天? Further, wouldn't I rather die in the arms of my disciples than in the arms of some retainers? Even though I do not get a grand state funeral, I am hardly dying by the roadside."

9.13 子貢曰：「有美玉於斯，韞匵而藏諸？求善賈而沽諸？」子曰：「沽之哉！沽之哉！我待賈者也。」

Zigong said, "We have an exquisite piece of jade here— should we box it up and put it away for safekeeping, or should we try to get a good price and sell it off?"

The Master replied, "Sell it! By all means, sell it! I am just waiting for the right price!"

9.14 子欲居九夷。或曰：「陋。如之何？」子曰：「君子居之，何陋之有？」

The Master wanted to go and live amongst the nine clans of the Eastern Yi Barbarians. Someone said to him, "What would you do about their crudeness?"

The Master replied, "Were an exemplary person (*junzi* 君子) to live among them, what crudeness could there be?"

9.15 子曰：「吾自衛反魯，然後樂正，《雅》、《頌》各得其所。」

The Master said, "It was only after my return to Lu from Wey that I revised the *Book of Music*, and put the 'Songs of the Kingdom' and the 'Ceremonial Hymns' in proper order."

9.16 子曰：「出則事公卿，入則事父兄，喪事不敢不勉，不爲酒困，何有於我哉？」

The Master said, "To serve the Duke and his ministers at court, and to serve my elders at home, in funerary matters not to presume to give less than my best efforts, and not to be overcome by drink—how could such things give me any trouble at all?"[137]

9.17 子在川上，曰：「逝者如斯夫！不舍晝夜。」

The Master was standing on the riverbank, and observed, "Isn't life's passing just like this, never ceasing day or night!"

9.18 子曰：「吾未見好德如好色者也。」

The Master said, "I have yet to meet the person who is fonder of excellence (*de* 德) than of physical beauty."[138]

9.19 子曰：「譬如爲山，未成一簣，止，吾止也。譬如平地，雖覆一簣，進，吾往也。」

The Master said, "As in piling up earth to erect a mountain, if, only one basketful short of completion, I stop, I have stopped. As in filling a ditch to level the ground, if, having dumped in only one basketful, I continue, I am progressing."[139]

9.20 子曰：「語之而不惰者，其回也與！」

The Master said, "If there was anyone who listened with full attention to what I had to say, it was surely Yan Hui."

9.21　子謂顏淵，曰：「惜乎！吾見其進也，吾未見其止也。」

The Master said about Yan Hui, "Such a pity! I only saw his progress; I never saw where he got to."

9.22　子曰：「苗而不秀者有矣夫！秀而不實者有矣夫！」

The Master said, "There are indeed seedlings that do not flower, and there are flowers that do not fruit."

9.23　子曰：「後生可畏，焉知來者之不如今也？四十、五十而無聞焉，斯亦不足畏也已。」

The Master said, "The young should be held in high esteem. After all, how do we know that those yet to come will not surpass our contemporaries? It is only when one reaches forty or fifty years of age and yet has done nothing of note that we should withhold our esteem."

9.24　子曰：「法語之言，能無從乎？改之為貴。巽與之言，能無說乎？繹之為貴。說而不繹，從而不改，吾末如之何也已矣。」

The Master said, "How could one but comply with what model sayings have to say? But the real value lies in reforming one's ways. How could one but find pleasure in polite language? But the real value lies in drawing out its meaning. What can possibly be done with people who find pleasure in polite language but do not draw out its meaning, or who comply with model sayings but do not reform their ways."

9.25　子曰：「主忠信，毋友不如己者，過則勿憚改。」

The Master said, "Take doing your utmost (*zhong* 忠) and making good on your word (*xin* 信) as your mainstay. Do not befriend anyone who is not as good as you are. And

where you have gone astray, do not hesitate to mend your
ways."

9.26 子曰：「三軍可奪帥也，匹夫不可奪志也。」

The Master said, "The Combined Armies can be deprived of
their commander, but common peasants cannot be deprived
of their purposes."

9.27 子曰：「衣敝縕袍，與衣孤貉者立，而不恥者，其由
也與？『不忮不求，何用不臧？』」子路終身誦之。子
曰：「是道也，何足以臧？」

The Master said, "If there is anyone who would feel no
shame in wearing a shabby old gown while standing next to
someone wearing fox and badger, it would have to be Zilu!

'Not jealous, not greedy,
How could he but be good?' "[140]

Zilu on hearing this praise of himself, kept repeating these
lines over and over again. The Master said to him, "How can
this remark deserve to be treasured so?"

9.28 子曰：「歲寒，然後知松柏之後彫也。」

The Master said, "It is only when the cold sets in that we realize the pine and the cypress are the last to fade."

9.29 子曰：「知者不惑，仁者不憂，勇者不懼。」

The Master said, "The wise (*zhi* 知) are not in a quandary;
the authoritative (*ren* 仁) are not anxious; the courageous
are not timid."[141]

9.30 子曰：「可與共學，未可與適道；可與適道，未可與
立；可與立，未可與權。」

The Master said, "You can study with some, and yet not necessarily walk the same path (*dao* 道); you can walk the same path as some, and yet not necessarily take your stand with them; you can take your stand with them, and yet not necessarily weigh things up in the same way."

9.31 「唐棣之華，偏其反而。豈不爾思？室是遠而。」子曰：「未之思也，未何遠之有？」

"The flowers of the wild cherry tree
Flutter and wave.
How could I not be thinking of you?
It is just that your home is so very far away."

The Master said, "He wasn't really thinking of her, or how could she be far away?"[142]

10.1　孔子於鄉黨，恂恂如也，似不能言者。其在宗廟朝
廷，便便言，唯謹爾。

In Confucius' home village, he was most deferential, as
though at a loss for words, and yet in the ancestral temple
and at court, he spoke articulately, though with deliberation.

10.2　朝，與下大夫言，侃侃如也；與上大夫言，誾誾如
也。君在，踧踖如也，與與如也。

At court, when speaking with lower officials, he was congenial, and when speaking with higher officials, straightforward
yet respectful. In the presence of his lord, he was reverent
though composed.

10.3　君召使擯，色勃如也，足躩如也。揖所與立，左右
手，衣前後，襜如也。趨進，翼如也。賓退，必復命
曰：「賓不顧矣。」

When summoned by his lord to receive a guest to the court,
his countenance would change visibly and his legs would
bend. He would salute the others standing in attendance, ges-
turing his clasped hands to the right and to the left, and with
his flowing robes swaying front and back with his move-
ments, he would glide forward briskly. When the guest retired, he would be certain to report to his lord, "Our guest no
longer looks back."

10.4　入公門，鞠躬如也，如不容。

> 立不中門，行不履閾。
>
> 過位，色勃如也，足躩如也，其言似不足者。
>
> 攝齊升堂，鞠躬如也，屏氣似不息者。
>
> 出，降一等，逞顏色，怡怡如也。
>
> 沒階，趨進，翼如也。
>
> 復其位，踧踖如也。

On passing through the entrance way to the duke's court, he would bow forward from the waist, as though the gateway were not high enough. While in attendance, he would not stand in the middle of the entranceway; on passing through, he would not step on the raised threshold. On passing by the empty throne, his countenance would change visibly, his legs would bend, and in his speech he would seem to be breathless. He would lift the hem of his skirts in ascending the hall, bow forward from the waist, and hold in his breath as though ceasing to breathe. On leaving and descending the first steps, he would relax his expression and regain his composure. He would glide briskly from the bottom of the steps, and returning to his place, would resume a reverent posture.

10.5　執圭，鞠躬如也，如不勝。上如揖，下如授。勃如戰色，足蹜蹜如有循。

> 享禮，有容色。
>
> 私覿，愉愉如也。

On grasping the jade tablet as the lord's envoy, he would bow forward from the waist as though it were too heavy to lift. He would hold the top of it as though saluting and the bottom of it as though offering it to someone. His countenance would change visibly as though going off to battle, and his steps were short and measured as though following a line. On the

135

occasion of presenting his credentials, his demeanor was dignified, and in private audience, he was affable.

10.6　君子不以紺緅飾，紅紫不以爲褻服。

　　　　當暑，袗絺綌，必表而出之。

　　　　緇衣，羔裘；素衣，麑裘；黃衣，狐裘。

　　　　褻裘長，短右袂。

　　　　必有寢衣，長一身有半。

　　　　狐貉之厚以居。

　　　　去喪，無所不佩。

　　　　非帷裳，必殺之。羔裘玄冠，不以弔。

　　　　吉月，必朝服而朝。

Persons of nobility[143] do not use reddish black or dark brown for the embroidered borders of their robes,[144] nor do they use red or purple in casual clothing. In the heat of summer, they wear an unlined garment made of fine or coarse hemp, but would invariably wear it over an undergarment to set it off. With black upper garments[145] they wear lambskin;[146] with undyed silk upper garments, fawn fur; with yellow-brown upper garments, fox fur. Casual fur robes were long overall, but the right sleeve was somewhat short. They are certain to have a nightcoat half the body in length.[147] They use the thick fur of the fox and badger for sitting rugs. Outside of the mourning period, they wear whatever girdle ornaments they please. Apart from pleated ceremonial skirts, they would invariably have their skirts tailored. A lambskin coat and a black cap could not be worn on funeral occasions. On New Year's Day, they would invariably go to court in full court attire.

10.7　齊，必有明衣，布。

　　　　齊必變食，居必遷坐。

In periods of purification, Confucius would invariably wear a spirit coat made of plain cloth. In such periods, he would invariably simplify his diet, and at home would change his resting-place.[148]

10.8 食不厭精，膾不厭細。食饐而餲，魚餒而肉敗，不食。色惡，不食。臭惡，不食。失飪，不食。不時，不食。割不正，不食。不得其醬，不食。肉雖多，不使勝食氣。唯酒無量，不及亂。沽酒市脯，不食。不撤薑食，不多食。

In his staple cereals, he did not object to them being polished, and in his dishes, he did not object to the food being cut up fine. When the cereal was damp and mildewed, and tasted unusual, and when the fish and meat had spoiled and gone bad, he would not eat them. If the food was off in color or smelled strange, he would not eat it. When the food was not properly cooked or the dining hour had not arrived, he would not eat. He would not eat food that was improperly prepared, or that was lacking the appropriate condiments and sauces. Even when meat was abundant, he would not eat it in disproportionate amount to the staple foods. Only in his wine[149] did he not limit himself, although he never got drunk. He would not eat store-bought wine or dried meats from the marketplace. When he had eaten his fill, he would not eat more, even if the ginger had not yet been cleared.

10.9 祭於公，不宿肉。祭肉不出三日。出三日，不食之矣。

After participating in public sacrifices, he would not keep the sacrificial meat for a second day. With other sacrificial meats, he would not keep it for more than three days, and if the three days had lapsed, he would not eat it.

10.10 食不語，寢不言。

While eating he would not converse, and having retired for the night he would not talk.

10.11 雖疏食菜羹，必祭，必齊如也。

Even with a simple meal of course grains and vegetable gruel, he invariably made an offering, and did so with solemnity.

10.12 席不正，不坐。

He would not sit unless the mats were properly placed in accord with custom.[150]

10.13 鄉人飲酒，杖者出，斯出矣。

When drinking wine at a village function, he would wait for those with canes to depart before taking his leave.[151]

10.14 鄉人儺，朝服而立於阼階。

When his fellow villagers were performing the *nuo* ritual to exorcise hungry ghosts, dressing in his court robes he would stand in attendance as host at the eastern stair.

10.15 問人於他邦，再拜而送之。

In asking after the well-being of a friend in another state,[152] he would bow twice before sending the messenger on his way.

10.16 康子饋藥，拜而受之。曰：「丘未達，不敢嘗。」

Ji Kangzi[153] sent a present of medicine, and Confucius, bowing to him, accepted it. He said, however, "Not knowing its effects, I dare not take it."

10.17 廄焚。子退朝，曰：「傷人乎？」不問馬。

When his stables caught fire, the Master hurried back from court and asked, "Was anyone hurt?" He did not inquire after the horses.

10.18 君賜食，必正席，先嘗之。君賜腥，必熟而薦之。君賜生，必畜之。侍食於君，君祭，先飯。

When his lord made a gift of prepared food, he would invariably place the mats properly according to custom and be the first to taste it. When his lord made a gift of raw meat, he would invariably cook it and make a display of it to his ancestors. When his lord made a gift of livestock, he would rear it. When waiting to dine with his lord and the lord was conducting the sacrifice, he would begin from the rice.

10.19 疾，君視之，東首，加朝服，拖紳。

When ill, and his lord came to see him, he would recline with his head facing east, and would have his court dress draped over him with his sash drawn.[154]

10.20 君命召，不俟駕行矣。

When his lord issued him a summons, he would set off on foot without waiting for the horses to be yoked to his carriage.[155]

10.21 入太廟，每事問。

The Master on entering the Grand Ancestral Hall asked questions about everything.[156]

10.22 朋友死，無所歸，曰：「於我殯。」

On the death of a friend, when there were no relatives to make the arrangements, the Master would say, "Let me take responsibility for laying him out."

10.23 朋友之饋，雖車馬，非祭肉，不拜。

The Master would not kowtow on receiving gifts from friends, even those as lavish as a horse and carriage, with the sole exception of sacrificial meat.

10.24 寢不尸，居不客。

In sleeping, he did not assume the posture of a corpse, and when at home alone, he did not kneel in a formal posture as though entertaining guests.[157]

10.25 見齊衰者，雖狎，必變。見冕者與瞽者，雖褻，必以貌。
　　凶服者式之。式負版者。有盛饌，必變色而作。迅雷風烈必變。

On meeting someone in mourning dress, even those on intimate terms, he would invariably take on a solemn appearance. On meeting someone wearing a ceremonial cap or someone who is blind, even though they were frequent acquaintances, he would invariably pay his respects.

On encountering a person in mourner's attire,[158] he would lean forward on the stanchion of his carriage. He would do the same on encountering an official with state census records on his back.

On being presented with a sumptuous feast, he would invariably take on a solemn appearance and rise to his feet.

On experiencing a sudden clap of thunder or fierce winds, he would invariably take on a solemn appearance.

10.26 升車，必正立，執綏。
　　車中，不內顧，不疾言，不親指。

To mount his carriage, he would invariably stand upright and grasp the cord.

While riding in the carriage, he would not turn his head to look back, speak hastily, or point at things.[159]

10.27   色斯舉矣，翔而後集。曰：「山梁雌雉，時哉時哉！」
子路共之，三嗅而作。

Sensing their approach, a bird took flight, and soared about before alighting. The Master said, "This hen-pheasant on the mountain bridge—how timely! how timely!" Zilu clasped his hands and saluted the bird which, flapping its wings three times, took to the air again.[160]

11.1　子曰：「先進於禮樂，野人也；後進於禮樂，君子
也。如用之，則吾從先進。」

The Master said, "The first to come to observing ritual propriety (*li* 禮) and to playing music (*yue* 樂) were the simple folk; those who came later were the nobility (*junzi* 君子).[161] In putting ritual and music to use, I would follow those who came to them first."[162]

11.2　子曰：「從我於陳、蔡者，皆不及門也。」

The Master said, "None of those who were with me during my difficulties in the states of Chen and Cai are with me now."[163]

11.3　德行：顏淵、閔子騫、冉伯牛、仲弓。言語：宰我、
子貢。政事：冉有、季路。文學：子游、子夏。

Those who excelled in their conduct: Yan Hui, Min Ziqian, Ran Boniu, and Zhonggong; in eloquence, Zaiwo and Zigong; in statesmanship, Ranyou and Zilu; in the study of culture, Ziyou and Zixia.[164]

11.4　子曰：「回也非助我者也，於吾言無所不說。」

The Master said, "Yan Hui is of no help to me. There is nothing that I say that he doesn't like."

11.5　子曰：「孝哉閔子騫！人不間於其父母、昆弟之言。」

The Master said, "Now Min Ziqian is a model of filial responsibility (*xiao* 孝). No one doubts the good things that his parents and his siblings have to say about him."

11.6 南容三復白圭，孔子以其兄之子妻之。

Nanrong frequently recited the *Book of Songs* verse on the White Jade Tablet.[165] Confucius gave him his elder brother's daughter to wed.[166]

11.7 季康子問弟子孰為好學。孔子對曰：「有顏回者好學，不幸短命死矣，今也則亡。」

Ji Kangzi inquired, "Which of your disciples truly loves learning (*haoxue* 好學)?"

Confucius replied, "There was one Yan Hui who truly loved learning. Unfortunately, he was to die young. Nowadays, there is no one."[167]

11.8 顏淵死，顏路請子之車以為之椁。子曰：「才不才，亦各言其子也。鯉也死，有棺而無椁。吾不徒行以為之椁。以吾從大夫之後，不可徒行也。」

When Yan Hui died, his father Yan Lu[168] asked Confucius for his carriage to provide an outer coffin for his son. Confucius replied, "Talented or not, a son is a son. My son, Boyu, also died,[169] and I provided him with an inner coffin, but no outer coffin. I could not go on foot in order to give him one—in my capacity as a retired official, it is not appropriate for me to travel on foot."[170]

11.9 顏淵死。子曰：「噫！天喪予！天喪予！」

When Yan Hui died, the Master cried, "Oh my! *Tian* 天 is the ruin of me! *Tian* is the ruin of me!"

11.10 顏淵死，子哭之慟。從者曰：「子慟矣！」曰：「有慟乎？非夫人之為慟而誰為？」

When Yan Hui died, the Master grieved for him with sheer abandon. His followers cautioned, "Sir, you grieve with such abandon." The Master replied, "I grieve with abandon? If I don't grieve with abandon for him, then for whom?"[171]

11.11 顏淵死，門人欲厚葬之。子曰：「不可。」

門人厚葬之。子曰：「回也視予猶父也，予不得視猶子也。非我也，夫二三子也。」

When Yan Hui died and his fellow students wanted to have a lavish burial for him, the Master said it would not be proper, and yet they did so anyway. The Master responded, "Yan Hui! You looked on me as a father, and yet I have not been able to treat you as a son. This was none of my doing—it was your fellow students who did it."

11.12 季路問事鬼神。子曰：「未能事人，焉能事鬼？」

曰：「敢問死？」曰：「未知生，焉知死？」

Zilu asked how to serve the spirits and the gods. The Master replied, "Not yet being able to serve other people, how would you be able to serve the spirits?" Zilu said, "May I ask about death?" The Master replied, "Not yet understanding life, how could you understand death?" [172]

11.13 閔子侍側，誾誾如也；子路，行行如也；冉有、子貢，侃侃如也。子樂。「若由也，不得其死然。」

Min Ziqian in attendance at the Master's side was straightforward yet respectful,[173] Zilu[174] was intent, and Ranyou and Zigong were congenial.[175] Although the Master was pleased, he said, "This Zilu—he will not meet a natural death."

11.14 魯人為長府。閔子騫曰：「仍舊貫，如之何？何必改作？」子曰：「夫人不言，言必有中。」

The leaders[176] of Lu were constructing the Long Treasury.
Min Ziqian said, "What about just restoring it to its old like-
ness? Why rebuild it?"

The Master remarked, "This man either says nothing or
is right on the mark in what he says."

11.15 子曰：「由之瑟奚為於丘之門？」門人不敬子路。子曰：「由也升堂矣，未入於室也。」

The Master said, "What is Zilu's zither doing inside my
gate?" And his other disciples ceased to treat Zilu with respect. The Master remarked, "As for Zilu, he has ascended
the hall, but he has not yet entered the inner chamber!"[177]

11.16 子貢問：「師與商也孰賢？」子曰：「師也過，商也不及。」

曰：「然則師愈與？」子曰：「過猶不及。」

Zigong inquired, "Who is of superior character (*xian* 賢),
Zizhang or Zixia?"[178] The Master replied, "Zizhang oversteps
the mark, and Zixia falls short of it."

"Does this make Zizhang better?" asked Zigong.

"One is as bad as the other," replied Confucius.

11.17 季氏富於周公，而求也為之聚斂而附益之。子曰：「非吾徒也。小子鳴鼓而攻之，可也。」

Even though the House of Ji is wealthier than the Duke of
Zhou,[179] Ranyou in gathering revenues for them added even
more to their coffers.[180] The Master said, "This man is no disciple of mine. You students have my permission to sound the
charge and attack him."[181]

11.18 柴也愚，參也魯，師也辟，由也喭。

Zigao is stupid; Zeng is thick; Zhuansun is biased; Zilu is rough and rude.

11.19 子曰：「回也其庶乎，屢空。賜不受命，而貨殖焉，億則屢中。」

The Master said, "Yan Hui is just about there, yet he has forever been in dire straits. Zigong is not content with his lot,[182] and has taken to hoarding and speculating. But in his ventures he is regularly on the mark."[183]

11.20 子張問善人之道。子曰：「不踐迹，亦不入於室。」

Zizhang asked about the way (*dao* 道) of the truly efficacious person (*shanren* 善人).[184]

The Master said, "Not following in the steps of others, one does not gain entrance to the inner chamber."

11.21 子曰：「論篤是與，君子者乎？色莊者乎？」

The Master said, "Allowing that a person is earnest in his words, the question is: is he an exemplary person (*junzi* 君子), or is he just pretending to be serious?"

11.22 子路問：「聞斯行諸？」子曰：「有父兄在，如之何其聞斯行之？」

冉有問：「聞斯行諸？」子曰：「聞斯行之。」

公西華曰：「由也問『聞斯行諸』，子曰：『有父兄在』；求也問『聞斯行諸？』子曰：『聞斯行之』。赤也惑，敢問。」子曰：「求也退，故進之；由也兼人，故退之。」

Zilu inquired, "On learning something, should one act upon it?" The Master said, "While your father and elder brothers are still alive, how could you, on learning something, act upon it?" Then Ranyou asked the same question. The Master replied, "On learning something, act upon it."

Gongxi Hua said, "When Zilu asked the question, you observed that his father and elder brothers are still alive, but when Ranyou asked the same question, you told him to act on what he learns. I am confused—could you explain this to me?"

The Master replied, "Ranyou is diffident, and so I urged him on. But Zilu has the energy of two, and so I sought to rein him in."

11.23　子畏於匡，顏淵後。子曰：「吾以女爲死矣。」曰：「子在，回何敢死？」

When the Master was surrounded in Kuang,[185] Yan Hui had fallen behind. The Master said to him, "I had given you up for dead." "While you are still living," Yan Hui replied, "how could I dare to die?"

11.24　季子然問：「仲由、冉求可謂大臣與？」子曰：「吾以子爲異之問，曾由與求之問。所謂大臣者，以道事君，不可則止。今由與求也，可謂具臣矣。」

　　曰：「然則從之者與？」子曰：「弑父與君，亦不從也。」

Ji Ziran inquired, "Can Zhongyu and Ranyou be called great ministers?" The Master replied, "I expected you to ask about other people, but then you ask about Zhongyu and Ranyou. What are called great ministers are those who serve their lord with the way (*dao* 道), and when they cannot, resign. Now as for Zhongyu and Ranyou, they can be called 'place-holder' ministers."

"Such being the case, can they be counted on to follow orders?" Ji Ziran asked.

The Master replied, "Even they would stop short of patricide or regicide."[186]

11.25   子路使子羔爲費宰。子曰：「賊夫人之子。」

子路曰：「有民人焉，有社稷焉，何必讀書，然後爲學？」

子曰：「是故惡夫佞者。」

When Zilu sent Zigao to be the prefect of Bi,[187] the Master said, "This is harming another man's son."

Zilu replied, "The prefecture has people in it and has the altars to the soil and grain in it. Why is it that only by reading books one can be considered learned?"

The Master said, "It is for this reason that I hate those with a glib tongue."

11.26   子路、曾皙、冉有、公西華侍坐。

子曰：「以吾一日長乎爾，毋吾以也。居則曰：『不吾知也！』如或知爾，則何以哉？」

子路率爾而對曰：「千乘之國，攝乎大國之間，加之以師旅，因之以饑饉；由也爲之，比及三年，可使有勇，且知方也。」

夫子哂之。

「求！爾何如？」

對曰：「方六七十，如五六十，求也爲之，比及三年，可使足民。如其禮樂，以俟君子。」

「赤！爾何如？」

對曰：「非曰能之，願學焉。宗廟之事，如會同，端章甫，願爲小相焉。」

「點！爾何如？」

鼓瑟希，鏗爾，舍瑟而作，對曰：「異乎三子者之撰。」

子曰：「何傷乎？赤各言其志也。」

曰：「莫春者，春服既成，冠者五六人，童子六七人，浴乎沂，風乎舞雩，詠而歸。」

夫子喟然歎曰：「吾與點也！」三子者出，曾皙後。曾皙曰：「夫三子者之言何如？」

子曰：「亦各言其志也已矣。」

曰：「夫子何哂由也？」

曰：「爲國以禮，其言不讓，是故哂之。」

「唯求則非邦也與？」

「安見方六七十如五六十而非邦也者？」

「唯赤則非邦也與？」

「宗廟會同，非諸侯而何？赤也爲之小，孰能爲之大？」

Zilu, Zengxi, Ranyou, and Zihua were all sitting in attendance on Confucius. The Master said, "Just because I am a bit older than you do not hesitate on my account. You keep saying, 'No one recognizes my worth!' but if someone did recognize your worth, how would you be of use to them?"

"As for me," Zilu hastily replied, "give me a state of a thousand chariots to govern, set me in among powerful neighbors, harass me with foreign armies, and add to that widespread famine, and at the end of three years, I will have imbued the people with courage, and moreover, provided them with a sure direction."

The Master smiled at him, and said, "Ranyou, what would you do?"

"Give me a small territory of sixty or seventy—or even fifty or sixty—*li* square, and at the end of three years, I will have made the people thrive. As for observing ritual propriety (*li* 禮) and the playing of music (*yue* 樂), these must wait upon an exemplary person (*junzi* 君子)."

"And what would you do, Zihua?" asked the Master.

"Not to say that I have the ability to do so, but I am willing to learn: in the events of the Ancestral Temple and in the forging of diplomatic alliances, donning the appropriate ceremonial robes and cap, I would like to serve as a minor protocol officer."

"And what about you, Zengxi?" asked the Master.

Zengxi plucked a final note on his zither to bring the piece to an end, and setting the instrument aside, he rose to his feet. "I would choose to do something somewhat different from the rest." he said.

"No harm in that," said the Master. "Each of you can speak your mind."

"At the end of spring, with the spring clothes having already been finished, I would like, in the company of five or six young men and six or seven children, to cleanse ourselves in the Yi River, to revel in the cool breezes at the Altar for Rain, and then return home singing."

The Master heaved a deep sigh, and said, "I'm with Zengxi!"

Zilu, Ranyou, and Zihua all left, but Zengxi waited behind, and asked the Master, "What do you think of what my three fellow students have said?"

"Each of you has simply spoken his mind, that's all," replied the Master.

"Why did you, sir, smile at Zilu?" said Zengxi.

"I smiled at him because in governing a state you need to observe ritual propriety, and yet in what he said there was no deference (*rang* 讓) at all," said the Master.

"Was it only Ranyou who did not speak of governing a state?" he asked.

"How can one speak of a territory of sixty or seventy—or even fifty or sixty—*li* square, and not be referring to a state?" replied the Master.

"Was it only Zihua, then, who did not speak of governing a state?" he asked.

"If the events of the Ancestral Temple and diplomatic alliances do not involve the various lords, then what are they? If he is only going to serve as a minor protocol officer, then who is able to take a major role?"

12.1   顏淵問仁。子曰：「克己復禮爲仁。一日克己復禮，
    天下歸仁焉。爲仁由己，而由人乎哉？」

        顏淵曰：「請問其目。」子曰：「非禮勿視，非
    禮勿聽，非禮勿言，非禮勿動。」

        顏淵曰：「回雖不敏，請事斯語矣。」

Yan Hui inquired about authoritative conduct (*ren* 仁). The
Master replied, "Through self-discipline and observing ritual
propriety (*li* 禮) one becomes authoritative in one's conduct.[188] If for the space of a day one were able to accomplish
this, the whole empire would defer to this authoritative
model. Becoming authoritative in one's conduct is self-originating—how could it originate with others?"

Yan Hui said, "Could I ask what becoming authoritative
entails?" The Master replied, "Do not look at anything that
violates the observance of ritual propriety; do not listen to
anything that violates the observance of ritual propriety; do
not speak about anything that violates the observance of
ritual propriety; do not do anything that violates the observance of ritual propriety."

"Though I am not clever," said Yan Hui, "allow me to act
on what you have said."

12.2   仲弓問仁。子曰：「出門如見大賓，使民如承大祭。
    己所不欲，勿施於人。在邦無怨，在家無怨。」

        仲弓曰：「雍雖不敏，請事斯語矣。」

Zhonggong[189] inquired about authoritative conduct (*ren* 仁). The Master replied, "In your public life, behave as though you are receiving important visitors; employ the common people as though you are overseeing a great sacrifice. Do not impose upon others what you yourself do not want, and you will not incur personal or political ill will."

"Though I am not clever," said Zhonggong, "allow me to act on what you have said."

12.3　司馬牛問仁。子曰：「仁者，其言也訒。」

曰：「其言也訒，斯謂之仁已乎？」子曰：「為之難，言之得無訒乎？」

Sima Niu inquired about authoritative conduct (*ren* 仁). The Master replied, "An authoritative person is slow to speak (*ren* 訒)."[190]

"Does just being slow to speak make one authoritative?" he asked.

The Master replied, "When something is difficult to accomplish, how can one but be slow to speak?"[191]

12.4　司馬牛問君子。子曰：「君子不憂不懼。」

曰：「不憂不懼，斯謂之君子已乎？」子曰：「內省不疚，夫何憂何懼？」

Sima Niu inquired about the exemplary person (*junzi* 君子). The Master replied, "The exemplary person is neither worried nor apprehensive."

"Does just being free from worry and apprehension make one an exemplary person?" he asked.

"If examining oneself there is nothing to be ashamed of, why be worried or apprehensive?" Confucius replied.

12.5　司馬牛憂曰：「人皆有兄弟，我獨亡。」子夏曰：「商聞之矣：死生有命，富貴在天。君子敬而無失，與人恭而有禮。四海之內，皆兄弟也。君子何患乎無兄弟也？」

Sima Niu lamented, "Everyone has brothers except for me."
Zixia said to him, "I have heard it said:

> Life and death are a matter of one's lot;
> Wealth and honor lie with *tian* 天.

Since exemplary persons (*junzi* 君子) are respectful and impeccable in their conduct, are deferential to others and observe ritual propriety (*li* 禮), everyone in the world is their brother. Why would exemplary persons worry over having no brothers?"[192]

12.6　子張問明。子曰：「浸潤之譖，膚受之愬，不行焉，可謂明也已矣。浸潤之譖，膚受之愬，不行焉，可謂遠也已矣。」

Zizhang inquired about perspicacity (*ming* 明). The Master replied, "A person who stays aloof from slander that pollutes the community and from rumor mongering that spreads like a rash can be said to be perspicacious. Such a person can also be said to be discerning."

12.7　子貢問政。子曰：「足食，足兵，民信之矣。」
　　　子貢曰：「必不得已而去，於斯三者何先？」
曰：「去兵。」
　　　子貢曰：「必不得已而去，於斯二者何先？」
曰：「去食。自古皆有死；民無信不立。」

Zigong asked about governing effectively (*zheng* 政). The Master said to him, "Make sure there is sufficient food to eat, sufficient arms for defense, and that the common people have confidence in their leaders."

154

"If you had to give up one of these three things," he said, "which should be given up first?"

"Give up the arms," he replied.

"If you had to give up one of the remaining two," he said, "which should be given up first?"

"Give up the food," he replied. "Death has been with us from ancient times, but if the common people do not have confidence in their leaders, community will not endure."

12.8 棘子成曰：「君子質而已矣，何以文爲？」子貢曰：「惜乎，夫子之說君子也！駟不及舌。文猶質也，質猶文也。虎豹之鞹猶犬羊之鞹。」

Ji Zicheng inquired, "Exemplary persons (*junzi* 君子) are determined by nothing other than the quality of their basic disposition (*zhi* 質); what need do they have of further refinement (*wen* 文)?"

Zigong replied, "It is a shame that the gentleman has spoken thus about the exemplary person—'A team of horses cannot retrieve his words.' Refinement is no different from one's basic disposition; one's basic disposition is no different from refinement. The skin of the tiger or leopard, shorn of its hair, is no different from the dog or sheep."[193]

12.9 哀公問於有若曰：「年饑，用不足，如之何？」

有若對曰：「盍徹乎？」

曰：「二，吾猶不足，如之何其徹也？」

對曰：「百姓足，君孰不足？百姓不足，君孰與足？」

Duke Ai inquired of Master You,[194] "The harvest has been bad and there is not enough in the government coffers. What should I do?"

Master You replied, "Have you not levied a tithe?"

"Never mind a tithe," said the duke, "I would not have enough even if I levied twice that amount."

"If the households of your people had sufficient, you could expect to have the same; but since the households do not have sufficient, how can you expect to have enough?"

12.10　子張問崇德、辨惑。子曰：「主忠信、徙義，崇德也。愛之欲其生，惡之欲其死。既欲其生，又欲其死，是惑也。『誠不以富，亦祇以異。』」

Zizhang inquired about accumulating excellence (*de* 德) and sorting things out when in a quandary. The Master replied, "To take doing one's utmost (*zhong* 忠), making good on one's word (*xin* 信), and seeking out what is appropriate (*yi* 義) as one's main concerns, is to accumulate excellence. To simultaneously love and hate someone, and thus to simultaneously want this person to live and to die, is to be in a quandary. 'You surely do not gain fortune this way; you only get something different.'"[195]

12.11　齊景公問政於孔子。孔子對曰：「君君，臣臣，父父，子子。」公曰：「善哉！信如君不君，臣不臣，父不父，子不子，雖有粟，吾得而食諸？」

Duke Jing of Qi asked Confucius about governing effectively (*zheng* 政). Confucius replied, "The ruler must rule, the minister minister, the father father, and the son son."

"Excellent!" exclaimed the Duke. "Indeed, if the ruler does not rule, the minister not minister, the father not father, and the son not son, even if there were grain, would I get to eat of it?"[196]

12.12　子曰：「片言可以折獄者，其由也與？」
　　　　子路無宿諾。

The Master said, "If there is anyone who can decide a case listening to only one side, it is Zilu!"[137] Zilu also never procrastinates on a promise made."[198]

12.13　子曰：「聽訟，吾猶人也。必也使無訟乎！」

The Master said, "In hearing cases, I am the same as anyone. What we must strive to do is to rid the courts of cases altogether."

12.14　子張問政。子曰：「居之無倦，行之以忠。」

Zizhang asked about governing effectively (*zheng* 政), and the Master replied, "Be unflagging in deliberating upon policy, and do your best in carrying it out."[199]

12.15　子曰：「博學於文，約之以禮，亦可以弗畔矣夫！」

The Master said, "Learn broadly of culture (*wen* 文), discipline this learning through observing ritual propriety (*li* 禮), and moreover, in so doing, remain on course without straying from it."[200]

12.16　子曰：「君子成人之美，不成人之惡。小人反是。」

The Master said, "The exemplary person (junzi 君子) helps to bring out the best in others, but does not help to bring out the worst. The petty person does just the opposite."

12.17　季康子問政於孔子。孔子對曰：「政者、正也。子帥以正，孰敢不正？」

Ji Kangzi asked Confucius about governing effectively (*zheng* 政), and Confucius replied to him, "Governing effectively is doing what is proper (*zheng* 正). If you, sir, lead by doing what is proper, who would dare do otherwise?"[201]

12.18 季康子患盜，問於孔子。孔子對曰：「苟子之不欲，
雖賞之不竊。」

Ji Kangzi was troubled by the number of thieves, and asked
Confucius for advice. Confucius replied to him, "If you yourself were not so greedy, the people could not be paid to
steal."

12.19 季康子問政於孔子曰：「如殺無道，以就有道，何
如？」孔子對曰：「子爲政，焉用殺？子欲善而民善
矣。君子之德風，小人之德草。草上之風，必偃。」

Ji Kangzi asked Confucius about governing effectively (*zheng*
政), saying, "What if I kill those who have abandoned the
way (*dao* 道) to attract those who are on it?"

   "If you govern effectively," Confucius replied, "what
need is there for killing? If you want to be truly adept (*shan*
善), the people will also be adept. The excellence (*de* 德) of
the exemplary person (*junzi* 君子) is the wind, while that of
the petty person is the grass. As the wind blows, the grass is
sure to bend."²⁰²

12.20 子張問：「士何如斯可謂之達矣？」子曰：「何哉，
爾所謂達者？」子張對曰：「在邦必聞，在家必聞。」
子曰：「是聞也，非達也。夫達也者，質直而好義，
察言而觀色，慮以下人。在邦必達，在家必達。夫聞
也者，色取仁而行違，居之不疑。在邦必聞，在家必
聞。」

Zizhang inquired, "What does the scholar-apprentice (*shi* 士)
have to do to be described as being 'prominent'?"

   "What can you possibly mean by being 'prominent'?" replied the Master.

   "One who is sure to be known, whether serving in public
office or in the house of a ruling family," answered Zizhang.

"That is being known," said the Master, "it is not being 'prominent.' Those who are prominent are true in their basic disposition, and seek after what is most appropriate (*yi* 義). They examine what is said, are keen observers of demeanor, and are thoughtful in deferring to others. They are sure to be prominent, whether serving in public office or in the house of a ruling family. As for being merely known, they put on appearances to win a reputation for being authoritative (*ren* 仁) while their conduct belies it. They are wholly confident that they are authoritative, and sure to be known, whether serving in public office or in the house of a ruling family."

12.21 樊遲從遊於舞雩之下，曰：「敢問崇德、脩慝、辨惑。」子曰：「善哉問！先事後得，非崇德與？攻其惡，無攻人之惡，非脩慝與？一朝之忿，忘其身，以及其親，非惑與？」

Fan Chi accompanied the Master on an excursion to the Altar for Rain, and resting beneath it, inquired, "May I ask about accumulating excellence (*de* 德), reforming corruption, and sorting things out when in a quandary?"

"A fine question," replied the Master. "Get[203] only once you have given—is this not accumulating excellence? Attack depravity itself rather than the depravity of others—is this not reforming corruption? In a moment of rage to forget not only one's own person but even one's parents—is this not being in a quandary?"

12.22 樊遲問仁。子曰：「愛人。」
問知。子曰：「知人。」樊遲未達。子曰：「舉直錯諸枉，能使枉者直。」
樊遲退，見子夏曰：「鄉也吾見於夫子而問知，子曰：『舉直錯諸枉，能使枉者直。』何謂也？」

子夏曰：「富哉言乎！舜有天下，選於眾，舉皋陶，不仁者遠矣。湯有天下，選於眾，舉伊尹，不仁者遠矣。」

Fan Chi inquired about authoritative conduct (*ren* 仁), and the Master said, "Love others." He inquired about realizing (*zhi* 知), and the Master said, "Realize others." Fan Chi did not understand and so the Master explained, "If you promote the true into positions above the crooked you can make the crooked true." Fan Chi withdrew, and on being received by Zixia, he asked, "Recently I was received by the Master and asked him about realizing. He replied, 'If you promote the true into positions above the crooked you can make the crooked true.' What does he mean?"

"Rich indeed are the Master's words!" said Zixia. "When Shun ruled the land, he selected Gao Yao from among the multitude and promoted him, and the perverse gave them a wide berth. When Tang ruled the land, he selected Yi Yin from among the multitude and promoted him, and the perverse gave them a wide berth."[204]

12.23　子貢問友。子曰：「忠告而善道之，不可則止，毋自辱焉。」

Zigong inquired about how to treat friends, and the Master replied, "Do your utmost (*zhong* 忠) to exhort them, and lead them adeptly (*shan* 善) along the way (*dao* 道). But if they are unwilling then desist—don't disgrace yourself in the process."[205]

12.24　曾子曰：「君子以文會友，以友輔仁。」

Master Zeng said, "The exemplary person (*junzi* 君子) attracts friends through refinement (*wen* 文), and thereby promotes authoritative conduct (*ren* 仁)."

13.1　子路問政。子曰：「先之勞之。」請益。曰：「無倦。」

Zilu inquired about governing effectively (*zheng* 政). The Master replied, "Set an example yourself and then urge the people on."

"Please elaborate," Zilu said.

"Be unflagging in your efforts," replied the Master.

13.2　仲弓爲季氏宰，問政。子曰：「先有司，赦小過，舉賢才。」

　　　曰：「焉知賢才而舉之？」曰：「舉爾所知；爾所不知，人其舍諸？」

Zhonggong was serving as steward in the House of Ji, and asked about governing effectively (*zheng* 政). The Master said to him, "Set an example yourself for those in office, pardon minor offenses, and promote those with superior character (*xian* 賢) and ability."

"How do you recognize those with superior character and ability in order to promote them?" Zhonggong asked.

The Master replied, "Promote those that you do recognize with the confidence that others will not spurn those that you do not."

13.3　子路曰：「衛君待子而爲政，子將奚先？」

　　　子曰：「必也正名乎！」

子路曰：「有是哉？子之迂也！奚其正？」

子曰：「野哉由也！君子於其所不知，蓋闕如也。名不正，則言不順；言不順，則事不成；事不成，則禮樂不興；禮樂不興，則刑罰不中；刑罰不中，則民無所錯手足。故君子名之必可言也，言之必可行也。君子於其言，無所苟而已矣。」

"Were the Lord of Wey to turn the administration of his state over to you, what would be your first priority?" asked Zilu.

"Without question it would be to insure that names are used properly (*zhengming* 正名)," replied the Master.

"Would you be as impractical as that?" responded Zilu. "What is it for names to be used properly anyway?"

"How can you be so dense!" replied Confucius. "An exemplary person (*junzi* 君子) defers on matters he does not understand. When names are not used properly, language will not be used effectively; when language is not used effectively, matters will not be taken care of; when matters are not taken care of, the observance of ritual propriety (*li* 禮) and the playing of music (*yue* 樂) will not flourish; when the observance of ritual propriety and the playing of music do not flourish, the application of laws and punishments will not be on the mark; when the application of laws and punishments is not on the mark, the people will not know what to do with themselves. Thus, when the exemplary person puts a name to something, it can certainly be spoken, and when spoken it can certainly be acted upon. There is nothing careless in the attitude of the exemplary person toward what is said."[206]

13.4 樊遲請學稼。子曰：「吾不如老農。」請學爲圃。曰：「吾不如老圃。」

樊遲出。子曰：「小人哉，樊須也！上好禮，則民莫敢不敬；上好義，則民莫敢不服；上好信，則民

莫敢不用情。夫如是，則四方之民襁負其子而至矣，
焉用稼？」

Fan Chi wanted to learn to farm. "A farmer would serve you better," said the Master. He wanted to learn to grow vegetables. "A vegetable grower would serve you better," said the Master.

When Fan Chi had left, the Master said, "This Fan Chi is certainly a petty person! If their superiors cherished the observance of ritual propriety (*li* 禮), none among the common people would dare be disrespectful;[207] if their superiors cherished appropriate conduct (*yi* 義), none among the common people would dare be disobedient; if their superiors cherished making good on their word (*xin* 信), none among the common people would dare be duplicitous. This being the case, the common people from all quarters would flock here with babies strapped to their backs. What need is there to talk of farming?"

13.5　子曰：「誦《詩》三百，授之以政，不達；使於四
方，不能專對；雖多，亦奚以爲？」

The Master said, "If people can recite all of the three hundred *Songs* and yet when given official responsibility, fail to perform effectively, or when sent to distant quarters, are unable to act on their own initiative, then even though they have mastered so many of them, what good are they to them?"

13.6　子曰：「其身正，不令而行；其身不正，雖令不從。」

The Master said, "If people are proper (*zheng* 正) in personal conduct, others will follow suit without need of command. But if they are not proper, even when they command, others will not obey."

13.7　子曰：「魯、衛之政，兄弟也。」

The Master remarked, "The governments of Lu and Wei are elder and younger brother respectively."[208]

13.8　子謂衛公子荊善居室。始有，曰：「苟合矣。」少有，曰：「苟完矣。」富有，曰：「苟美矣。」

The Master observed about Zijing, Duke of Wey, that he made the most of his living accommodations: "When he was starting out, he said that they were quite adequate, when he was better off, that they were quite all he needed, and when he prospered, that they were quite luxurious."

13.9　子適衛，冉有僕。子曰：「庶矣哉！」
　　　冉有曰：「既庶矣，又何加焉？」曰：「富之。」
　　　曰：「既富矣，又何加焉？」曰：「敎之。」

Ranyou drove the Master's carriage on a trip to Wey. The Master remarked, "What a teeming population!" Ranyou asked, "When the people are already so numerous, what more can be done for them?" The Master said, "Make them prosperous." "When the people are already prosperous," asked Ranyou, "what more can be done for them?" "Teach them," replied the Master.[209]

13.10　子曰：「苟有用我者，期月而已可也，三年有成。」

The Master said, "If someone were to make use of me in governing, in the course of one year I could make a difference, and in three years I would really have something to show for it."

13.11　子曰：「『善人爲邦百年，亦可以勝殘去殺矣。』誠哉是言也！」

The Master said, "'If truly efficacious people (shanren 善人)[210] were put in charge of governing for a hundred years, they would be able to overcome violence and dispense with killing altogether.' These words could not be more true!"

13.12　子曰：「如有王者，必世而後仁。」

The Master said, "Were a Genuine King to arise, it would still take a generation before authoritative conduct (*ren* 仁) would prevail."

13.13　子曰：「苟正其身矣，於從政乎何有？不能正其身，如正人何？」

The Master said, "If proper (*zheng* 正) in their own conduct, what difficulty would they have in governing (*zheng* 政)? But if not able to be proper in their own conduct, how can they demand such conduct from others?"

13.14　冉子退朝。子曰：「何晏也？」對曰：「有政。」子曰：「其事也。如有政，雖不吾以，吾其與聞之。」

Ranyou returned from court, and the Master asked him, "Why are you working so late?" Ranyou replied, "There were affairs of state." "Routine business, perhaps," remarked the Master. "Even though I am not in office, if there were affairs of state, I would know about it."

13.15　定公問：「一言而可以興邦，有諸？」
　　　　孔子對曰：「言不可以若是其幾也。人之言曰：『為君難，為臣不易。』如知為君之難也，不幾乎一言而興邦乎？」
　　　　曰：「一言而喪邦，有諸？」
　　　　孔子對曰：「言不可以若是其幾也。人之言曰：『予無樂乎為君，唯其言而莫予違也。』如其善而莫之違也，不亦善乎？如不善而莫之違也，不幾乎一言而喪邦乎？」

Duke Ding inquired, "Is there any one saying that can make a state prosper?"[211] "A saying itself cannot have such effect," said the Master, "but there is the saying, 'Ruling is difficult, and ministering is not easy either.' If the ruler really does understand the difficulty of ruling, is this not close to a saying making a state prosper?"

"Is there any one saying that can ruin a state?" Duke Ding asked. "A saying itself cannot have such effect," replied Confucius, "but there is the saying, 'I find little pleasure in ruling, save that no one will take exception to what I say.' If what one has to say is efficacious (*shan* 善) and no one takes exception, fine indeed. But if what one has to say is not efficacious and no one takes exception, is this not close to a saying ruining a state?"

13.16　葉公問政。子曰：「近者說，遠者來。」

The Governor of She asked about governing effectively (*zheng* 政), and the Master replied, "Those near at hand are pleased, and those at a distance are drawn to you."

13.17　子夏爲莒父宰，問政。子曰：「無欲速，無見小利。欲速，則不達；見小利則大事不成。」

Zixia was made the prefect of Jufu, and asked about governing effectively (*zheng* 政). The Master replied, "Don't try to rush things, and don't get distracted by small opportunities. If you try to rush things, you won't achieve your ends; if you get distracted by small opportunities, you won't succeed in the more important matters of government."

13.18　葉公語孔子曰：「吾黨有直躬者，其父攘羊，而子證之。」孔子曰：「吾黨之直者異於是：父爲子隱，子爲父隱。直在其中矣。」

The Governor of She in conversation with Confucius said, "In our village there is someone called 'True Person.' When his father took a sheep on the sly,[212] he reported him to the authorities."

Confucius replied, "Those who are true in my village conduct themselves differently. A father covers for his son, and a son covers for his father. And being true lies in this."[213]

13.19 樊遲問仁。子曰：「居處恭，執事敬，與人忠。雖之夷狄，不可棄也。」

Fan Chi inquired about authoritative conduct (*ren* 仁), and the Master replied, "At home be deferential, in handling public affairs be respectful, and do your utmost (*zhong* 忠) in your relationships with others. Even if you were to go and live among the Yi or Di barbarians, you could not do without such an attitude."

13.20 子貢問曰：「何如斯可謂之士矣？」子曰：「行己有恥，使於四方，不辱君命，可謂士矣。」

曰：「敢問其次。」曰：「宗族稱孝焉，鄉黨稱弟焉。」

曰：「敢問其次。」曰：「言必信，行必果，硜硜然小人哉！抑亦可以爲次矣。」

曰：「今之從政者何如？」子曰：「噫！斗筲之人，何足算也！」

Zigong inquired, "What must one be like to be called a scholar-apprentice (*shi* 士)?"

The Master replied, "Those who conduct themselves with a sense of shame and who, when sent to distant quarters, do not disgrace the commission of their lord, deserve to be called a scholar-apprentice."

"May I ask what kind of person would rank next?" asked Zigong.

"Persons whom family and clan would praise for filial conduct (*xiao* 孝) and whom fellow villagers would praise as being deferential to their elders," he replied.

"And next?"

"Persons who always make good on their word (*xin* 信) and follow through in what they do, in spite of their stubborn pettiness, can still be considered to be next."

"What about those who are presently carrying out the offices of government?"

"Indeed! Those trifling bureaucrats hardly amount to much!"

13.21　子曰：「不得中行而與之，必也狂狷乎！狂者進取，狷者有所不爲也。」

The Master said, "If one cannot find the company of temperate colleagues, one has no choice but to turn to the more rash and the more timid. The rash will forge ahead in their actions, and the timid will not do what they think is wrong."[214]

13.22　子曰：「南人有言曰：『人而無恆，不可以作巫醫。』善夫！『不恆其德，或承之羞。』」子曰：「不占而已矣。」

The Master said, "People from the south have a saying: 'A person who lacks constancy will not even make a shaman medicine man.' Apt words indeed! The *Book of Changes* hexagram 32 states: 'A person who is not constant in his character will perhaps suffer shame on account of it.'" The Master remarked on it: "This simply means that such persons need not divine to know their future."[215]

13.23　子曰：「君子和而不同，小人同而不和。」

The Master said, "Exemplary persons seek harmony not sameness; petty persons, then, are the opposite."[216]

13.24　子貢問曰：「鄉人皆好之，何如？」子曰：「未可也。」

　　　「鄉人皆惡之，何如？」子曰：「未可也；不如鄉人之善者好之，其不善者惡之。」

Zigong inquired, saying, "What do you think about someone who is loved by everyone in his village?"

"It is not enough," said the Master.

"What if everyone in the village despises a person?"

"It is not enough. It would be better that the best villagers love, and the worst despise, this person."

13.25　子曰：「君子易事而難說也。說之不以道，不說也；及其使人也，器之。小人難事而易說也。說之雖不以道，說也；及其使人也，求備焉。」

The Master said, "Exemplary persons (*junzi* 君子) are easy to serve but difficult to please. If one tries to please them with conduct that is not consistent with the way (*dao* 道), they will not be pleased. In employing others, they use them according to their abilities. Petty persons are difficult to serve but easy to please.[217] If one tries to please them with conduct that is not consistent with the way, they will be pleased anyway. But in employing others, they expect them to be good at everything."

13.26　子曰：「君子泰而不驕，小人驕而不泰。」

The Master said, "Exemplary persons (*junzi* 君子) are distinguished but not arrogant; petty persons are the opposite."

13.27　子曰：「剛、毅、木、訥近仁。」

The Master said, "Being firm, resolute, honest, and deliberate in speech is close to authoritative conduct (*ren* 仁)."

13.28　子路問曰：「何如斯可謂之士矣？」子曰：「切切偲偲，怡怡如也，可謂士矣。朋友切切偲偲，兄弟怡怡。」

Zilu inquired, "What must one be like to be called a scholar-apprentice (*shi* 士)?"

The Master replied, "Persons who are critical and demanding yet amicable can be called scholar-apprentices. They need to be critical and demanding with their friends, and amicable with their brothers."

13.29　子曰：「善人教民七年，亦可以即戎矣。」

The Master said, "It is only once a truly efficacious person (*shanren* 善人) has instructed the people for seven years that the subject of battle can be broached."[218]

13.30　子曰：「以不教民戰，是謂棄之。」

The Master said, "To go into battle with people who have not been properly trained is to forsake them."

14.1　憲問恥。子曰：「邦有道、穀，邦無道、穀，恥也。」

　　　「克、伐、怨、欲不行焉，可以爲仁矣？」子曰：
「可以爲難矣，仁則吾不知也。」

Yuansi[219] inquired about shameful conduct, and the Master
replied, "To receive a stipend of grain when the way (*dao* 道)
prevails in the state and to be still receiving this stipend when
it does not, is shameful conduct."[220]

He again inquired, "If in one's conduct one refrains from
intimidation, from self-importance, from ill will, and from
greed, can one be considered authoritative (*ren* 仁)?"

"I would say that this is hard to do," replied the Master,
"but I don't know that it makes one's conduct authoritative."

14.2　子曰：「士而懷居，不足以爲士矣。」

The Master said, "The scholar-apprentice (*shi* 士) who cher-
ishes worldly comforts is not worthy of the name."[221]

14.3　子曰：「邦有道，危言危行；邦無道，危行言孫。」

The Master said, "When the way prevails be perilously high-
minded[222] in your speech and conduct; when it does not prevail, be perilously high-minded in your conduct, but be prudent in what you say."

14.4　子曰：「有德者必有言，有言者不必有德。仁者必有
勇，勇者不必有仁。」

The Master said, "The person of excellence (*de* 德) is certain to have something to say, but someone who has something to say is not necessarily an excellent person. The authoritative person (*ren* 仁) is certain to be bold, but someone who is bold[223] is not necessarily authoritative."

14.5   南宮适問於孔子曰：「羿善射，奡盪舟，俱不得其死然。禹、稷躬稼而有天下。」夫子不答。

　　　　南宮适出，子曰：「君子哉若人！尚德哉若人！」

Nangong Kuo asked Confucius, "How is it that Yi was a master (*shan* 善) at archery and Ao was strong enough to push a boat on dry land, and yet both met an unnatural end, while Yu and Ji personally farmed the land, and yet came to rule the world?"[224]

At the time, the Master did not reply, but after Nangong Kuo's departure, he remarked, "There is an exemplary person (*junzi* 君子)! There is someone who really esteems excellence (*de* 德)!"[225]

14.6   子曰：「君子而不仁者有矣夫，未有小人而仁者也。」

The Master said, "There have been occasions on which an exemplary person (*junzi* 君子) fails to act in an authoritative manner (*ren* 仁), but there has never been an instance of a petty person being able to act authoritatively."[226]

14.7   子曰：「愛之，能勿勞乎？忠焉，能勿誨乎？」

The Master said, "Can you really love the people without urging them on? Can you do your utmost (*zhong* 忠) for your lord without instructing him?"[227]

14.8   子曰：「為命，裨諶草創之，世叔討論之，行人子羽脩飾之，東里子產潤色之。」

The Master said, "In the drawing up of a diplomatic treaty, Pi Chen would make a first draft of it, Shi Shu would comment on it and discuss it, the diplomat Ziyu would revise and polish it, and Zichan of Dongli would then add the final touches."[228]

14.9　或問子產。子曰：「惠人也。」

問子西。曰：「彼哉！彼哉！」

問管仲。曰：「人也。奪伯氏駢邑三百，飯疏食，沒齒無怨言。」

Someone asked about Zichan. The Master replied, "He was kind and good."

"Zixi?" he asked.

"That man! That man!"[229]

"And Guanzhong?" he asked.

"His conduct was authoritative (*ren* 仁).[230] He seized three hundred households from the Bo clan in the town of Pian, and although the Bo clan was left with only coarse rice to eat, they lived out their days without ever speaking ill of Guanzhong."

14.10　子曰：「貧而無怨、難，富而無驕、易。」

The Master said, "To be poor without feeling ill will is much more difficult than to be wealthy without being arrogant."

14.11　子曰：「孟公綽爲趙、魏老則優，不可以爲滕、薛大夫。」

The Master said, "Were Meng Gongchuo to serve the Zhao or Wei families as household steward, he would be well within his reach, but he could not serve as a minister even to the likes of Teng or Xue."

14.12 子路問成人。子曰：「若臧武仲之知，公綽之不欲，卞莊子之勇，冉求之藝，文之以禮樂，亦可以爲成人矣。」曰：「今之成人者何必然？見利思義，見危授命，久要不忘平生之言，亦可以爲成人矣。」

Zilu inquired about consummate persons (*chengren* 成人). The Master replied, "Persons who are as wise as Zang Wuzhong, as free from desires as Meng Gongchuo, as bold as Bian Zhuangzi, and as cultivated as Ranyou, and who in addition, have become refined through observing ritual propriety (*li* 禮) and playing music (*yue* 樂)—such persons can be said to be consummate. But," he continued, "need consummate persons of today be all of this? If on seeing a chance to profit they think of appropriate conduct (*yi* 義), on seeing danger they are ready to give their lives, and when long in desperate straits, they still do not forget the words they live by—such persons can also be said to be consummate."

14.13 子問公叔文子於公明賈曰：「信乎，夫子不言、不笑、不取乎？」

公明賈對曰：「以告者過也。夫子時然後言，人不厭其言；樂然後笑，人不厭其笑；義然後取，人不厭其取。」

子曰：「其然？豈其然乎？」

The Master asked Gongming Jia about Gongshu Wenzi, "Are we to believe that your master never spoke, never laughed, and never took anything?"

Gongming Jia replied, "Whoever told you that is exaggerating. Because my master only spoke at the proper time, no one grew tired of what he had to say; because he only laughed when he was happy, no one grew tired of his laughter; because he only took what was appropriate for him to take, no one ever grew tired of his taking."

14.14 子曰：「臧武仲以防求爲後於魯，雖曰不要君，吾不信也。」

The Master said, "Zang Wuzhong appealed to the House of Lu to have his fief at Fang passed on to his descendents. Even though it is said that he did not pressure them, I do not believe it."

14.15 子曰：「晉文公譎而不正，齊桓公正而不譎。」

The Master said, "Duke Wen of Jin being devious in his conduct was not proper (*zheng* 正), while Duke Huan of Qi being proper in his conduct was not devious."

14.16 子路曰：「桓公殺公子糾，召忽死之，管仲不死。」曰：「未仁乎？」子曰：「桓公九合諸侯，不以兵車，管仲之力也。如其仁，如其仁。」

Zilu said, "When Duke Huan had his elder brother Prince Qiu killed, the tutor Shao Hu died with him, but Guanzhong did not."[231] "In this instance," he added, "did Guanzhong fall short of authoritative conduct (*ren* 仁)?"

The Master said, "Many times did Duke Huan assemble the various feudal lords, and it was always through Guanzhong's influence rather than a resort to arms. Such was his authoritative conduct, such was his authoritative conduct."[232]

14.17 子貢曰：「管仲非仁者與？桓公殺公子糾，不能死，又相之。」子曰：「管仲相桓公，霸諸侯，一匡天下，民到于今受其賜。微管仲，吾其被髮左衽矣。豈若匹夫匹婦之爲諒也，自經於溝瀆而莫之知也？」

Zigong said, "Was it that Guanzhong really was not authoritative (*ren* 仁)? When Duke Huan had his elder brother

Prince Qiu killed, not only did Guanzhong not die with him, he became the prime minister for Duke Huan!"

The Master replied, "When Guanzhong served as prime minister for Duke Huan, he enabled the duke to become leader of the various feudal lords, uniting and bringing order to the empire. Even today the people[233] still benefit from his largesse. If there were no Guanzhong, we would likely be wearing our hair loose and folding our robes to the left.[234] Should we expect that he would have the earnestness of some country yokel, managing to strangle himself in an irrigation ditch with no one the wiser?"

14.18 公叔文子之臣大夫僎，與文子同升諸公。子聞之，曰：「可以爲『文』矣。」

The household steward of Gongshu Wenzi, Zhuan, together with Wenzi, climbed to high public office. On hearing of this, the Master commented, "Gongshu Wenzi certainly deserved the posthumous title 'refined (*wen* 文)' conferred upon him."

14.19 子言衛靈公之無道也，康子曰：「夫如是，奚而不喪？」孔子曰：「仲叔圉治賓客，祝鮀治宗廟，王孫賈治軍旅。夫如是，奚其喪？」

The Master said of Duke Ling of Wey that he had lost the way (*wu dao* 無道). Kangzi asked, "If this was so, why did he not come to ruin?"

The Master replied, "He had Zhongshu Yu to take care of visiting envoys and court guests, the priest Tuo to conduct the affairs of the ancestral temple, and Wangsun Jia to command the armies. This being so, why would he come to ruin?"

14.20 子曰：「其言之不怍，則爲之也難。」

The Master said, "If one talks big with no sense of shame, it will be hard indeed to make good on one's words."

14.21 陳成子弒簡公。孔子沐浴而朝，告於哀公曰：「陳恆弒其君，請討之。」公曰：「告夫三子！」

孔子曰：「以吾從大夫之後，不敢不告也。君曰『告夫三子』者！」

之三子，告，不可。孔子曰：「以吾從大夫之後，不敢不告也。」

Chen Chengzi assassinated Duke Jian. Confucius having cleansed himself ceremonially went to court and reported to Duke Ai, saying, "Chen Chengzi has assassinated his lord. I implore you to send an army to punish him."

The duke replied, "Report this to the heads of the Three Families."

The Master on withdrawing said, "Ranking below the high ministers, I had no choice but to report this. And the duke said to me, 'Report this to the heads of the Three Families.'"

On going to the heads of the Three Families and reporting this, they refused his petition. Confucius said, "Ranking below the high ministers, I had no choice but to report this to you."[235]

14.22 子路問事君。子曰：「勿欺也而犯之。」

Zilu asked how to serve one's lord properly. The Master replied, "Let there be no duplicity when taking a stand against him."

14.23 子曰：「君子上達，小人下達。」

The Master said, "The exemplary person (*junzi* 君子) takes the high road, while the petty person takes the low."[236]

14.24 子曰：「古之學者爲己，今之學者爲人。」

The Master said, "Scholars of old would study for their own sake, while those of today do so to impress others."[237]

14.25 蘧伯玉使人於孔子。孔子與之坐而問焉，曰：「夫子何爲？」對曰：「夫子欲寡其過而未能也。」

使者出。子曰：「使乎！使乎！」

Qu Boyu, a minister of Wey, sent an envoy to see Confucius. Confucius sitting together with him asked him a question: "How is the Minister doing these days?" The envoy replied, "The Minister has been trying to reduce his faults, but with no success."

When the envoy had departed, the Master said, "That is an envoy! That is an envoy!"[238]

14.26 子曰：「不在其位，不謀其政。」

曾子曰：「君子思不出其位。」

The Master said, "Do not plan the policies of an office you do not hold."[239]

Master Zeng commented, "The thoughts of exemplary persons (*junzi* 君子) do not wander beyond their station."[240]

14.27 子曰：「君子恥其言而過其行。」

The Master said, "Exemplary persons would feel shame if their words were better than their deeds."

14.28 子曰：「君子道者三，我無能焉：仁者不憂，知者不惑，勇者不懼。」子貢曰：「夫子自道也。」

The Master said, "The path (*dao* 道) of the exemplary person (*junzi* 君子) has three conditions that I am unable to find in myself: The authoritative (*ren* 仁) are not anxious; the wise (*zhi* 知) are not in a quandary; the courageous are not timid."

Zigong replied, "This is the path that you yourself walk, sir."[241]

14.29　子貢方人。子曰：「賜也賢乎哉？夫我則不暇。」

Zigong was given to judging other people. The Master said, "It is because Zigong is of such superior character (*xian* 賢) himself that he has time for this. I myself have none."

14.30　子曰：「不患人之不己知，患其不能也。」

The Master said, "Don't worry about not being recognized by others; worry about not having any reason for them to recognize you."[242]

14.31　子曰：「不逆詐，不億不信，抑亦先覺者，是賢乎！」

The Master said, "Without anticipating duplicity or suspecting dishonesty, to still be the first to become aware of such conduct—is this not a mark of superior character (*xian* 賢)?"

14.32　微生畝謂孔子曰：「丘何爲是栖栖者與？無乃爲佞乎？」孔子曰：「非敢爲佞也，疾固也。」

Weisheng Mou said to Confucius, "Why do you flit from perch to perch? Are you aspiring to be an eloquent talker?"

Confucius replied, "It is not that I aspire to be an eloquent talker, but rather that I hate inflexibility."

14.33　子曰：「驥不稱其力，稱其德也。」

The Master said, "A fine steed is praised for its excellence (*de* 德), not for its strength."

14.34　或曰：「『以德報怨』，何如？」子曰：「何以報德？『以直報怨，以德報德。』」

Someone asked, "What do you think about the saying: 'Repay ill will with beneficence (*de* 德)'?"[243]

The Master replied, "Then how would one repay beneficence? Repay ill will by remaining true. Repay beneficence with gratitude (*de* 德)."[244]

14.35　子曰：「莫我知也夫！」子貢曰：「何爲其莫知子也？」子曰：「不怨天，不尤人，下學而上達。知我者其天乎！」

The Master sighed, saying, "No one appreciates me!"[245]

Zigong replied, "Why doesn't anyone appreciate you, sir?"

The Master said, "I don't hold any ill will against *tian* 天 nor blame other people. I study what is near at hand and aspire to what is lofty. It is only *tian* who appreciates me!"

14.36　公伯寮愬子路於季孫。子服景伯以告，曰：「夫子固有惑志於公伯寮，吾力猶能肆諸市朝。」

子曰：「道之將行也與，命也；道之將廢也與，命也。公伯寮其如命何！」

Gongbo Liao maligned Zilu to Ji Sun. Zifu Jingbo reported it to the Master, and moreover said, "My master Ji Sun has certainly been led astray by Gongbo Liao, but I still have enough influence to have Gongbo Liao's corpse displayed in the marketplace."

The Master replied, "If the way (*dao* 道) is going to prevail in the world, it is because circumstances (*ming* 命) would have it so; if it is not going to prevail, it is because they won't. What effect is the likes of Gongbo Liao going to have on these circumstances?"

14.37　子曰：「賢者辟世，其次辟地，其次辟色，其次辟言。」

子曰：「作者七人矣。」

The Master said, "Those of the highest character (*xian* 賢) avoid office in such an age altogether, the next avoid the specific place, the next avoid people with decadent manners, and the next avoid those with decadent things to say."

The Master said, "There were seven who took such initiatives."[246]

14.38 子路宿於石門。晨門曰：「奚自？」子路曰：「自孔氏。」曰：「是知其不可而爲之者與？」

Zilu spent the night at Stone Gate. The morning gatekeeper asked him, "Where are you from?" "From the residence of Confucius," replied Zilu. "Isn't he the one who keeps trying although he knows that it is in vain?" asked the gatekeeper.

14.39 子擊磬於衞，有荷蕢而過孔氏之門者，曰：「有心哉，擊磬乎！」既而曰：「鄙哉，硜硜乎！莫己知也，斯已而已矣。『深則厲，淺則揭。』」
　　　子曰：「果哉！末之難矣。」

The Master while in Wey was playing on the stone chimes. A person, toting his baskets and passing by the gate of the Confucius family residence, exclaimed, "How moving!" At the end of the piece, he continued, "How common! And so stubborn! If no one appreciates him, he should simply give it up![247]

If the water is deep, you take the plunge,
If it is shallow, you lift your skirts."[248]

The Master remarked, "That would certainly be decisive! And so easy, too!"

14.40 子張曰：「《書》云：『高宗諒陰，三年不言。』何謂也？」子曰：「何必高宗，古之人皆然。君薨，百官總己以聽於冢宰三年。」

Zizhang said, "The *Book of Documents* says: 'When the Shang dynasty king Gaozong dwelt in the mourning shed, for three years he did not speak.'[249] What is the meaning of this passage?"

The Master said, "It was not only Gaozong[250]—all of the ancients did the same. When the ruler died, all of the various ministers would come together and place themselves under the command of the prime minister for a period of three years."[251]

14.41　子曰：「上好禮，則民易使也。」

The Master said, "If those in high station cherish the observance of ritual propriety (*li* 禮), the common people will be easy to deal with."[252]

14.42　子路問君子。子曰：「脩己以敬。」
　　　　曰：「如斯而已乎？」曰：「脩己以安人。」
　　　　曰：「如斯而已乎？」曰：「脩己以安百姓。脩己以安百姓，堯、舜其猶病諸？」

Zilu asked about exemplary persons (*junzi* 君子). The Master replied, "They cultivate themselves by being respectful."

"Is that all?" asked Zilu.

"They cultivate themselves by bringing accord to their peers."[253]

"Is that all?" asked Zilu.

"They cultivate themselves by bringing accord to the people. Even a Yao or a Shun would find such a task daunting."

14.43　原壤夷俟。子曰：「幼而不孫弟，長而無述焉，老而不死，是為賊。」以杖叩其脛。

Yuanrang[254] was sitting on the floor with his legs stretched out, waiting. The Master scolded him, saying, "In one's youth to be neither modest nor respectful to one's elders, to grow up without having accomplished anything at all to pass on, and on growing old, not to have the courtesy to die—such a person is a thief." He then rapped Yuanrang on the shin with his cane.

14.44　闕黨童子將命。或問之曰：「益者與？」子曰：「吾見其居於位也，見其與先生並行也。非求益者也，欲速成者也。」

A youth from the Que village would carry messages for the Master. Someone asked Confucius, "Is he making any progress?" The Master replied, "I have seen him sitting[255] in places reserved for his seniors, and have seen him walking side by side with his elders. This is someone intent on growing up quickly rather than on making progress."

15.1 衛靈公問陳於孔子。孔子對曰：「俎豆之事，則嘗聞之矣；軍旅之事，未之學也。」明日遂行。

Duke Ling of Wey asked Confucius about military formations. Confucius replied, "I have heard something about the use of ritual vessels, but I have never studied military matters." On the following day, he left the state.[256]

15.2 在陳絕糧，從者病，莫能興。子路慍見曰：「君子亦有窮乎？」子曰：「君子固窮，小人窮斯濫矣。」

While in the state of Chen, their provisions were exhausted, and Confucius' followers became so feeble they could not stand up. Zilu met with the Master, and indignantly said, "Do even exemplary persons (*junzi* 君子) find themselves in such adversity?" The Master replied, "Exemplary persons are steadfast in the face of adversity, while petty persons are engulfed by it."

15.3 子曰：「賜也，女以予爲多學而識之者與？」對曰：「然，非與？」曰：「非也，予一以貫之。」

The Master said, "Zigong, do you take me to be someone who has learned a great deal and who can remember it all?" Zigong replied, "I do indeed. Is it not so?"

"No, it is not," said the Master, "I just pull it together on one continuous strand."[257]

15.4 子曰：「由！知德者鮮矣。」

The Master said, "Zilu, those who realize (*zhi* 知) excellence (*de* 德) are rare indeed."[258]

15.5 子曰：「無爲而治者其舜也與？夫何爲哉？恭己正南面而已矣。」

The Master said, "If anyone could be said to have effected proper order while remaining nonassertive,[259] surely it was Shun. What did he do? He simply assumed an air of deference and faced due south."

15.6 子張問行。子曰：「言忠信，行篤敬，雖蠻貊之邦，行矣。言不忠信，行不篤敬，雖州里，行乎哉？立則見其參於前也，在輿則見其倚於衡也，夫然後行。」子張書諸紳。

Zizhang asked about proper conduct. The Master replied, "If you do your utmost (*zhong* 忠) to make good on your word (*xin* 信), and you are earnest and respectful in your conduct, even though you are living in the barbarian states of Man or Mo, your conduct will be proper. If, on the other hand, you do not do your utmost to make good on your word, and you are not earnest and respectful in your conduct, even if you never leave your own neighborhood, how can your conduct be proper? When standing, see these words—'do your utmost to make good on your word, be earnest and respectful in your conduct'—in front of you, and when riding in your carriage, see them propped against the stanchion. Only then will your conduct be proper."

Zizhang wrote the words down on his sash.

15.7 子曰：「直哉史魚！邦有道，如矢；邦無道，如矢。君子哉蘧伯玉！邦有道，則仕；邦無道，則可卷而懷之。」

The Master said, "How true was Shiyu! When the way (*dao* 道) prevailed in the state, he was as true as an arrow; when it did not, he was still as true as an arrow. And Qu Boyu was indeed an exemplary person (*junzi* 君子)! When the way prevailed in the state, he gave of his service, and when it did not, he rolled it up and tucked it away."[260]

15.8　子曰：「可與言而不與言，失人；不可與言而與之言，失言。知者不失人，亦不失言。」

The Master said, "To fail to speak with someone who can be engaged is to let that person go to waste; to speak with someone who cannot be engaged is to waste your words. The wise (*zhi* 知) do not let people go to waste, but they do not waste their words either."

15.9　子曰：「志士仁人，無求生以害仁，有殺身以成仁。」

The Master said, "For the resolute scholar-apprentice (*shi* 士) and the authoritative person (*renren* 仁人), while they would not compromise their authoritative conduct to save their lives, they might well give up their lives in order to achieve it."

15.10　子貢問爲仁。子曰：「工欲善其事，必先利其器。居是邦也，事其大夫之賢者，友其士之仁者。」

Zigong inquired about authoritative conduct (*ren* 仁). The Master replied, "Tradesmen wanting to be good at (*shan* 善) their trade must first[261] sharpen their tools. While dwelling in this state, then, we should serve those ministers who are of the highest character (*xian* 賢), and befriend those scholar-apprentices (*shi* 士) who are most authoritative in their conduct."

15.11 顏淵問爲邦。子曰：「行夏之時，乘殷之輅，服周之冕，樂則《韶》《舞》。放鄭聲，遠佞人。鄭聲淫，佞人殆。」

Yan Hui asked about a viable state. The Master replied, "Introduce the calendar of the Xia dynasty,[262] ride on the large yet plain chariot of the Yin, wear the ceremonial cap of the Zhou, and as for music, play the *shao* and *wu*.[263] Abolish the 'music' from the state of Zheng and keep glib talkers at a distance, for the Zheng music is lewd and glib talkers are dangerous."[264]

15.12 子曰：「人無遠慮，必有近憂。」

The Master said, "The person who does not consider what is still far off will not escape being alarmed at what is near at hand."

15.13 子曰：「已矣乎！吾未見好德如好色者也。」

The Master said, "I have yet to meet the person who is fonder of excellence (*de* 德) than of physical beauty, and I am afraid I never will."[265]

15.14 子曰：「臧文仲、其竊位者與！知柳下惠之賢而不與立也。」

The Master said, "Does not Zang Wenzhong hold his own office under false pretenses? While knowing the superior character (*xian* 賢) of the man known as Liu Xiahui—'the kind man under the willow tree'[266]—he failed to give him a place."

15.15 子曰：「躬自厚而薄責於人，則遠怨矣。」

The Master said, "To demand much from oneself personally, and not overmuch from others, will keep ill will at a distance."

15.16 子曰：「不曰『如之何、如之何』者，吾末如之何也已矣。」

The Master said, "There is nothing that I can do for someone who is not constantly asking himself: 'What to do? What to do?'"

15.17 子曰：「群居終日，言不及義，好行小慧，難矣哉！」

The Master said, "Those who would get together all day long and, occupying themselves with witty remarks, never once get to the topic of appropriate conduct (*yi* 義)—such persons are hard to deal with."

15.18 子曰：「君子義以爲質，禮以行之，孫以出之，信以成之。君子哉！」

The Master said, "Having a sense of appropriate conduct (*yi* 義) as one's basic disposition (*zhi* 質), developing it in observing ritual propriety (*li* 禮), expressing it with modesty, and consummating it in making good on one's word (*xin* 信): this then is an exemplary person (*junzi* 君子)."[267]

15.19 子曰：「君子病無能焉，不病人之不己知也。」

The Master said, "Exemplary persons (*junzi* 君子) are distressed by their own lack of ability, not by the failure of others to acknowledge them."

15.20 子曰：「君子疾沒世而名不稱焉。」

The Master said, "Exemplary persons (*junzi* 君子) despise the thought of ending their days without having established a name."

15.21　子曰：「君子求諸己，小人求諸人。」

The Master said, "Exemplary persons (*junzi* 君子) make demands on themselves, while petty persons make demands on others."

15.22　子曰：「君子矜而不爭，群而不黨。」

The Master said, "Exemplary persons (*junzi* 君子) are self-possessed but not contentious; they gather together with others, but do not form cliques."

15.23　子曰：「君子不以言舉人，不以人廢言。」

The Master said, "Exemplary persons (*junzi* 君子) do not promote others because of what they say, nor do they reject what is said because of who says it."

15.24　子貢問曰：「有一言而可以終身行之者乎？」子曰：「其恕乎！己所不欲，勿施於人。」

Zigong asked, "Is there one expression that can be acted upon until the end of one's days?"

　　　The Master replied, "There is *shu* 恕: do not impose on others what you yourself do not want."[268]

15.25　子曰：「吾之於人也，誰毀誰譽。如有所譽者，其有所試矣。斯民也，三代之所以直道而行也。」

The Master said, "When it comes to other people, I am not usually given to praise or blame.[269] But if I do praise people, you can be sure they have proven themselves to be worthy of it. It is because of such people that the Three Ages—Xia, Shang, and Zhou—steadfastly continued on the true path (*dao* 道)."

15.26　子曰：「吾猶及史之闕文也。有馬者借人乘之，今亡矣夫！」

The Master said, "I still encounter places where scribes have given us problematic text. Today you never see someone who has a horse lending it to someone else to ride."[270]

15.27　子曰：「巧言亂德。小不忍，則亂大謀。」

The Master said, "Clever words undermine excellence (*de* 德). If one is impatient with the details, great plans will come to naught."

15.28　子曰：「眾惡之，必察焉；眾好之，必察焉。」

The Master said, "Where everyone despises a person, you must look into the matter carefully; where everyone celebrates a person, you must also look into it carefully."[271]

15.29　子曰：「人能弘道，非道弘人。」

The Master said, "It is the person who is able to broaden the way (*dao* 道), not the way that broadens the person."

15.30　子曰：「過而不改，是謂過矣。」

The Master said, "Having gone astray, to fail to get right back on track is to stray indeed."[272]

15.31　子曰：「吾嘗終日不食，終夜不寢，以思，無益，不如學也。」

The Master said, "Once, lost in my thoughts, I went a whole day without eating and a whole night without sleeping. I got nothing out of it, and would have been better off devoting the time to learning."[273]

15.32　子曰：「君子謀道不謀食。耕也，餒在其中矣；學也，祿在其中矣。君子憂道不憂貧。」

The Master said, "Exemplary persons (*junzi* 君子) make their plans around the way (*dao* 道) and not around their sustenance. Tilling the land often leads to hunger as a matter of course; studying often leads to an official salary as a matter of course.[274] Exemplary persons are anxious about the way, and not about poverty."

15.33　子曰：「知及之，仁不能守之；雖得之，必失之。知及之，仁能守之。不莊以涖之，則民不敬。知及之，仁能守之，莊以涖之，動之不以禮，未善也。」

The Master said, "When persons come to a realization (*zhi* 知) but are not authoritative (*ren* 仁) enough to sustain its implementation, even though they had it, they are sure to lose it. When persons come to a realization, are sufficiently authoritative to implement it, but nevertheless fail to guide the common people with proper dignity, the people will not be respectful. When persons come to a realization, are authoritative enough to implement it, guide the common people with proper dignity, but fail to inspire them by observing ritual propriety (*li* 禮), they are still not good enough at it."[275]

15.34　子曰：「君子不可小知而可大受也，小人不可大受而可小知也。」

The Master said, "Exemplary persons (*junzi* 君子) cannot be given trivial assignments but can be relied upon for important responsibilities. Petty persons, then, are the opposite."

15.35　子曰：「民之於仁也，甚於水火。水火、吾見蹈而死者矣，未見蹈仁而死者也。」

The Master said, "Authoritative conduct (*ren* 仁) is more vital to the common people than even fire and water. I have seen persons lose their lives after walking[276] into fire or into water, but I have yet to see a casualty from authoritative conduct."[277]

15.36　子曰：「當仁，不讓於師。」

The Master said, "In striving to be authoritative in your conduct (*ren* 仁), do not yield even to your teacher."[278]

15.37　子曰：「君子貞而不諒。」

The Master said, "Exemplary persons (*junzi* 君子) are proper, but not fastidious."

15.38　子曰：「事君，敬其事而後其食。」

The Master said, "In serving your lord, compensation comes second to full attention to one's duties."

15.39　子曰：「有教無類。」

The Master said, "In instruction, there is no such thing as social classes."[279]

15.40　子曰：「道不同，不相爲謀。」

The Master said, "People who have chosen different ways (*dao* 道) cannot make plans together."

15.41　子曰：「辭達而已矣。」

The Master said, "In expressing oneself, it is simply a matter of getting the point across."

15.42　師冕見，及階，子曰：「階也。」及席，子曰：「席也。」皆坐，子告之曰：「某在斯，某在斯。」
　　　師冕出。子張問曰：「與師言之道與？」子曰：「然；固相師之道也。」

The blind Master of Music, Mian, had an interview with Confucius, and, on reaching the steps, the Master said, "Here are the steps," and on reaching the mat, the Master said, "Here is the mat." When they had all sat down together, the

Master informed him of who was present: "So-and-so is here, and so-and-so is there."

When Master of Music Mian had departed, Zizhang asked Confucius, "Is this the way (*dao* 道) that one should speak with a blind music master?"

Confucius replied, "Indeed, this has been the traditional way of assisting a music master."

16.1 　季氏將伐顓臾。冉有、季路見於孔子曰：「季氏將有事於顓臾。」

孔子曰：「求！無乃爾是過與？夫顓臾，昔者先王以爲東蒙主，且在邦域之中矣，是社稷之臣也。何以伐爲？」

冉有曰：「夫子欲之，吾二臣者皆不欲也。」

孔子曰：「求！周任有言曰：『陳力就列，不能者止。』危而不持，顛而不扶，則將焉用彼相矣？且爾言過矣，虎兕出於柙，龜玉毀於櫝中，是誰之過與？」

冉有曰：「今夫顓臾，固而近於費。今不取，後世必爲子孫憂。」

孔子曰：「求！君子疾夫舍曰欲之而必爲之辭。丘也聞有國有家者，不患寡而患不均，不患貧而患不安。蓋均無貧，和無寡，安無傾。夫如是，故遠人不服，則脩文德以來之。既來之，則安之。今由與求也，相夫子，遠人不服而不能來也；邦分崩離析而不能守也；而謀動干戈於邦內。吾恐季孫之憂，不在顓臾，而在蕭牆之內也。」

The Ji clan was about to attack its vassal state, Zhuanyu. Ranyou and Zilu had an interview with Confucius, and informed him, "The Ji clan is going to make trouble with Zhuanyu."

The Master replied, "Ranyou! Shouldn't you take the blame for this? The people of Zhuanyu in ancient times were put in charge of the sacrifices to Dongmeng mountain, and further, residing within the borders of our state, are subject to our sacrifices to the gods of the soil and grain. Why would we want to attack them?"

Ranyou replied, "Our lord wants to attack Zhuanyu, but Zilu and I are dead set against it."

The Master rejoined, "Ranyou! The ancient historian Zhouren has said:

To show off your strength you deploy your ranks,
If you are lacking, you cease and desist.

If when one's lord encounters danger his ministers do not support him, or when he is about to fall his ministers do not catch him, then what on earth are his ministers for? And besides, what you say is not so. When a tiger or rhinoceros escapes from its cage, or when a precious tortoise shell or piece of jade is destroyed in its case, who is to blame for this?"

Ranyou replied, "Now then, Zhuanyu is heavily fortified, and is near to the Ji clan's fief, Bei. If we do not annex it today, in the course of time it is certain to become a source of concern for our descendents."

Confucius said, "Ranyou! What the exemplary person (*junzi* 君子) hates most is having to declare in favor of something that he has already rejected, and then to have to come up with some excuse for doing so. As for me, I have heard that the ruler of a state or the head of a household:

Does not worry that his people are poor,
But that wealth is inequitably distributed;
Does not worry that his people are too few in number,
But that they are disharmonious.

Does not worry that his people are unstable,
But that they are insecure.

For if the wealth is equitably distributed, there is no poverty; if the people are harmonious, they are not few in number; if the people are secure, they are not unstable.[280] Under these circumstances, if distant populations are still not won over, they persuade them to join them through the cultivation of their refinement (*wen* 文) and excellence (*de* 德), and once they have joined them, they make them feel secure.

Now, with you and Zilu as ministers to your lord, you are unable to persuade distant populations who are not won over, you are unable to shore up your own state that is divided and crumbling around you, but instead resort to the use of arms within the state itself. I fear that the real worry for Ji Sun does not lie with Zhuanyu, but within the screen of reverence at the Lu court."[281]

16.2 孔子曰：「天下有道，則禮樂征伐自天子出；天下無道，則禮樂征伐自諸侯出。自諸侯出，蓋十世希不失矣；自大夫出，五世希不失矣；陪臣執國命，三世希不失矣。天下有道，則政不在大夫。天下有道，則庶人不議。」

Confucius said, "When the way (*dao* 道) prevails in the world, ritual propriety (*li* 禮), music (*yue* 樂), and punitive campaigns are initiated by the emperor. If the way does not prevail in the world, then they are initiated by the various nobles. When they are initiated by the various nobles, it is unlikely that the state will survive beyond ten generations. When they are initiated by the ministers, it is unlikely that the state will survive beyond five generations. When the household stewards of the ministers seize command of the state, it is unlikely that the state will survive beyond three generations. When the way prevails in the world, governing does not lie in the hands of the ministers; when the way prevails in the world, the common people do not debate affairs of state."[282]

16.3　孔子曰：「祿之去公室五世矣，政逮於大夫四世矣，故夫三桓之子孫微矣。」

Confucius said, "It has been five generations since ranks and emoluments have been determined by the ducal house of Lu, and it has been four generations since governance devolved to the ministers. It is thus that the power of the descendents of the Three Families who came to prominence under Duke Xuan is steadily declining."

16.4　孔子曰：「益者三友，損者三友。友直，友諒，友多聞，益矣。友便辟，友善柔，友便佞，損矣。」

Confucius said, "Having three kinds of friends will be a source of personal improvement; having three other kinds of friends will be a source of personal injury. One stands to be improved by friends who are true, who make good on their word, and who are broadly informed; one stands to be injured by friends who are ingratiating, who feign compliance, and who are glib talkers."

16.5　孔子曰：「益者三樂，損者三樂。樂節禮樂，樂道人之善，樂多賢友，益矣。樂驕樂，樂佚遊，樂宴樂，損矣。」

Confucius said, "Finding enjoyment in three kinds of activities will be a source of personal improvement; finding enjoyment in three other kinds of activities will be a source of personal injury. One stands to be improved by the enjoyment found in attuning oneself to the rhythms of ritual propriety (*li* 禮) and music (*yue* 樂),[283] by the enjoyment found in talking about what others do well (*shan* 善), and by the enjoyment found in having a circle of many friends of superior character (*xian* 賢); one stands to be injured by finding enjoyment in being arrogant, by finding enjoyment in dissolute diversions, and by finding enjoyment in the easy life."

16.6　孔子曰：「侍於君子有三愆：言未及之而言謂之躁，言及之而不言謂之隱，未見顏色而言謂之瞽。」

Confucius said, "There are three mistakes that are easily made in attendance on one's lord: to speak first without waiting for the lord to speak is called being rash; to not speak when you should speak up is called holding back; to speak up without taking into account the lord's countenance is called being blind."

16.7　孔子曰：「君子有三戒：少之時，血氣未定，戒之在色；及其壯也，血氣方剛，戒之在鬪；及其老也，血氣既衰，戒之在得。」

Confucius said, "Exemplary persons (*junzi* 君子) have three kinds of conduct that they guard against: when young and vigorous, they guard against licentiousness; in their prime when their vigor is at its height, they guard against conflict; in their old age when their vigor is declining, they guard against acquisitiveness."

16.8　孔子曰：「君子有三畏：畏天命，畏大人，畏聖人之言。小人不知天命而不畏也，狎大人，侮聖人之言。」

Confucius said, "Exemplary persons (*junzi* 君子) hold three things in awe: the propensities of *tian* (*tianming* 天命), persons in high station, and the words of the sages (*shengren* 聖人). Petty persons, knowing nothing of the propensities of *tian*, do not hold it in awe; they are unduly familiar with persons in high station, and ridicule the words of the sages."

16.9 孔子曰：「生而知之者上也，學而知之者次也；困而學之，又其次也；困而不學，民斯爲下矣。」

Confucius said, "Knowledge (*zhi* 知) acquired through a natural propensity for it is its highest level;[284] knowledge acquired through study is the next highest; something learned in response to difficulties encountered is again the next highest. But those among the common people who do not learn even when vexed with difficulties—they are at the bottom of the heap."

16.10 孔子曰：「君子有九思：視思明，聽思聰，色思溫，貌思恭，言思忠，事思敬，疑思問，忿思難，見得思義。」

Confucius said, "Exemplary persons (*junzi* 君子) always keep nine things in mind: in looking they think about clarity, in hearing they think about acuity, in countenance they think about cordiality, in bearing and attitude they think about deference, in speaking they think about doing their utmost (*zhong* 忠), in conducting affairs they think about due respect, in entertaining doubts they think about the proper questions to ask, in anger they think about regret, in sight of gain they think about appropriate conduct (*yi* 義)."

16.11 孔子曰：「見善如不及，見不善而探湯。吾見其人矣，吾聞其語矣。隱居以求其志，行義以達其道。吾聞其語矣，未見其人也。」

Confucius said, "'On seeing ability (*shan* 善), I go after it as though I cannot catch up to it; on seeing a lack of ability, I recoil from it as though testing boiling water.' I have heard such words, and have even seen such persons. 'I dwell in seclusion to pursue my ends, and act on my sense of what is appropriate (*yi* 義) to extend my way (*dao* 道).' I have heard such words, but I have yet to see such persons."

16.12 齊景公有馬千駟，死之日，民無得而稱焉。伯夷、叔齊餓于首陽之下，民到于今稱之。其斯之謂與？

Duke Jing of Qi had a thousand teams of horses, and on the day he died, the common people felt no sense of gratitude (*de* 德) out of which to praise him. On the other hand, Bo Yi and Shu Qi died of starvation at the foot of Shouyang Mountain, and the common people praise them down to the present day. Is this not what it means?"[285]

16.13 陳亢問於伯魚曰：「子亦有異聞乎？」

對曰：「未也。嘗獨立，鯉趨而過庭。曰：『學《詩》乎？』對曰：『未也。』『不學《詩》，無以言。』鯉退而學《詩》。他日，又獨立，鯉趨而過庭。曰：『學禮乎？』對曰：『未也。』『不學禮，無以立。』鯉退而學禮。聞斯二者。」

陳亢退而喜曰：「問一得三，聞《詩》，聞禮，又聞君子遠其子也。」

Chen Gang asked the son of Confucius, Boyu: "Have you been given any kind of special instruction?"

"Not yet," he replied. "Once when my father was standing alone and I hastened quickly and deferentially across the courtyard, he asked me, 'Have you studied the *Songs*?' I replied, 'Not yet,' to which he remarked, 'If you do not study the *Songs*, you will be at a loss as to what to say.' I deferentially took my leave and studied the *Songs*.

"On another day when he was again standing alone, I hastened quickly and deferentially across the courtyard. He asked me, 'Have you studied the *Rites*?' I replied, 'Not yet,' to which he remarked, 'If you do not study the *Rites*, you will be at a loss as to where to stand.' I deferentially took my leave and studied the *Rites*. What I have learned from him, then, are these two things."

Chen Gang, taking his leave, was delighted, and said, "I asked one question and got three answers. I learned the importance of the *Songs* and of the *Rites*, and I also learned that exemplary persons (*junzi* 君子) do not treat their own sons as a special case."

16.14　邦君之妻，君稱之曰夫人，夫人自稱小童；邦人稱之曰君夫人，稱諸異邦曰寡小君；異邦人稱之亦曰君夫人。

The official wife of the ruler of a state is addressed by the ruler as "My Lady." She calls herself, "Little Child." The people of the state refer to her as "Lady of the Lord." In speaking of her with those of other states, the Lord calls her "My Little Lord," and they refer to her as "Lady of the Lord."

17.1　陽貨欲見孔子，孔子不見，歸孔子豚。

孔子時其亡也，而往拜之。

遇諸塗。

謂孔子曰：「來！予與爾言。」曰：「懷其寶而
迷其邦，可謂仁乎？」曰：「不可。好從事而亟失
時，可謂知乎？」曰：「不可。日月逝矣，歲不我
與。」

孔子曰：「諾；吾將仕矣。」

Yang Huo[286] wanted Confucius to come and see him, and
when Confucius would not oblige him, he sent Confucius the
gift of a suckling pig. Confucius, waiting for a time when
Yang Huo would not be home, went to acknowledge the gift.
Confucius however happened to meet up with him on the
road.

Yang Huo said to Confucius, "Come with me! I have
something I would like to speak to you about." Continuing,
he said, "Can you call someone authoritative (*ren* 仁) who
hoards his treasure of talent while his country loses its way? I
should say not. Can you call someone wise (*zhi* 知) who has
always wanted to serve in office but who repeatedly misses
the opportunity to do so? I should say not. The days and
months are passing; the years will not wait for us."

Confucius replied, "All right, all right. I will serve in
office then."[287]

子曰：「性相近也，習相遠也。」

The Master said, "Human beings are similar in their natural tendencies (*xing* 性),[288] but vary greatly by virtue of their habits."

17.3 子曰：「唯上知與下愚不移。」

The Master said, "Only the most wise (*zhi* 知) and the most stupid do not move."

17.4 子之武城，聞弦歌之聲。夫子莞爾而笑，曰：「割雞焉用牛刀？」

子游對曰：「昔者偃也聞諸夫子曰：『君子學道則愛人，小人學道則易使也。』」

子曰：「二三子！偃之言是也。前言戲之耳。」

The Master, on traveling to the walled town of Wu,[289] heard the sounds of stringed instruments and singing. He smiled, saying, "Why would one use an ox cleaver to kill a chicken?"[290]

Ziyou responded, "In the past I have heard you, Master, say, 'Exemplary persons (junzi 君子) who study the way (*dao* 道) love others; petty persons who study the way are easier to employ.'"

The Master replied, "My young friends, what Ziyou has said is right. What I was saying was just in fun."

17.5 公山弗擾以費畔，召，子欲往。

子路不說，曰：「末之也已，何必公山氏之之也？」

子曰：「夫召我者，而豈徒哉？如有用我者，吾其為東周乎？」

Gongshan Furao[291] was plotting rebellion with the Bi stronghold,[292] and summoned Confucius to join him. Confucius wanted to go.

Zilu was upset, and said to Confucius, "So we have nowhere to go—why on earth must we go to this man Gongshan?"

The Master replied, "How could this person who is summoning me be doing so for no reason? If there were someone who would use me, I would give him a 'Zhou of the east.'"

17.6　子張問仁於孔子。孔子曰：「能行五者於天下爲仁
矣。」

　　「請問之。」曰：「恭、寬、信、敏、惠。恭則不
侮，寬則得眾，信則人任焉，敏則有功，惠則足以使
人。」

Zizhang asked Confucius about authoritative conduct (*ren* 仁). Confucius replied, "A person who is able to carry into practice[293] five attitudes in the world can be considered authoritative."

"What are these five attitudes?" asked Zizhang.

Confucius replied, "Deference, tolerance, making good on one's word (*xin* 信), diligence, and generosity. If you are deferential, you will not suffer insult; if tolerant, you will win over the many; if you make good on your word, others will rely upon you; if diligent, you will get results; if generous, you will have the status to employ others effectively."

17.7　佛肸召，子欲往。

　　子路曰：「昔者由也聞諸夫子曰：『親於其身爲
不善者，君子不入也。』佛肸以中牟畔，子之往也，
如之何？」

　　子曰：「然，有是言也。不曰堅乎磨而不磷；不
曰白乎涅而不緇。吾豈匏瓜也哉？焉能繫而不食？」

Bixi summoned Confucius, and Confucius wanted to go. Zilu said, "In the past I have heard you, Master, say, 'Exemplary persons (*junzi* 君子) will have nothing to do with someone who personally behaves badly (*bushan* 不善).' Bixi is plotting rebellion with the Zhongmou stronghold. How could you justify going to him?"

"You are right," said the Master. "It is as you say. But is it not said, 'With the hardest, grinding will not wear it thin.' Is it not said, 'With the whitest, dying will not turn it black.' Am I just some kind of gourd? How can I allow myself to be strung up on the wall and not be eaten?"[294]

17.8 子曰：「由也！女聞六言六蔽矣乎？」對曰：「未也。」

「居！吾語女。好仁不好學，其蔽也愚；好知不好學，其蔽也蕩；好信不好學，其蔽也賊；好直不好學，其蔽也絞；好勇不好學，其蔽也亂；好剛不好學，其蔽也狂。」

The Master said, "Zilu, have you heard of the six flaws that can accompany the six desirable qualities of character?"

"No, I have not," replied Zilu.

"Sit down," said the Master, "and I'll tell you about them. The flaw in being fond of acting authoritatively (*ren* 仁) without equal regard for learning is that you will be easily duped; the flaw in being fond of acting wisely (*zhi* 知) without equal regard for learning is that it leads to self-indulgence; the flaw in being fond of making good on one's word (*xin* 信) without equal regard for learning is that it leads one into harm's way; the flaw in being fond of candor without equal regard for learning is that it leads to rudeness; the flaw in being fond of boldness without equal regard for learning is that it leads to unruliness; the flaw in being fond of firmness without equal regard for learning is that it leads to rashness."[295]

17.9　子曰：「小子！何莫學夫《詩》？《詩》，可以興，可以觀，可以群，可以怨。邇之事父，遠之事君；多識於鳥獸草木之名。」

The Master said, "My young friends, why don't any of you study the *Songs*? Reciting the *Songs* can arouse your sensibilities, strengthen your powers of observation, enhance your ability to get on with others, and sharpen your critical skills. Close at hand it enables you to serve your father, and away at court it enables you to serve your lord. It instills in you a broad vocabulary for making distinctions in the world around you."

17.10　子謂伯魚曰：「女爲《周南》、《召南》矣乎？人而不爲《周南》、《召南》，其猶正牆面而立也與？」

The Master said to his son, Boyu, "Have you mastered the 'Zhounan' and 'Shaonan' sections of the *Book of Songs*? Striving to become a person without doing so is like trying to take your stand with your face to the wall."[296]

17.11　子曰：「禮云禮云，玉帛云乎哉？樂云樂云，鍾鼓云乎哉？」

The Master said, "In referring time and again to observing ritual propriety (*li* 禮), how could I just be talking about gifts of jade and silk? And in referring time and again to making music (*yue* 樂), how could I just be talking about bells and drums?"

17.12　子曰：「色厲而內荏，譬諸小人，其猶穿窬之盜也與？」

The Master said, "As for the person who would give the outward appearance of being stern while being pulp inside, if we were to look to petty people for an example of this kind of deceit, it is the house burglar who bores holes in walls or scales over them."

17.13　子曰：「鄉原、德之賊也。」

The Master said, "The 'village worthy' is excellence (*de* 德) under false pretenses."[297]

17.14　子曰：「道聽而塗說，德之棄也。」

The Master said, "Those who repeat whatever they hear in the streets and alleyways are at odds with excellence (*de* 德)."

17.15　子曰：「鄙夫可與事君也與哉？其未得之也，患不得之。既得之，患失之。苟患失之，無所不至矣。」

The Master said, "How can one possibly join with a common fellow in serving one's lord? Before such a person has been appointed to office, he is desperate that he will not be.[298] Once he has been appointed, he is desperate that he will lose his position. And in his desperation that he might lose his position, he will stop at nothing to hang on to it."

17.16　子曰：「古者民有三疾，今也或是之亡也。古之狂也肆，今之狂也蕩；古之矜也廉，今之矜也忿戾；古之愚也直，今之愚也詐而已矣。」

The Master said, "In the old days, the common people had three faults that people of today perhaps have done away with. Of old, rash people were merely reckless, but nowadays they have managed to overcome all restraint. Of old, proud people were merely smug, but nowadays they are quarrelsome and easily provoked. Of old, stupid people were frank and direct, but nowadays they are positively deceitful."

17.17　子曰：「攷言令色，鮮矣仁。」

The Master said, "It is a rare thing for glib speech and an in-sinuating appearance to accompany authoritative conduct (*ren* 仁)."[299]

17.18 子曰：「惡紫之奪朱也，惡鄭聲之亂雅樂也，惡利口之覆邦家者。」

The Master said, "I detest the fact that purple has stolen the place of red in noble dress;[300] I detest the fact that the sounds of Zheng are corrupting our classical court music;[301] I detest the fact that glib-tongued talkers bring down states and fami-lies."

17.19 子曰：「予欲無言。」子貢曰：「子如不言，則小子何述焉？」子曰：「天何言哉！四時行焉，百物生焉，天何言哉？」

The Master said, "I think I will leave off speaking."

"If you do not speak," Zigong replied, "how will we your followers find the proper way?"[302]

The Master responded, "Does *tian* 天 speak? And yet the four seasons turn and the myriad things are born and grow within it. Does *tian* speak?"

17.20 孺悲欲見孔子，孔子辭以疾。將命者出戶，取瑟而歌，使之聞之。

Ru Bei sought a meeting with Confucius, but Confucius de-clined to entertain him, feigning illness. Just as the envoy car-rying the message was about to depart, Confucius got out his lute and sang, making sure that the messenger heard him.[303]

17.21 宰我問：「三年之喪，期已久矣。君子三年不爲禮，禮必壞；三年不爲樂，樂必崩。舊穀既沒，新穀既升，鑽燧改火，期可已矣。」

　　子曰：「食夫稻，衣夫錦，於女安乎？」

曰：「安。」

「女安，則爲之！夫君子之居喪，食旨不甘，聞樂
不樂，居處不安，故不爲也。今女安，則爲之！」

宰我出。子曰：「予之不仁也！子生三年，然後
免於父母之懷。夫三年之喪，天下之通喪也，予也有
三年之愛於其父母乎！」

Zaiwo inquired, "The three-year mourning period on the
death of one's parents is already too long. If for three years
exemplary persons (*junzi* 君子) were to give up observing
ritual propriety (*li* 禮), the rites would certainly go to ruin.
And if for three years they were to give up the performance
of music (*yue* 樂), music would certainly collapse. The old
grain has been used up, the new crop is ready for harvest,
and the different woods used ceremonially as drills for making fire have gone through their full cycle[304]—surely a year is
good enough."

The Master replied, "Would you then be comfortable
eating fine rice and wearing colorful brocade?"

"I would indeed," responded Zaiwo.

"If you are comfortable, then do it," said the Master.
"When exemplary persons (*junzi* 君子) are in the mourning
shed,[305] it is because they can find no relish in fine-tasting
food, no pleasure in the sound of music, and no comfort in
their usual lodgings, that they do not abbreviate the mourning period to one year. Now if you are comfortable with these
things, then by all means, enjoy them."

When Zaiwo had left, the Master remarked, "Zaiwo is really perverse (*bu ren* 不仁)! It is only after being tended by
his parents for three years that an infant can finally leave
their bosom. The ritual of a three-year mourning period for
one's parents is practiced throughout the empire. Certainly

Zaiwo received this three years of loving care from his parents!"[306]

17.22　子曰：「飽食終日，無所用心，難矣哉！不有博弈者乎？爲之，猶賢乎已。」

The Master said, "There are problems ahead for those who spend their whole day filling their stomachs without ever exercising their heart-and-mind (*xin* 心). Are there not diversions such as the board games of *bo* and *weiqi*? Even playing these games would be better than nothing."[307]

17.23　子路曰：「君子尙勇乎？」子曰：「君子義之爲上，君子有勇而無義爲亂，小人有勇而無義爲盜。」

Zilu said,[308] "Does the exemplary person (*junzi* 君子) give first priority to boldness?"

"In fact," the Master replied, "the exemplary person gives first priority to appropriate conduct (*yi* 義). An exemplary person who is bold yet is lacking a sense of appropriateness will be unruly, while a petty person of the same cut will be a thief."

17.24　子貢曰：「君子亦有惡乎？」子曰：「有惡：惡稱人之惡者，惡居下流而訕上者，惡勇而無禮者，惡果敢而窒者。」

　　　　曰：「賜也亦有惡乎？」「惡徼以爲知者，惡不孫以爲勇者，惡訐以爲直者。」

Zigong said, "Do exemplary persons (*junzi* 君子) have things they detest?"

"They do indeed," said the Master. "They detest those who announce what is detestable in others; they detest those subordinates who would malign their superiors; they detest those who are bold yet do not observe ritual propriety; they detest those who, being determined to get what they want, are unrelenting. But Zigong, don't you, too, have things you detest?"

Zigong replied,[309] "I detest those who think that details and distinctions are the substance of wisdom; I detest those who think that immodesty is boldness; I detest those who think that revealing the secrets of others is being true."[310]

17.25 子曰：「唯女子與小人爲難養也，近之則不孫，遠之則怨。」

The Master said, "It is only women and petty persons who are difficult to provide for. Drawing them close, they are immodest, and keeping them at a distance, they complain."

17.26 子曰：「年四十而見惡焉，其終也已。」

The Master said, "The person who at age forty still evokes the dislike of others is a hopeless case."

18.1 微子去之，箕子爲之奴，比干諫而死。孔子曰：「殷
有三仁焉。」

Viscount Wei abandoned him, Viscount Ji served him as his
slave, and Bi Gan lost his life in remonstrating with him.[311]
Confucius observed, "There were three authoritative persons
(*ren* 仁)[312] during the Shang dynasty."

18.2 柳下惠爲士師，三黜。人曰：「子未可以去乎？」
曰：「直道而事人，焉往而不三黜！枉道而事人，何
必去父母之邦？」

The man known as Liu Xiahui—"the kind man under the
willow tree"[313]—served as a magistrate, and repeatedly he was
dismissed from office. Others said to him, "Can't you quit
the state of Lu?" He replied, "If one follows the straight and
narrow in the service of others, where could one go and not
be repeatedly dismissed from office? If, on the other hand,
one were willing to take a crooked path in the service of others, why leave the state of one's parents?"

18.3 齊景公待孔子曰：「若季氏，則吾不能；以季、孟之
間待之。」曰：「吾老矣，不能用也。」孔子行。

Duke Jing of Qi in hosting Confucius, observed, "I cannot
treat him on a par with the head of the Ji clan—I will treat
him as ranking between the heads of the Ji and Meng clans."

"I am old," he continued, "and cannot make use of him," whereupon Confucius took his leave.[314]

18.4　齊人歸女樂，季桓子受之，三日不朝，孔子行。

The Qi kinsmen[315] made a gift of young singing and dancing girls to the throne. Ji Huanzi[316] accepted them, and for three days he did not hold court, whereupon Confucius took his leave.

18.5　楚狂接輿歌而過孔子曰：「鳳兮鳳兮！何德之衰？往者不可諫，來者猶可追。已而，已而！今之從政者殆而！」

　　　孔子下，欲與之言。趨而辟之，不得與之言。

A madman of Chu, Carriage Groom,[317] was singing as he passed by Confucius:

> "Phoenix! Phoenix![318]
> Excellence (*de* 德) has waned!
> No use rebuking what has already past;
> But you can still give chase to what is yet to come!
> Give it up! Give it up!
> Those who seek office these days are in real danger."[319]

Confucius got down from his carriage, wanting to speak with him. But hastening on his way, the madman avoided him, and Confucius did not get the chance.

18.6　長沮、桀溺耦而耕，孔子過之，使子路問津焉。

　　　長沮曰：「夫執輿者爲誰？」

　　　子路曰：「爲孔丘。」

　　　曰：「是魯孔丘與？」

　　　曰：「是也。」

　　　曰：「是知津矣。」

　　　問於桀溺。

桀溺曰：「子爲誰？」

曰：「爲仲由。」

曰：「是魯孔丘之徒與？」

對曰：「然。」

曰：「滔滔者天下皆是也，而誰以易之？且而與其從辟人之士也，豈若從辟世之士哉？」耰而不輟。

子路行以告。

夫子憮然曰：「鳥獸不可與同群，吾非斯人之徒與而誰與？天下有道，丘不與易也。」

Old Marsh and Boldly Sunk were out in harness ploughing the field. Confucius, passing their way, sent Zilu to ask them where to ford.

Old Marsh asked him, "Who is that man holding the reins of your carriage?"

"He is Confucius," replied Zilu.

"The Confucius of Lu?"

"Indeed."

"Then he already knows where the ford is."

Zilu turned and asked Boldly Sunk where to ford.

"Who are you?" asked Boldly Sunk.

"I am Zilu."

"You are that follower of Confucius of Lu?"

"The very one."

He then said, "We are inundated like floodwaters. And the whole world is the same. Who then is going to change it into a new world? You follow after a teacher who avoids people selectively. Wouldn't you be better off following a teacher who avoids the world altogether?" As he spoke he continued to turn the earth over the seeds.

Zilu left to inform Confucius. Confucius, with some frustration, replied, "We cannot run with the birds and beasts. Am I not one among the people of this world? If not them, with whom should I associate? If the way (*dao* 道) prevailed in the world, I wouldn't need to change it."

18.7　子路從而後，遇丈人，以杖荷蓧。

子路問曰：「子見夫子乎？」

丈人曰：「四體不勤，五穀不分。孰爲夫子？」
植其杖而芸。

子路拱而立。

止子路宿，殺雞爲黍而食之，見其二子焉。

明日，子路行以告。

子曰：「隱者也。」使子路反見之。至，則行
矣。

子路曰：「不士無義。長幼之節，不可廢也；君
臣之義，如之何其廢之？欲絜其身，而亂大倫。君子
之仕也，行其義也。道之不行，已知之矣。」

Zilu was accompanying the Master when he fell behind. He came across an old man using his staff to tote his baskets on his shoulder.

"Have you seen my Master?" asked Zilu.

The old man replied,

"You—'a person who does no work

And who can't tell one grain from another—'[320]

who would your Master be?" He then stuck his staff in the ground and continued his weeding.

Zilu stood by him with his hands cupped respectfully in a salute. The old man invited Zilu to spend the night. He killed a chicken and prepared some special millet for the occasion, and presented his two sons to his guest. On the following day, Zilu took his leave, and reported the event to Confucius.

"He is a recluse," said the Master, and sent Zilu back to see him again. On Zilu's arrival, he discovered the old man had already left.[321]

Zilu remarked, "To refuse office is to fail to do what is important and appropriate (*yi* 義). If the differentiation between young and old cannot be abandoned, how could one think of abandoning what is appropriate between ruler and subject? This is to throw the most important relationships into turmoil in one's efforts to remain personally untarnished. The opportunity of the exemplary person (*junzi* 君子) to serve in office is the occasion to effect what is judged to be important and appropriate. That the way (*dao* 道) does not prevail—this is known already."

18.8 逸民：伯夷、叔齊、虞仲、夷逸、朱張、柳下惠、少連。子曰：「不降其志，不辱其身，伯夷、叔齊與！」謂「柳下惠、少連，降志辱身矣，言中倫，行中慮，其斯而已矣。」謂「虞仲、夷逸，隱居放言，身中清，廢中權。我則異於是，無可無不可。」

Examples of those whose talents were lost to the people are the following: Bo Yi, Shu Qi, Yu Zhong, Yi Yi, Zhu Zhang, Liu Xiahui, and Shao Lian.

The Master observed, "Bo Yi and Shu Qi were two men who were unwilling to compromise their purposes or bring disgrace on their own persons."[322]

With respect to Liu Xiahui—"the kind man under the willow tree"[323]—and Shao Lian, he observed, "Even though they compromised their purposes and suffered disgrace, they were reasonable in what they had to say and deliberate in what they did. That is all there was to it."

As for Yu Zhong and Yi Yi, he said, "They lived in seclusion and said what came to mind. They were flawless in their own persons and their being set aside was at their own discretion. But I am different from all of these people[324] in that I do not have presuppositions as to what may and may not be done."

18.9 大師摯適齊，亞飯干適楚，三飯繚適蔡，四飯缺適秦，鼓方叔入於河，播鼗武入於漢，少師陽、擊磬襄入於海。

The Grand Musician Zhi fled to the state of Qi; the Music Master Gan who played for the second course, fled to Chu; the Music Master Liao from the third course fled to Cai; the Music Master Que from the fourth course fled to Qin. The drummer Fang Shu went to live on the north bank of the Yellow River; the tambour drummer Wu went to live on the north bank of the Han River; the Music Apprentice Yang and the stonechimes player Xiang went to live at the sea's edge.[325]

18.10 周公謂魯公曰：「君子不弛其親，不使大臣怨乎不以。故舊無大故，則不棄也。無求備於一人！」

The Duke of Zhou addressed his son, the Duke of Lu, saying: "Exemplary persons (*junzi* 君子) are not remiss in family relations, nor do they give the great ministers occasion to harbor ill will because they are ignored. They do not, without some compelling reason, dismiss officials who have given long service, and do not seek all things from any one man."

18.11 周有八士：伯達、伯适、仲突、仲忽、叔夜、叔夏、季隨、季騧。

Zhou had eight worthy scholar-apprentices (*shi* 士): the eldest twins Da and Kuo; the middle twins Tu and Hu; the younger twins Ye and Xia, and the youngest twins Sui and Kuo.[326]

19.1 子張曰：「士見危致命，見得思義，祭思敬，喪思哀，其可已矣。」

Zizhang said, "Those scholar-apprentices (*shi* 士) are quite acceptable who on seeing danger are ready to put their lives on the line, who on seeing an opportunity for gain concern themselves with what is appropriate (*yi* 義), who in performing sacrifice concern themselves with proper respect, and who in participating in a funeral concern themselves with grief."

19.2 子張曰：「執德不弘，信道不篤，焉能為有？焉能為亡？」

Zizhang said, "Those who lack a firm grip on excellence (*de* 德) and who are not earnest in living up to the way (*dao* 道)—it makes no difference if they live or die."

19.3 子夏之門人問交於子張。子張曰：「子夏云何？」

對曰：「子夏曰：『可者與之，其不可者拒之。』」

子張曰：「異乎吾所聞：君子尊賢而容眾，嘉善而矜不能。我之大賢與，於人何所不容？我之不賢與，人將拒我，如之何其拒人也？」

The disciples of Zixia asked Zizhang about making acquaintances. Zizhang queried, "What has Zixia told you?" They replied, "Join together with those who are worthy of association; spurn those who aren't."

Zizhang responded, "This is different from what I have learned. The exemplary person (*junzi* 君子) exalts those of superior character (*xian* 賢) and is tolerant of everyone, praises those who are truly efficacious (*shan* 善) and is sympathetic with those who are less so. If, in comparison with others, I am truly superior in character, who am I unable to tolerate? If I am not superior in the comparison, and people are going to spurn me, on what basis do I spurn others?"

19.4　子夏曰：「雖小道，必有可觀者焉；致遠恐泥，是以君子不爲也。」

Zixia said, "Even along byways, there are bound to be worthwhile things to see. The reason that exemplary persons (*junzi* 君子) do not pay attention to such things is because they have a long way to go and are afraid of being bogged down."

19.5　子夏曰：「日知其所亡，月無忘其所能，可謂好學也已矣。」

Zixia said, "A person can be said to truly love learning (*haoxue* 好學) who, on a daily basis, is aware of what is yet to be learned, and who, from month to month, does not forget what has already been mastered."

19.6　子夏曰：「博學而篤志，切問而近思，仁在其中矣。」

Zixia said, "Learn broadly yet be focused in your purposes; inquire with urgency yet reflect closely on the question at hand—authoritative conduct (*ren* 仁) lies simply in this."

19.7　子夏曰：「百工居肆以成其事，君子學以致其道。」

Zixia said, "The various craftsmen stay in their shops so that they may master their trades; exemplary persons (*junzi* 君子) study that they might promote their way (*dao* 道)."

19.8 子夏曰：「小人之過也必文。」

Zixia said, "Petty persons are sure to gloss over where they have gone astray."

19.9 子夏曰：「君子有三變：望之儼然，即之也溫，聽其言也厲。」

Zixia said, "Exemplary persons (*junzi* 君子) impress one differently: Seen from far off, they appear stately; on approaching, they appear cordial; on hearing them speak, they appear stern."

19.10 子夏曰：「君子信而後勞其民；未信，則以爲厲己也。信而後諫；未信，則以爲謗己也。」

Zixia said, "Only once exemplary persons (*junzi* 君子) have won the confidence (*xin* 信) of the common people do they work them hard; otherwise, the people would think themselves exploited. Only once they have won the confidence of their lord do they remonstrate with him; otherwise, their lord would think himself maligned."

19.11 子夏曰：「大德不踰閑；小德出入可也。」

Zixia said, "In matters which demand surpassing excellence (*de* 德), one never oversteps the mark; in minor affairs one has some latitude."

19.12 子游曰：「子夏之門人小子，當洒掃、應對、進退，則可矣，抑末也。本之則無，如之何？」

子夏聞之，曰：「噫！言游過矣！君子之道，孰先傳焉？孰後倦焉？譬諸草木，區以別矣。君子之道，焉可誣也？有始有卒者，其唯聖人乎！」

Ziyou said, "The disciples and young friends of Zixia are quite all right when it comes to housekeeping, taking care of guests, and standing in attendance, but these are just the tips of the branches. What do you do about the fact that they have no roots?"

Zixia heard about this, and responded, "Ah! Ziyou is mistaken! On the path (*dao* 道) of the exemplary person (*junzi* 君子), what is passed on first and what must wait until maturity, can be compared to plants which must be nurtured differently according to kind. How can he so misrepresent the path of the exemplary person? And it is the sage (*shengren* 聖人) alone who walks this path every step from start to finish."

19.13 子夏曰：「仕而優則學，學而優則仕。」

Zixia said, "If while serving in public office one has a surplus of energy, it should be directed toward study; if while studying one has a surplus of energy, it should be directed at seeking public office."[327]

19.14 子游曰：「喪致乎哀而止。」

Ziyou said, "In mourning one does not go beyond the full expression of one's grief."

19.15 子游曰：「吾友張也為難能也，然而未仁。」

Ziyou said, "My good friend Zizhang is laudable in his abilities, but even so, he is not yet authoritative in his conduct (*ren* 仁)."

19.16 曾子曰：「堂堂乎張也，難與並為仁矣。」

Master Zeng said, "So lofty and distant is Zizhang that it is difficult indeed to work shoulder to shoulder with him in becoming authoritative in one's conduct (*ren* 仁)."[328]

19.17　曾子曰：「吾聞諸夫子：人未有自致者也，必也親喪乎！」

Master Zeng said, "I have heard the Master say: 'Even those who have yet to give of themselves utterly[329] are sure to do so in the mourning of their parents.'"

19.18　曾子曰：「吾聞諸夫子：孟莊子之孝也，其他可能也；其不改父之臣與父之政，是難能也。」

Master Zeng said, "I have heard the Master say: 'While in most respects others could attain Meng Zhuangzi's degree of filial piety (*xiao* 孝), it would be difficult indeed for them to follow the way in which he refrained from reforming his father's ministers and his father's policies.'"[330]

19.19　孟氏使陽膚爲士師，問於曾子。曾子曰：「上失其道，民散久矣。如得其情，則哀矜而勿喜！」

When the head of the Meng clan appointed Yang Fu as a magistrate, he sought advice from Master Zeng. Master Zeng said, "With their superiors having lost the way (*dao* 道), the common people have long since scattered. In uncovering what really happened in criminal cases, you should take pity on them and show them sympathy rather than being pleased with yourself."

19.20　子貢曰：「紂之不善，不如是之甚也。是以君子惡居下流，天下之惡皆歸焉。」

Zigong said, "The perversities (*bushan* 不善) of the Shang tyrant Zhou were nowhere near the extreme of what is now reported. That is why the exemplary person (*junzi* 君子)

hates to dwell in the sewer—all of the world's filth finds its way there."

19.21　子貢曰：「君子之過也，如日月之食焉：過也，人皆見之；更也，人皆仰之。」

Zigong said, "When exemplary persons (*junzi* 君子) go astray, it is like an eclipse of the sun and moon. When they stray, everyone sees it, and when they correct their course, everyone looks up to them."

19.22　衛公孫朝問於子貢曰：「仲尼焉學？」子貢曰：「文武之道，未墜於地，在人。賢者識其大者，不賢者識其小者。莫不有文武之道焉。夫子焉不學？而亦何常師之有？」

Gongsun Chao of Wei asked Zigong, "With whom did Confucius study?"

　　Zigong replied, "The way (*dao* 道) of Kings Wen and Wu has not collapsed utterly—it lives in the people. Those of superior character (*xian* 賢) have grasped the greater part, while those of lesser quality have grasped a bit of it. Everyone has something of Wen and Wu's way in them. Who then does the Master not learn from? Again, how could there be a single constant teacher for him?"

19.23　叔孫武叔語大夫於朝曰：「子貢賢於仲尼。」
　　　　子服景伯以告子貢。
　　　　子貢曰：「譬之宮牆，賜之牆也及肩，闚見屋家之好。夫子之牆數仞，不得其門而入，不見宗廟之美，百官之富。得其門者或寡矣。夫子之云，不亦宜乎！」

Shusun Wushu said to the other ministers at court, "Zigong is a better man than Confucius."

Zifu Jingbo reported this to Zigong.

Zigong replied, "Let us take a perimeter wall as an analogy. My wall is shoulder high, so one can catch a glimpse of the charm of the buildings inside. The Master's wall, on the other hand, is massive, rising some twenty or thirty feet in the air. Without gaining entry through the gate, one cannot see the magnificence of the ancestral temple or the lavishness of the estate inside. Since those who gain entry are few, is it surprising that the minister speaks as he does?"

19.24　叔孫武叔毀仲尼。子貢曰：「無以爲也！仲尼不可毀也。他人之賢者，丘陵也，猶可踰也；仲尼、日月也，無得而踰焉。人雖欲自絕，其何傷於日月乎？多見其不知量也。」

Shusun Wushu spoke disparagingly of Confucius. Zigong responded, "Do not do this! Confucius cannot be disparaged. The superior character (*xian* 賢) of other people is like a mound or a hill which can still be scaled, but Confucius is the sun and moon which no one can climb beyond. When people cut themselves off from the sun and moon, what damage does this do to the sun and moon? It would only demonstrate that such people do not know their own limits."

19.25　陳子禽謂子貢曰：「子爲恭也，仲尼豈賢於子乎？」

子貢曰：「君子一言以爲知，一言以爲不知，言不可不慎也。夫子之不可及也，猶天之不可階而升也。夫子之得邦家者，所謂立之斯立，道之斯行，綏之斯來，動之斯和。其生也榮，其死也哀，如之何其可及也？」

Chen Ziqin said to Zigong, "You are only being deferential—how could Confucius be superior in character (*xian* 賢) to you?"

Zigong replied, "Exemplary persons (*junzi* 君子) must be ever so careful about what they say. On the strength of a word others can deem them either wise (*zhi* 知) or foolish. The Master cannot be matched just as a ladder cannot be used to climb the sky. Were he to have become a head of state or of a clan, it would have illustrated the saying:

> He gave them a place and they took a stand,
> He led them forward and they followed,
> He brought peace and they flocked to him,
> He aroused them and they achieved harmony.
> In life he was glorious,
> And in death he was mourned.

How could anyone be his match?"

20.1　堯曰：「咨！爾舜！天之厤數在爾躬，允執其中。四
海困窮，天祿永終。」

舜亦以命禹。

曰：「予小子履敢用玄牡，敢昭告于皇皇后帝：
有罪不敢赦。帝臣不蔽，簡在帝心。朕躬有罪，無以
萬方；萬方有罪，罪在朕躬。」

周有大賚，善人是富。「雖有周親，不如仁人。
百姓有過，在予一人。」

謹權量，審法度，脩廢官，四方之政行焉。興滅
國，繼絕世，舉逸民，天下之民歸心焉。

所重：民、食、喪、祭。

寬則得眾，信則民任焉，敏則有功，公則說。

Yao said,

> "Oh—you Shun!
>
> The line of succession conferred by *tian* 天 rests on your
>   person.
>
> Grasp it sincerely and without deviation.
>
> If all within the four seas sink into dire straits,
>
> *Tian*'s charge will be severed utterly."

In just this manner, Shun in due course also ceded his throne
to Yu.

[Tang] said, "I, Lu, dare to humbly offer in sacrifice a
black bull, and dare to call upon the August High Ancestor.
Those who do wrong will not be pardoned. I will not shield

your subjects from your sight, but will let all decisions rest
with you. If I, your subject, personally do wrong, let not the
many states be implicated; if any of the many states do
wrong, the guilt lies with me personally."[331]

The House of Zhou made great gifts, and truly efficacious
(*shan* 善) persons were enriched therefrom.

> I certainly have my immediate relatives,
> But better to have authoritative persons (*renren* 仁人).
> Where the people go astray
> Let the blame rest with me alone.[332]

Carefully calibrate the scales and measures, review the laws
and statutes, and revive those offices that have fallen into dis-
use, and government policies will be carried out everywhere.
Restore those states that have been destroyed, continue those
lineages that have been broken, lift up those subjects whose
talents have been lost to the people,[333] and you will win over
the hearts-and-minds of the common people throughout the
land.

Priorities: the common people, sufficient food, mourning
practices, and the sacrifices.

Those who are tolerant will win over the many; if they
make good on their word (*xin* 信), others will rely upon
them; if diligent, they will get results;[334] if impartial, the
people will be happy."

20.2　子張問於孔子曰：「何如斯可以從政矣？」

　　　　子曰：「尊五美，屏四惡，斯可以從政矣。」

　　　　子張曰：「何謂五美？」

　　　　子曰：「君子惠而不費，勞而不怨，欲而不貪，
泰而不驕，威而不猛。」

　　　　子張曰：「何謂惠而不費？」

子曰：「因民之所利而利之，斯不亦惠而不費乎？擇可勞而勞之，又誰怨？欲仁而得仁，又焉貪？君子無眾寡，無小大，無敢慢，斯不亦泰而不驕乎？君子正其衣冠，尊其瞻視，儼然人望而畏之，斯不亦威而不猛乎？」

子張曰：「何謂四惡？」

子曰：「不教而殺謂之虐，不戒視成謂之暴，慢令致期謂之賊，猶之與人也，出納之吝謂之有司。」

Zizhang inquired of Confucius, saying, "What kind of a person is it that can be given the reins of government?"

The Master replied, "A person who honors the five virtues (*mei* 美) and rejects the four vices (*e* 惡) can be given the reins of government."

"What are the five virtues?" asked Zizhang.

The Master replied, "Exemplary persons (*junzi* 君子) are generous and yet not extravagant, work the people hard and yet do not incur ill will, have desires and yet are not covetous, are proud and yet not arrogant, and are dignified and yet not fierce."

"What does it mean to be generous and yet not extravagant?" asked Zizhang.

The Master replied, "Give the common people those benefits that will really be beneficial to them—is this not being generous without being extravagant? If you select those projects which the people can handle and make them work at them, who will feel ill will? Desire to be authoritative (*ren* 仁) and become authoritative—how is this being covetous? Exemplary persons, regardless of whether dealing with the many or the few, the great or the small, do not dare to neglect anyone. Is this not being proud and yet not arrogant? Exemplary persons wear their caps and robes correctly, and are always polite in their gaze. With such an air of dignity, persons seeing them from far off hold them in awe. Is this not being dignified and yet not fierce?"

"What then are the four vices?" asked Zizhang.

The Master replied, "To execute a person who has not first been educated is cruel; to expect a job to be finished without having first given notice is oppressive; to enforce a timetable when slow in giving direction is injurious; when something is to be given to someone, to be niggardly in carrying it out is officious."

20.3 孔子曰：「不知命，無以爲君子也；不知禮，無以立也；不知言，無以知人也。」

The Master said, "Someone who does not understand the propensity of circumstances (*ming* 命) has no way of becoming an exemplary person (*junzi* 君子); someone who does not understand the observance of ritual propriety (*li* 禮) has no way of knowing where to stand; a person who does not understand words has no way of knowing others."[335]

NOTES
TO THE
TRANSLATION

BOOK 1   1. Gilbert Ryle (1949) makes a distinction between "task" or "process" words such as "study," and "achievement" or "success" words such as "learn." Given the priority of process and change over form and stasis as the natural condition of things in classical Chinese cosmology, the language tends to favor the former. See Hall and Ames (1998):229–30 and Hall and Ames (1995):183–97.

2. For the distinction between *peng* 朋 and *you* 友 see Hall and Ames (1994):77–94 and (1998):257–69. *Peng* here means *menxia* 門下, students of the same master, and would probably refer to the many followers of Confucius who came from foreign places. *You* is more like mentor.

3. Master You: see Lau pp. 261–62. Master You was always referred to with the honorific by Confucius' inner circle. He was said to resemble Confucius, probably in terms of what he had to say. In *Liji* 3.70/18/8, Ziyou says that Master You's words resemble those of the Master.

4. We follow the *ren* 仁 variant for this passage.

5. This passage is repeated as 17.17.

6. "Peers (*ren* M)" here stands in contrast with "the common people (*min* 民)" and refers to a particular class of people. Compare 14.42.

7. Several texts read: "and be intimate with your peers (*ren* 人)," but we follow the *ren* 仁 variant here.

8. Zixia was a man of letters, and is remembered by tradition as having had an important role in establishing the Confucian canon. He has a major place in the last five chapters, where he underscores the importance of learning. Confucius allows that he himself has gotten a great deal from his conversations with Zixia. Although Zixia tries to compensate for his image as a pedant by insisting that virtuous conduct in one's personal relationships is what learning is all about, Confucius criticizes him at times for being petty and narrow in his aspirations.

9. The point being made here is that gravity does not preclude flexibility.

10. See Hall and Ames (1994) and (1998) for the Confucian notion of "friendship." See note 2 above.

11. The performative function of language is most effective in societies that are stabilized through the observance of propriety (*li* 禮).

12. Zigong excelled as a statesman and as a merchant, and was perhaps second only to Yan Hui in Confucius' affections. Confucius was respectful of Zigong's abilities, and in particular, his intellect, but was less impressed with his use of this intellect to amass personal wealth. Putting the many references to Zigong together, it is clear that Confucius was not entirely comfortable with his lack of commitment to the well-being of others, choosing to increase his own riches rather than taking on the responsibilities of government office. Zigong was aloof, and not a generous spirit. And in his readiness to pass judgment on others, he acted superior. Coming from a wealthy, educated home, Zigong was well spoken, and as such, Confucius' most persistent criticism of him was that his deeds could not keep pace with his words. Even so, much of the flattering profile of Confucius collected in the *Analects* is cast in the words of the eloquent Zigong.

13. Note the distinction between "attitude" and "conduct"—the expectation is that conduct itself would not be open to question while the father is alive, but attitude might be.

14. *Gai* 改 means to "change" in the sense of revising and adjusting. This term is often glossed as *geng* 更, which also means to change in the sense of "revise, alter, amend." See also Appendix II, pp. 279–81.

15. See 4.20 where this same passage is repeated.

16. Master You is making an important distinction here between simply enforcing order and achieving harmony.

17. *Xue* 學 is usually associated with cultivating appropriate conduct in affairs of the world rather than simply book learning. It is defined paronomastically as *jue* 覺, "to be aware," and entials both learning and teaching—the priority of situation over agency. See Hall and Ames (1987):43–46, and Introduction, p. 61–62.

18. Many of the redactions, including the Dingzhou strips, have "poor but happy (*le* 樂)" rather than "poor but enjoying the way (*ledao* 樂道)." Parallel structure would recommend the latter.

19. *Songs* 55. Compare Legge IV:55.

BOOK 2 20. The Dingzhou text has "proper (*zheng* 正)" for "governing (*zheng* 政)." The use of this cognate character in the extended and specific sense of "governing properly" is familiar in the classical texts. See 12.17.

21. This is the Confucian version of the Daoist "nonassertive action (*wuwei* 無爲)" where patterns of deference make governing "noncoer-

cive," and "authority" is authoritative rather than authoritarian. Compare 2.3.

22. This expression occurs in the *Book of Songs* 297:

> Sturdy are the stallions, in the distant open grounds;
> Among those sturdy ones, there are dark-and-white ones,
> There are red-and-white ones, there are hairy-legged ones,
> There are fish-eyed ones;
> With their chariots, they go vigorously without swerving;
> The horses are fleet.

Compare Legge IV:612. This song seems simply to celebrate good horses, and has nothing to do with human morality. Zhu Xi observes: "Those who are good (*shan* 善) can arouse the hearts-and-minds of people to be good; those who are not can be a warning to the wayward purposes of people. Their function lies in causing people to be correct in their character, and nothing else." He seems to be interpreting this phrase as literally "have no wanton thoughts," and by extension, "make people correct in their hearts-and-minds." However, Confucius is given to citing the *Songs* creatively and out of context so often that there seems to be no good reason to be literal here.

23. This passage again gives us a Confucian version of "noncoercive" governing through participation in a ritually constituted community, a Confucian version of the Daoist "nonassertive action (*wuwei* 無爲)."

24. The vocabulary in this passage entails the "path (*dao* 道)" metaphor: striking out in a direction, taking one's place, knowing which way to go, realizing the terrain around one, following along (there has been speculation that "ear" here might be a corruption, but the Dingzhou text has this character), and then journeying wherever one wants without going astray. See also Fingarette (1972): Chapter 2.

25. A minister in the state of Lu.

26. Fan Chi comes across as an avid enquirer, asking about authoritative conduct (*ren* 仁) and "realizing" (*zhi* 知) in 12.22 and 13.19. He is not a quick study, repeatedly asking what Confucius means by his comments. On one occasion when Fan Chi asks Confucius how to grow a garden (13.4), Confucius gets impatient with him. The lineage drawn by filial conduct is another expression of the image of the moving line (*dao* 道) that pervades Chinese culture.

27. The son of Meng Yizi who appears in the previous passage.

28. This passage is ambiguous; it can also mean "Give your mother and father nothing to worry about beyond their own physical well-being."

29. If Zixia erred on the side of book learning, Ziyou was too much like Ziyu, emphasizing the formal side of the Confucian teachings, the rites and rituals, at the expense of warmth and good humor.

30. Note the hermeneutical attitude toward learning that is the signature of classical Confucianism.

31. Confucius is keen to maintain a distinction between education and training. Personal cultivation is a matter of developing character, not acquiring specific skills.

32. The Dingzhou text is more succinct: "Having taken action, their words follow from it."

33. The medieval philosopher, Chengzi, comments on this passage: "Learn broadly, ask searchingly, reflect carefully, distinguish clearly, and act earnestly. To be lacking in one of these is to fail to learn."

34. Here we follow the Dingzhou text which has "to be accomplished in, to specialize in *(gong* 功)" rather than "to attack *(gong* 攻)" as found in the received editions. Because the character *gong* "to attack" appears three other times in the *Analects* and in each case means "to attack," Yang Bojun, ignoring the fact that *gong* here is followed by the prepositional particle "in *hu* (乎)," rejects the commentaries that would read this as "to pursue study in." He reads this passage as "If one attacks heterodox doctrines, it will put an end to their harm." The Dingzhou text seems to resolve this debate.

35. Zilu was another of Confucius' best-known and favorite protégés. He was a person of courage and action who was sometimes upbraided by Confucius for being too bold and impetuous. When he asked Confucius if courage was indeed the highest virtue, Confucius tried to rein him in by replying that a person who is bold without a sense of appropriateness will be a troublemaker, and a lesser person will be a thief.

Confucius' feelings for Zilu were mixed. On the one hand, he was constantly critical of Zilu's rashness and immodesty, and impatient with his seeming indifference to book learning. On the other hand, Confucius appreciated Zilu's unswerving loyalty and directness—he never delayed on fulfilling his commitments.

But being nearer Confucius in age, Zilu with his military temper was not one to take criticism without giving it back. On several occasions, especially in the apocryphal literature, Zilu challenges Confucius' judgment in associating with political figures of questionable character and immodest reputation—the concubine of Duke Ling of Wei, for example, where Confucius is left defending himself. At the end of the day, enormous affection for the irrepressible Zilu comes through the text.

36. We follow the Dingzhou text here. An alternative reading found in the received text would be:

> The Master said: "Zilu, shall I instruct you in what it means to know something? To know what you know and know what you do not know—this then is what it means to know."

37. Zizhang seems to be rash, caring more for appearances than for substance. He is criticized by other protégés.

38. Ji Kangzi was head of the Three Families, who were de facto rulers of Lu. He died in 469 BCE.

39. The character *shan* 善 is formulaically translated as "good," but importantly it is first a relational term and only derivatively an essential attribute. It means "good at, good to, good with, good for, good in," and so on, and hence, "adeptness, efficaciousness, competency." In this passage, "those who are adept" stand in contrast to "those who are not (*buneng* 不能)."

40. Like the carriage pins, making good on one's word (*xin* 信) is the link between saying and doing.

41. This passage reflects the emphasis on both change and continuity that we find in Confucius. A novel future emerges out of a continuing past. Yin is an alternative name for the Shang dynasty.

BOOK 3

42. The Ji clan was usurping a royal prerogative in so doing.

43. *Songs* 282. Compare Legge IV:589.

44. Note how this passage follows two in which Confucius criticizes impudent rulers for their inappropriate use of ritual. Such associations among contiguous passages is a common feature in the editing of this text.

45. Lin Fang appears as well in 3.6, where Confucius castigates him for not protesting against the Ji clan sacrificing to Mount Tai. The implication of that passage is: do they really think they are fooling Mount Tai!

46. The Yi and Di were tribes that bordered the proto-Chinese states to the east and north. The Chinese language might reflect a certain contempt for such bordering tribes: the Di 狄 tribes are classified under the "dog (*quan* 犬)" radical, the Man 蠻 tribes to the south are classified under the "beast/insect (*hui* 虫)" radical, and the Mo 貊 tribes in the north are classified under the "reptile/beast (*chi* 豸)" radical. An alternative explanation would be that these tribes, like other proto-Chinese

peoples, used animals as emblems, and that the *long* 龍, conventionally translated "dragon," is a totemic accumulation of such tribal symbolism. See Tu Wei-ming (1997):14.

47. At this time, Ranyou, a student of Confucius, was in the service of the Ji clan. Confucius saw Ranyou as a rather mediocre student lacking in initiative (11.22).

48. See note 8.

49. The first two lines are from *Songs* 57. Compare Legge IV:94.

50. The implication here is that the *di* sacrifice which is held in the state of Lu every five years, associated as it is with the imperial lineage, is not being done properly.

51. This refers to Confucius' father, who had been an official in the town of Zou.

52. The Dingzhou text has "Zigong dispensed with the sacrifice . . ."

53. The Zhu Xi commentary states that the emperor would present the various nobles with a sheep to sacrifice in the ancestral temple. Although beginning with Duke Wen, Lu ceased observing this sacrifice, an official still presented Lu with the sheep.

54. *Songs* 1. Compare Legge IV:1.

55. Zaiwo was devoted to Confucius, yet on numerous occasions Confucius criticized him roundly for a lack of character. Confucius in a metaphorical reference to attempting to educate Zaiwo, said, "You cannot carve rotten wood, and cannot trowel over a wall of manure." (5.10).

56. The altar pole is the center of the community. These poles would function at all levels of the political life of the people, from neighborhood (*lishe* 里社) to state (*guoshe* 國社). The modern expression "society (*shehui* 社會)" means literally "to gather at the altar pole."

The Dingzhou text has "ruler (*zhu* 主)" as a cognate variant of "altar pole (*she* 社)," both of them representing authority.

57. A pun can be made, perhaps, on each of these three kinds of wood. For *song* 松 there is *song* 悚: "to frighten." For *bo* 柏 there is *po* 迫, "to press," or, more likely, *pa* 怕, originally "quiet, passive" and later, "to fear." For *li* 栗 there is *li* 慄, meaning "to fear."

58. The Dingzhou text has *guo* 國 instead of *bang* 邦, observing the taboo on the founding Han dynasty ruler's given name, Liu Bang 劉邦. Guanzhong was a famous seventh-century BCE minister of the state of Qi who strengthened it both economically and militarily. See also 14.9, 14.16, and 14.17.

59. The Dingzhou text has "sincerity (*yun* 允)" in place of "flow (*yi* 繹)."

60. The Dingzhou text does not have the phrase, "On taking his leave, he said." Although the border official's comments are still directed at the followers of Confucius, they are made within the context of the interview itself.

61. See note 39. *Shan* here means "productive of good relationships."

62. In *Mencius* 2A7 this passage from Confucius is repeated, and commented upon at length.

> Mencius said, "How could the arrow maker be less authoritative (*ren*) than the shield maker? The only worry of the arrow maker is that his arrows will fail to hurt others; the only worry of the shield maker is that his shield will fail to protect others. The medical practitioner and the coffin maker are another case in point. One has to take great care in the quality of one's art. Confucius said, 'In taking up one's residence, it is the presence of authoritative persons that is the greatest attraction. How can anyone be called wise who, in having the choice, does not dwell among authoritative persons?'
>
> Now being authoritative is that status most revered by *tian* 天, and that residence most comfortable for the human being. One who fails to live among authoritative persons when nothing stands in the way is not a wise person. A person who is neither authoritative nor wise, who respects neither ritual propriety (*li* 禮) nor appropriateness (*yi* 義), is in fact a servant to others. To be a servant and to be ashamed of serving others is like the bow maker being ashamed of making his bows, or the arrow maker being ashamed of making his arrows. If you are truly ashamed of being a servant, nothing is as good as becoming authoritative. An authoritative person can be likened to an archer. The archer shoots only after having corrected his posture. When he misses the mark, he does not resent those who have beaten him, but simply turns inward to find his error."

The movement from servant (*yi* 役) to authoritative person (*ren* 仁) entails the movement from serving others to serving oneself—correcting one's posture and looking inward for the source of one's errors.

63. See *Great Learning* 10. Being disliked in the right way and by the right person can be constructive.

64. See also 7.30.

65. We follow the *ren* 仁 variant for *ren* 人 here.

66. This passage is perhaps metaphorical with "dawn" meaning early in one's life.

67. The distinction here seems to be what is appropriate versus what is to one's particular benefit. It seems to reinforce the previous passage, and the one that follows.

68. This same passage appears in 1.11.

69. See note 29.

70. Compare 12.23.

BOOK 5   71. See note 12. Zigong is being criticized here as "the best kind of functionary."

72. Compare 2.12 where this would be taken as a stern criticism; hence, Zigong's further question.

73. The *hu* and the *lan* were sacrificial vessels used in the ancestral halls of the Xia and Shang dynasties respectively.

74. See note 35.

75. See 2.6.

76. See 11.24.

77. Zihua has the image of a diplomat, careful and concise in his speech and proper in his decorum.

78. See note 12.

79. See note 55.

80. The Dingzhou text divides the text into two passages at this point.

81. Compare 9.1 and 9.4. Graham (1990) in "The Background of the Mencian Theory of Human Nature" claims that *xing* 性 only became a philosophical topic after Confucius' death.

82. This might also be "hear it again (*you* 又)" [before he acted on what he had already been told].

83. D. C. Lau (1992) points out that the *Yi Zhou Shu* 54/28/2 逸周書 has a passage that says: "diligence in learning and seeking advice is called '*wen*.'"

Waley provides a profile of Kong Wenzi: a minister of Wei who died between 484 and 480 BCE. He was a disloyal and self-serving minister; hence, Zigong's surprise.

84. Confucius is criticizing a minister for usurping the trappings of royalty.

85. The Dingzhou text has *guo* 國 instead of *bang* 邦, observing the taboo on the founding Han dynasty ruler's given name, Liu Bang 劉邦.

86. See *Mencius* 7B37:

> Wan Zhang inquired, "When the Master, Confucius, was in Chen he said, 'Why don't we go home? My young friends at home are rash and ambitious, while perhaps careless in the details. They keep forging ahead, and do not forget their beginnings.' Why would the Master while in Chen be reflecting on the rash scholar-apprentices of Lu?"
>
> Mencius replied, "For the Master, 'If one cannot find the company of temperate colleagues, one has no choice but to turn to the more rash and the more timid. The rash will forge ahead in their actions, and the timid will not do what they think is wrong.' (13.21) Surely the Master wanted temperate colleagues, but because he wasn't guaranteed of getting them he reflected on the next best thing."
>
> "May I ask what kind of persons would be called 'rash and ambitious'?" he inquired.
>
> "Persons such as Qin Zhang, Zengxi, and Mu Pi are what the Master means by 'rash and ambitious,'" Mencius replied.
>
> "Why would he call them 'rash and ambitious'?"
>
> "They are so grand in their ambitions," he replied. "They are forever saying 'The Ancients this! And the Ancients that!' but if one looks at their conduct, it doesn't measure up. And if the Master still could not find such rash and ambitious scholars, then he would need to associate with those who are too timid to do wrong. These are cautious people, and belong to the next lower group. The Master said, 'The only person who gives me no regret in passing by my gate without coming in is the 'village worthy.' The village worthy claims excellence under false pretenses.' (17.13)"
>
> "What kind of persons would be called a 'village worthy'?"
>
> "The village worthy would say: 'What is the point of the rash scholar's grand ambitions? With no relation between word and deed, nor any between deed and word, I simply say "The Ancients this! And the Ancients that!" And why the timid scholar's unsociable airs? Born into this world, act on behalf of this world. As long as you are

good at it, it's fine.' At home anywhere, toadying to all around—such is the village worthy."

"If the entire village praises him as an honorable man," said Wan Zhang, "and everywhere he goes he acts as an honorable man, why would the Master regard him as claiming excellence under false pretenses?"

"If you want to condemn the village worthy," said Mencius, "you have nothing on him; if you want to criticize him, there is nothing to criticize. He chimes in with the practices of the day and blends in with the common world. Where he lives he seems to be conscientious and to live up to his word, and in what he does, he seems to have integrity. His community all like him, and he even sees himself as being right. Yet one cannot walk the way of Yao or Shun with such a person. This is why the Master says that he claims excellence under false pretenses. The Master said, 'As for my dislike and condemnation of what is specious: I dislike weeds lest they be confused with grain; I dislike flattery lest it be confused with what is proper for one to say; I dislike a glib tongue lest it be confused with integrity; I dislike the tunes of Zheng lest they be confused with music; I dislike purple lest it be confused with red; I dislike the village worthy lest he be confused with the excellent. The exemplary person simply reverts to the standard. Where the standard is upheld, the common people will flourish, and where they flourish, there will be no perversity or ugliness.'"

87. See also 7.15, 16.12, and 18.8 for Bo Yi and Shu Qi.

BOOK 6   88. Zhonggong, like Yan Hui, was three decades younger than Confucius. Although Zhonggong was of humble origins, Confucius thought so highly of him and his refinement that he believed Zhonggong could be king—high praise indeed! See 6.2 and 6.6.

89. See note 77.

90. Following the "functional" rather than "anatomic" implications of *xin* 心, it can be translated as "thoughts and feelings" rather than just as "heart-and-mind."

91. Ji Kangzi was the head of the Three Families, who were de facto rulers of Lu.

92. The Dingzhou text has "He is near the end (*mo* 末)," clarifying the meaning of the received text.

93. We have added the phrase "and there is nothing we can do" from the Dingzhou text. This reading is also found in the biography of Confucius' disciples in Sima Qian (1959):2189.

94. The Dingzhou text has "without the authoritative conduct (*ren* 仁) of Priest Tuo" rather than "without the eloquence (*ning* 佞) of Priest Tuo" as found in the received text. In the *Zuo Commentary to the Spring and Autumn Annals* Ding 4, Priest Tuo recites eulogies at a gathering of the various nobles, suggesting that he was known for his eloquence. However, we follow the Dingzhou text here because Confucius throughout the *Analects* consistently expresses suspicion of what might otherwise be a neutral term, "eloquence," most often interpreting it as "glibness." See 5.5 for the Master's view on eloquence. See also 11.25, 14.32, 15.11, and 16.4 where *ning* 佞 has to be translated as "glibness" rather than "eloquence."

95. The key to this passage is *you* 由: "to go out from." The analogy with *dao* is that it is not a way provided that you then walk; it is rather a way that you go out from.

96. This use of "love (*hao* 好)" evokes the expression "to love learning (*haoxue* 好學)" that pervades the text. The worth of knowledge is a direct consequence of its efficacy: to what degree does it conduce to human happiness and enjoyment?

97. See note 26.

98. See note 55.

99. The authoritative person (*renzhe* 仁者) and the exemplary person (*junzi* 君子) are used interchangeably in this passage. The exemplary person would not be able to rescue the person in the well if he were to jump in after him.

There is an important difference between being deceived, which involves quite properly having taken people at their word, and being duped, which involves having done something that would diminish one as a person. This distinction is pursued in *Mencius* 5A2:

> "Some time ago," said Mencius, "a gift of a live fish was made to Zichan of Zheng, and Zichan sent it to his ponds-keeper to put in his pond. In fact, the pondskeeper cooked it up, and then reported back, 'When I first let the fish go, it seemed listless, but in a little while it came to life, and plunged into the depths.' Zichan replied, 'It found its element! It found its element!' The pondskeeper withdrew,

and said, 'Who said that Zichan was a wise person? I have already cooked and eaten his fish, and he says "It found its element! It found its element!"' Indeed the exemplary person can be deceived in how things are done, but he cannot be duped into taking the wrong road (*dao* 道)...."

100. This passage is repeated in 12.15.

101. Nanzi was the concubine of Duke Ling of Wei who had a rather colorful and unseemly reputation.

102. This same strategy for becoming an authoritative person is repeated in 12.1: "Through self-discipline and observing ritual propriety (*li* 禮) one becomes authoritative in one's conduct." The method of becoming authoritative is full participation in those personal relations near at hand.

BOOK 7   103. Translating *shu* 述 as "to follow the proper way" enables us to maintain the "path (*dao* 道)" metaphor.

104. Throughout the early corpus, *zuo* 作 is associated with "sageliness"; hence Confucius' description of himself is an expression of modesty.

105. See *Mozi* 63/39/19 and 81/46/50 for a parody critiquing this passage.

106. See *Songs* 195 for the earliest use of these expressions. Compare Legge IV:330.

107. See also 5.23, 16.12, and 18.8. Because Confucius was living in Wey at this juncture, it would not be prudent to ask him this question directly.

108. The received version of the *Analects* has 亦 rather than 易, the latter usually interpreted as a reference to the *Book of Changes* (*Yijing*). This association is reinforced by the biography of Confucius in Sima Qian (1959):1937 which recounts the interest that Confucius invested in this text in his later years, and by the new commentaries to the *Book of Changes* recovered at Mawangdui. See Shaughnessy (1996). The Dingzhou text is consistent with the *Lulun* 魯論 in 亦, which we follow here.

109. *She* was a district in the state of Chu.

110. The Dingzhou text has "and does not even realize that old age has arrived."

111. *Sheng* 生, what we have translated here as "through a natural propensity for it," has a multivalent range of meanings: "birth, life, and growth." This, then, is not some claim to a priori knowledge, but a recognition that the circumstances of one's birth such as family and community as well as native ability have a direct yet often imperceptible bearing on one's education. See also 16.9.

112. Confucius discusses *shanren* 善人 several times: see also 11.20, 13.11, and 13.29.

113. The observance of ritual propriety (*li* 禮) is important in all matters, even in recreation.

114. See 7.1.

115. See 2.14 and 15.22.

116. In *Xunzi* 104/29/19ff, it recounts a similar story in which the person asking the question is in fact offending against ritual propriety because there are circumstances under which one is not free to speak ill of a superior, or in this case, a deceased lord. See Yang Bojun (1980):75.

117. See 7.2 for a similar description.

118. The Dingzhou text has *cheng* 誠 rather than *zheng* 正. The Zheng Xuan commentary states that the *Lulun* had the former, while the *Gulun* version had the latter.

119. Compare *Mencius* 2A2:

> Gongsun Chou said to Mencius . . . , "Zaiwo and Zigong were adept in their rhetorical skills, while Ranniu, Minzi, and Yan Hui were adept in speaking on excellent conduct. Although Confucius excelled at both, he said of himself, 'I have no ability when it comes to rhetorical persuasion.' Even so, have you, sir, already become a sage (*sheng* 聖)?"
>
> "What!" exclaimed Mencius, "Such nonsense! In times past Zigong asked Confucius, 'Are you, sir, a sage?' Confucius replied, 'I cannot claim to be a sage— I only study without respite and instruct others without growing weary.'
>
> 'To study without respite is to be wise,' said Zigong. 'To instruct others without growing weary is to be an authoritative person (*ren* 仁). And in being both authoritative and wise, you, sir, are already a sage.' If even Confucius will not accept this title—such nonsense!"

BOOK 8

120. Yang Bojun's note identifies Taibo as the eldest son of the ancestor of the Zhou court, Gugong Tanfu. Gugong had three sons, Taibo, Zhongyong, and Jili. The son of Jili was Jichang (King Wen). According to tradition, Gugong had a premonition of Jichang's sagacity, and wanted to break the lineage by giving the throne to his youngest son, Jili, who in turn would pass it on to Jichang. In order to insure his father's wishes, Taibo together with Zhongyong fled to Gouwu (the first ancestor of the state of Wu), and in the end the throne was given to Jili and Jichang.

Jichang expanded the power of his state, occupying two thirds of the territory of the empire. His son, Jifa (King Wu) overthrew the Shang dynasty, and unified the empire.

121. Master Zeng is best remembered as a proponent of filial piety—devotion and service to one's parents. A natural extension of this affection for one's family is friendship, and Master Zeng is portrayed as being able to distinguish between the sincerity of Yan Hui, and the rashness of Zizhang.

122. *Songs* 195. Compare Legge IV:564.

123. Usually understood as a reference to Yan Hui.

124. It is possible to read the songs, rites, and music as either the titles of the classical texts or the actual performance of the songs, rituals, and music.

125. The *Guodian* 郭店 *Zundeyi* 尊德義 text has *dao* 道 for *you* 由, "The common people can be made to take it as their way. . . ." See Jingmen Municipal Museum (1998): 174. Compare 15.29 in which the way is something being built and extended by the cultural heroes of every generation. It is both made and followed. The point here is that everyone can find a place on the way, even when they don't participate in constructing it.

Compare also *Mencius* 3A4: "There are those who use their hearts-and-minds and those who use their muscles; the former rule, the latter are ruled."

126. The Dingzhou text has: "there is nothing to recommend the rest of him."

127. See 14.26. Alternatively, "Unless you hold office, you don't get to plan policy."

128. *Songs* 1. Compare Legge IV:1.

129. See 17.16. Waley (1937):135 comments that "in the old days people at any rate had the merits of their faults."

130. The metaphor of "way" is strong here.

131. In the *Zuo Commentary to the Spring and Autumn Annals* Zhao 20, it quotes the "Great Oath" from the *Book of Documents* as stating: "I have ten ministers who can bring proper order to the world and who are of like mind and excellence."

BOOK 9   132. See 5.13. An argument can be made that Confucius seldom spoke of "personal advantage" and "the propensity of things," but it is hard to say that some 108 references to "authoritative conduct" is "rare." In the commentarial tradition, many attempts have been made to explain this problematic passage, none of them winning consensus.

133. A *dang* 黨 is a village of five hundred households.

134. The *Guodian* 郭店 *Collected Sayings* 3 語叢三 has this passage in a different order, with "he did not claim or demand certainty" at the end. See Jingmen Municipal Museum (1998):212.

135. See 19.22.

136. According to the biography of Confucius in Sima Qian (1959):1919, Confucius had left Wey and was on route to Chen when he passed through Kuang. The people of Kuang had recently been ravaged by Yang Huo, also from the state of Lu, and mistook Confucius for him. See also 11.23.

137. Yang Bojun (1982):92 thinks that this last phrase should have the opposite meaning to preserve Confucius' modesty—"how could I live up to these things!".

138. This passage is repeated in 15.13.

139. This passage illustrates 12.1: "Becoming authoritative in one's person is self-originating—how could it originate with others?"

140. *Songs* 33. Compare Legge IV:52.

141. This passage also occurs as part of 14.28.

142. See 7.30 and 9.11. Yang Bojun (1982):95–96 suggests that this is a metaphor for authoritative conduct (*ren* 仁) and the way (*dao* 道).

BOOK 10

143. Although *junzi* 君子 is used here, it retains its pre-Confucian meaning, referring specifically to persons of nobility who have responsibilities at court.

144. Black was the formal ritual color, and these colors are too close to it.

145. In ancient times, the fur faced outward, with the skin on the inside. The *yi* 衣 is an upper garment that contrasts with and is independent of an apron or skirt worn below.

146. The Dingzhou text has "beautiful (*mei* 美)" in the place of "lamb (*gao* 羔)," but the similarity of the characters suggests a copying error.

147. It is an *yi* 衣 which covers the upper part of the body.

148. He would not sleep with his wife.

149. Most "wine" was made from grains, with millet being predominant.

150. The placement of the mat would be determined by the status and purposes of other people in the room relative to his own rank and obligations. See 10.18.

151. What the received text has as passages 11, 12, and 13, the Dingzhou text has combined as one passage.

152. The Dingzhou text has *guo* 國 instead of *bang* 邦, observing the taboo on the founding Han dynasty ruler's given name, Liu Bang 劉邦.

153. Ji Kangzi was the head of the Three Families, who were the de facto rulers of Lu.

154. In ancient times, the bed for the master of the house was usually on the western side of the southern window, so when the lord would come, he would approach by ascending the stairs from the east. The eastern stair is the place of the host, but since the lord is the host of the entire country, he would ascend and descend from the eastern steps. The Dingzhou text has passages 18 and 19 combined as one passage.

155. Presumably the carriage would pick him up on the way. See *Mencius* 5B7 for a discussion of the appropriateness of Confucius' conduct:

> Mencius said, ". . . Wanting to meet with a person of superior character while not following his path is like inviting him in while barring the gate against him. Being appropriate (*yi* 義) is the roadway; observing ritual propriety (*li* 禮) is the gate. Only the exemplary person (*junzi* 君子) is able to set off on this roadway and to come and go by this gate. The *Book of Songs* 203 says:
>
> > The way of Zhou is as flat as a grindstone
> > And is as straight as an arrow;
> > It is walked by the nobleman
> > And admired by the commoner."
>
> "When Confucius' lord issued him a summons," said Wan Zhang, "he would set off on foot without waiting for the horses to be yoked to his carriage. If so, was Confucius wrong in this?"
>
> "That was because Confucius was in service and had the responsibilities of office," said Mencius. "His lord summoned him in this official capacity."

156. This passage is also part of 3.15.

157. According to Yang Bojun (1982):107, in ancient times there were three postures for sitting that entailed a varying degree of formality. The first and most formal for entertaining guests was to kneel down with the buttocks resting on one's feet. The second way to sit was to squat with feet planted, knees in the air, and the buttocks hanging down between them. The third, and most informal way, was to sit on the ground with the legs stretched out like a fan—hence, called "fan-sitting."

158. The Dingzhou text has "six (*liu/lu* 六)" in place of "mourner (*xiong* 凶)," which the commentators suggest might be "execution attire" with the homophone *lu* 戮.

159. The Dingzhou text has passages 25 and 26 combined as one.

160. This final passage ties the whole chapter, which details a ritualized lifestyle, into the natural world.

BOOK 11 161. Confucius seems to be using *junzi* 君子 in a political sense here—and as the historical point at which this term was undergoing transition from a political to a moral category, it is not unlikely that it can have both values in this text.

162. Compare *Mencius* 3A3 for the contrast. See *Analects* 6.18, 12.8, and 12.20 for the interdependence of one's basic disposition and refinement.

163. See *Mencius* 7B18 for a reference to these trials in Chen and Cai:

> Mencius said, "That this exemplary person, Confucius, fell into difficult straits between Chen and Cai was because he had no acquaintances in either court."

See also Confucius' biography in Sima Qian (1959):1930 which recounts these adventures. It reports that the state of Chu had sent an envoy to enlist Confucius. The ministers of Chen and Cai were afraid that Confucius would punish their misdeeds, and so on his way to Chu, they waylaid him. John Makeham (1998) has analyzed the various accounts of this story that appear throughout the early corpus.

Some of the commentators suggest that this passage should be read: "None are in office."

164. Yang Bojun (1982):110–11 cites the *History of the Later Han* which records that the classics of history, ritual, and music were established by Confucius, and that the editing of them was begun with Zixia. In his commentary on this passage, Zhu Xi suggests that these ten disciples were all with Confucius in Chen and Cai, but given the available detail in the historical records, this is patently not the case. For example, since the event occurred in Confucius' sixty-first year (Duke Ai 4), Ziyou would have been sixteen and Zixia seventeen years old.

165. See *Songs* 256, Karlgren (1950):

> Be cautious about the words you utter, be careful about your demeanor; in all things be mild and good; a flaw in a white *kuei* tessera can still be ground away; a flaw in those words of yours, for that nothing can be done.

166. See 5.2.

167. A more extended version of this passage appears in 6.3, where Duke Ai asks the question. Commentators attribute meaning to the fact that Confucius answers the legitimate Duke Ai in more detail than he does the patriarch of the usurping Ji clan.

168. According to the biography of the disciples in Sima Qian (1959), Yan Lu was also a student of Confucius.

169. Confucius' son, Boyu, died at age fifty when Confucius was seventy. See also 16.13 and 17.10.

170. The two reasons for Confucius not to oblige: Yan Hui did not have the status, and Confucius did.

171. Confucius insists on following convention, but also is sincere in grieving beyond constraint. There is no duplicity here. The ultimate standard is sincerity.

172. David Keightley (1990), in his reflections on the broader meaning and value of death in classical China, allows that death was perceived as "unproblematic." Of course, he is not claiming that the end of life was not approached with some trepidation. He means rather that death was not considered unnatural, perverse, or horrible. Chinese "natural" death is contrasted with the enormity of death in the Judeo-Christian tradition, where mortality is conceived as divine punishment meted out for human hubris and disobedience. While there is an uneasiness manifested in visions of the "Yellow Springs," a name for the netherworld, there is a marked absence of the morbidity and gloom that we associate with the Greek, Roman, and medieval European conceptions of death. See also Ames (1998).

173. This was the same attitude expressed by Confucius in his dealing with superior officials in 10.2.

174. See note 35.

175. As was Confucius in dealing with subordinate officials—see 10.2.

176. Yang Bojun (1982):114 thinks that *ren* 人, here translated as "leaders," entails a class distinction between them and the common people (*min* 民), and hence cannot be rendered "people." Given the structure of governance, this makes sense. See also 1.5 and 14.42.

177. This story is elaborated upon in *Shuoyuan* 19.44/172/19 in which it is not the instrument that Confucius objects to, but the quality of the music.

178. See notes 12, 37, and 8 for Zigong, Zizhang, and Zixia, respectively.

179. Yang Bojun (1982):115 cites two possible interpretations of "the Duke of Zhou," but the *Xunzi* seems to support one reading. See *Xunzi* 23/8/70; Knoblock (1992):77 where it refers to the wealth of the more famous Duke of Zhou.

180. See the *Zuo Commentary on the Spring and Autumn Annals* Ai 11 (compare Legge V:826) in which this incident is discussed:

> The head of the House of Ji Sun wanted to use the land tax system to increase their revenues, and sent Ranyou to solicit Confucius' advice. Confucius said to him, "I know nothing of these matters." Several times inquires were made of him, and finally the head of the Ji clan said to him, "You are a senior adviser to the state, and I am waiting for you to carry out its business. What is the meaning of your silence?"
>
> Confucius did not reply, but privately said to Ranyou, "The exemplary ruler in his conduct observes ritual propriety. In what he gives he is generous, in carrying out his affairs he does what is fitting, and in what he exacts in taxation he tries to be moderate. This being the case, according to the Qiu ordinance the taxes being levied are quite enough. If they do not act in accordance with ritual propriety, but instead are insatiable in their greed, even if they exact a land tax, it will not be enough. If the Ji Sun clan wants to act lawfully, there are the statutes of the Duke of Zhou; if they want to act otherwise, why are they seeking advice from me?"
>
> He was not heeded in this matter.

Ranyou continues to listen to the House of Ji and implements the tax system.

> In the *Book of Rites* (*Liji*) 43.2/166/21 it says clearly:
>
> A family of a hundred chariots is not entitled to a revenue collector. Rather than having one, wouldn't they be better off employing a robber.

181. *Mencius* 4A14 has a fuller statement of this passage:

> Mencius said, "Ranyou was the household steward of the Ji clan, and although he had no success in reforming the quality of their conduct, he was able to double their tax revenues. Confucius said, 'This man Ranyou is no disciple

of mine. You students have my permission to sound the charge and attack him.' From this we can see that ministers who would enrich rulers not given to authoritative government (*renzheng* 仁政) were all rejected by Confucius—how much more so those ministers who would strengthen such a ruler's ability to wage war. When they contend for land by waging war, the carnage fills the fields; when they contend for cities by waging war, the carnage fills the cities. This is what is called teaching the land to devour human flesh—death is too good for such people. Thus, those who are skilled at waging war should suffer the harshest punishment, those who forge alliances among the feudal lords should suffer the next, and those who open up the frontiers for homesteading should be next."

Although it might seem that this last category of minister is advising the ruler to do something that would redound to the benefit of the people, in fact, his motivation lies in benefiting the ruler, and by extension, himself. The main reason for poverty among the people was not inadequate farmland, but excessive taxation and protracted wars.

182. Although some translate this *ming* 命 as "not receiving an official commission," historically Zigong did in fact serve in government.

183. Confucius is being facetious.

184. Confucius discusses *shanren* 善人 several times: see also 7.26, 13.11, 13.29.

185. See 9.5.

186. The Dingzhou text has "Even they would stop short of killing their fathers and rulers."

187. Bi was the stronghold of the Ji clan that had usurped political power in Lu.

BOOK 12　　188. This passage occurs in the *Zuo Commentary to the Spring and Autumn Annals* Zhao 12 (compare Legge V:641) where Confucius says,

> There is an ancient record which states, "Through self-discipline and observing ritual propriety one becomes authoritative in one's conduct." This is well said indeed. If King Ling of Chu had been able to live up to this, how could he have come to such disgrace at Ganqi?

The context is a king who comes to a bad end because he has no "self-control (*zike* 自克)." Waley (1937):162 notes that *ke* can also mean "able," but the *Zuo* passage is rather clear evidence that it means "self-discipline" in this instance. It is important not to "naturalize" a notion of "ego-self" that then has to be overcome. Rather, this is an inchoate, incipient, and radically embedded "self" that needs cultivation and extension.

189. Zhonggong, like Yan Hui, was three decades younger than Confucius. Although Zhonggong was of humble origins, Confucius thought so highly of him and his refinement that he said in effect: Zhonggong could be king—high praise indeed! See 6.1, 6.2, and 6.6.

190. Confucius is defining "authoritative conduct (*ren* 仁)" paronomastically as "to be slow to speak (*ren* 訒)."

191. According to Sima Qian (1959):2214–5, Sima Niu was garrulous and impulsive. Confucius is speaking specifically to this condition, thereby criticizing those who do not treat their words seriously as having the force of action.

192. We know that, historically, Sima Niu did have a brother— Huan Tui—the man who threatened Confucius' life. See the *Zuo Commentary to the Spring and Autumn Annals* Ai 14 and *Analects* 7.23. Sima Niu here disowns him, altering the unalterable by refusing to interpret "brotherliness" in terms of "facticity." Zixia trumps him by insisting that the reverse can also be effected—a brotherless person can alter his "propensity of circumstances (*ming* 命)" which has rendered him brotherless by redefining what it means to have brothers—that is, changing the name (*ming* 名). He asserts that the criterion of brotherhood can be ethical and religious rather than biological. This passage, far from justifying fatalism, demonstrates the fluidity of circumstances and the inseparability of fact and value in the description of these same circumstances. See Hall and Ames (1987):214–15.

Yang Bojun disputes the identification of Sima Niu with the person of the same name who appears in the *Zuozhuan Commentary*. Kong Anguo is the first commentator to identify the two, yet he says that Sima Niu's name is Li 犁, while the *Record of the Historian* states that his name is Geng 耕.

193. The text offers a similar position with respect to the difference between the cultured Chinese and the barbarians. When Confucius is asked how he would deal with the crudeness of the barbarians were he to dwell among them, his response is "Were an exemplary person (*junzi* 君子) to live among them, what crudeness could there be?" (9.14). Basic disposition and refinement, nature and nurture, cannot be separated.

194. See note 3.

195. The parallel structure seems to demand "accumulating" rather than just "celebrating."

From *Songs* 188. See Legge IV:302. Most commentators think that this is an interpolation here. But this song tells the story of a forsaken wife who says to her husband that in taking up with a new mate, he gains not in fortune, but only in difference. This would also seem to relate to the loving and hating someone simultaneously referenced in this passage.

196. Compare 1.2 and 2.21 in which the argument is that the root of both community and polity is effective familial relations.

197. Zilu had the trust of people, and no one would cheat him. Hence he could decide the case without dispute.

198. Zilu made good on his promises, giving him the relationship he needed to enjoy the trust and confidence of the people.

199. The contrast here is between "sitting down (*ju* 居)" and "walking (*xing* 行)"—between sitting and deliberating over policy and then putting it into practice.

200. This passage also occurs in 6.27.

201. "Governing effectively (*zheng* 政)" is defined paronomastically by "doing what is proper (*zheng* 正)."

202. This same passage occurs in *Mencius* 3A2. We translate this passage in its entirety because it also has relevance to 14.40 and 17.21.

> Duke Ding of Teng died, and the Crown Prince said to his tutor, Ranyou: "In the past while I was in Song, Mencius spoke with me frequently and I have never forgotten what he said. Today I am truly unfortunate in having to deal with my father's passing, and would like you to go and seek advice from Mencius before we carry out the funeral."
>
> Ranyou went to Zou and inquired of Mencius.
>
> "Wonderful!" replied Mencius. "In the death of one's parents, one ought to give of oneself utterly. [Compare *Analects* 19.17.] Master Zeng said, 'A person can be called filial who, while they are living, serves his parents according to the observances of ritual propriety (*li* 禮), and when they are dead, buries and sacrifices to them according to the observances of ritual propriety. [*Analects* 2.5.] I have not made a study of the ritual propriety observed by the various nobles, but even so, I have heard something about it. Three years of mourning, coarse clothing cut and hemmed, and thin gruel for sustenance—the Xia, Shang, and Zhou dynasties all followed this regimen from the Son of Heaven down to the common people."

Ranyou returned and reported this to his lord, who then fixed his mourning period at three years. His older relatives and various ministers all objected, counseling him thus: "The rulers of our ancestral lineage in Lu did not follow such a custom, nor did our own ancestral rulers. Now that tradition has come down to your person, we do not think you should go against them. Moreover, the *Records* state: 'In matters of mourning and sacrifice, one should follow the practices of one's ancestors.' We have a tradition to respect," they insisted.

The Crown Prince said to Ranyou, "In the past I have not been much of a student, being fonder of racing horses and wielding a sword. Now my older relatives and our ministers do not think all that much of me, and I am concerned that they will not do their utmost for me. Please go and consult Mencius for me."

Ranyou again went to Zou to ask Mencius his advice.

"I understand," said Mencius, "but the Crown Prince cannot take his standard from others in this matter. Confucius said, 'When the ruler died, the Crown Prince would have all of the various ministers place themselves under the command of the prime minister. [Compare *Analects* 14.40.] He would eat only thin gruel, his face would turn ink-black, and taking his proper place, he would weep. That the various ministers and officers of the court would not dare but grieve was because he stood before them. When a superior shows a passion for something, those below are sure to be even more zealous. The excellence of the exemplary person is the wind, while that of the petty person is the grass. As the wind blows, the grass is sure to bend.' [*Analects* 12.19.] This matter lies with the Crown Prince."

Ranyou returned and reported his conversation to the Crown Prince.

"He is right," said the Crown Prince. "This matter really does lie with me alone."

For five months the Crown Prince stayed in the mourning shed, and issued no orders or prohibitions. All of his ministers and clansmen praised him, and said of him that he understood the observance of ritual propriety.

When the time came for the burial ceremony, people came from all over to observe it. The agony shown in his countenance and the anguish felt through his tears moved all of the mourners deeply.

203. There is a play here on the paronomastic relationship between "to get (*de* 得)" and "excellence (*de* 德)."

204. Compare 2.19.

205. Compare 4.26. If the person does not comply and yet is associated with you, his conduct can disgrace you.

BOOK 13   206. The *Zuo Commentary to the Spring and Autumn Annals* Cheng 2 (compare Legge V:344) recounts a story of Wey rewarding a commander who had come to their aid, giving him the use of certain musical instruments and the right to appear at court using emblems of a prince:

> It was a person of Xinzhu, Zhongshu Yuxi, who went to the aid of Sun Huanzi, and it was because of him that Sun Huanzi escaped with his life. Subsequently, the Wey kinsmen of Sun rewarded Zhongshu with a city, but he declined. He asked instead to be permitted to use the hanging musical bells reserved for the various lords and to appear at court with tassels on his horse trappings, which they allowed.
>
> Confucius on hearing of this said, "What a pity! It would have been better to give him many cities. It is insignias of office and titles alone that cannot be conceded to pretenders—they must be managed by the ruler. Proper titles give rise to confidence, and confidence is what protects the insignias of office. It is insignias in which the meaning of ritual propriety is invested, and it is ritual propriety that carries appropriate conduct (*yi* 義) into practice, appropriate conduct is what gives rise to benefit, and it is benefit that brings equanimity to the people. Such things are what structure government, and if you concede them to pretenders, you concede the government along with them. If the government is lost, the country will follow, and there can be no stopping it."

Hanshi waizhuan 5.34/41/19 also records a story in which Confucius, in attendance on Ji Sun (see 14.36), worries over the appropriate use of names.

207. The Dingzhou text has "none of the people would be disrespectful." Compare 14.41.

208. Waley (1938) points out that when the Zhou dynasty rose to power, the states of Lu and Wey were given to the fourth and seventh sons of King Wen respectively.

209. Confucius advocates the priority of economic well-being over education in governing the people. This same theme is carried through both *Mencius* and *Xunzi*, and down to the priority of economic and welfare rights over political rights in the contemporary human rights discourse.

210. Confucius discusses *shanren* 善人 three other times: see also 7.26, 11.20, and 13.29.

211. The Dingzhou text has *guo* 國 instead of *bang* 邦, observing the taboo on the founding Han dynasty ruler's given name, Liu Bang 劉邦.

212. According to the Zhu Xi commentary, *rang* 攘 means "to steal when in difficult straits."

213. See interesting and amusing developments of this anecdote in *Han Feizi* 49.9.2, *Lüshi chunqiu* (Xu Weiyu):449, and *Huainanzi* 13/125/14. In the tension between family and the Governor's law, Confucius is saying that the law does not trump the family. Order begins at home.

214. There is extensive and explicit commentary on this passage and 5.22 in *Mencius* 7B37. See note 86 above.

215. See 7.26. The *Book of Changes* is not actually cited by name in this passage, and Confucius usually does refer to a text by name when he is quoting directly from it: for example, the *Book of Songs*. The quote here, however, is identical with the commentary on the third line of hexagram 32 as we have it today, and the use of "to divine (*zhan* 占)" in this same passage suggests that the Master indeed had some familiarity with at least sections of the *Book of Changes*.

216. See also 2.14 and 15.22. For extended commentary on this passage, see the *Zuo Commentary to the Spring and Autumn Annals* Zhao 20 (compare Legge V:684):

> The Marquis of Qi had returned from the hunt, and was being attended by Master Yan at the Chuan pavilion when Ju of Liangqiu galloped up to them. The Marquis said, "Only Ju is in harmony (*he* 和) with me!"
>
> "All that Ju does is agree (*tong* 同) with you," said Master Yan. "Wherein is the harmony?"
>
> "Is there a difference between harmony and agreement?" asked the Marquis.

"There is," replied Master Yan. "Harmony is like making congee. One uses water, fire, vinegar, sauce, salt, and plum to cook fish and meat, and burns firewood and stalks as fuel for the cooking process. The cook blends these ingredients harmoniously to achieve the appropriate flavor. Where it is too bland, he adds flavoring, and where it is too concentrated, he dilutes it with water. When you partake of this congee, sir, it lifts your spirits.

"The relationship between ruler and minister is another case in point. Where the ruler considers something right and yet there is something wrong about it, the minister should point out what is wrong as a way of achieving what is right. Where the ruler considers something wrong and yet there is something right about it, the minister should point out what is right as a way of setting aside what is wrong. In such a way governing will be equitable without violating ritual propriety (*li* 禮) and the common people will not be contentious. Thus the *Book of Songs* says:

> There is indeed harmoniously blended congee;
> The kitchen has already been cautioned to bring out a
>   balanced and even flavor.
> The spirits will come to partake of it without finding
>   blame,
> And above and below will be free of contest.

"The Former Kings blended the five flavors and harmonized the five notes to lift their spirits and to achieve success in their governing. Music functions similarly to flavoring. There is one field of sound; the two kinds of music: martial and civil; the three kinds of songs: airs of the states, odes, and hymns; the four quarters from which materials are gathered for making instruments; the five-note pentatonic scale; the six-pitch pipes; the seven sounds; the winds of the eight directions; and the nine ballads—all of which complement each other. There are the distinctions between clear and turbid, small and great, short and long, quick and slow, plaintive and joyous, hard and soft, delayed and rapid, high and low, beginning and ending, and intimate and distant—all of which augment each other. You listen to these, sir, and it lifts your spirits, which in turn enables you to excel harmoniously. Hence the *Book of Songs* says, 'There are no imperfections in the sound of excellence.'

"Now Ju is not acting in this way. Whatever you say is right, Ju also says is right; whatever you say is wrong, Ju also says is wrong. If you season water with water, who is going to eat it? If you keep playing the same note on your lute, who is going to listen to it? The inadequacy of 'agreement' lies in this."

They were drinking wine and enjoying themselves when the Marquis observed, "If from ancient times there had been no death, what then would be the extent of our joy!"

"If from ancient times there had been no death," ventured Master Yan, "there would be the joy of the ancients, and what would you, sir, get out of that! In ancient times, the Shuangjiu clan first settled this territory, then came the Jice clan, followed by Youfeng Boling, the Pugu clan, and finally by your first ancestor. If from ancient times there had been no death, there would be the joy of the Shuangjiu clan, and I doubt that you would want that!"

This portion of the *Zuo Commentary* continues with a further illustration of the importance of harmony and balance:

Zichan of the state of Zheng was ill, and said to Zitai Shu, "When I die, you are sure to come to power. Only those with real moral excellence are able to win over the people with leniency. For all others, they had best be strict. When fire blazes, people will watch it from a distance in awe, and thus few die from it. But water is soft and pliant. People take it lightly and play about in it, and thus many die in it. Thus, governing with lenience is difficult."

Zichan was ill for several months and then died. And Zitai Shu did come to power. But he was lenient, being unable to bear being strict with people. Robbers overran the state of Zheng, picking their victims in the marshlands of Huanfu. Zitai Shu regretted this, saying, "If earlier I had followed Zichan's advice, it would not have come to this." He marshaled his troops to attack the robbers in the marshlands of Huanfu, and obliterated them. Robberies declined and then desisted altogether.

Confucius remarked, "Excellent! When government is lenient, the common people scorn it, and you need to dis-

cipline them with strictness. But with strictness, you injure
the people, and this injury must be treated with leniency.
With leniency you temper strictness, and with strictness
you discipline leniency, and as a consequence, governing
functions harmoniously. The *Book of Songs* says,

> The people indeed toil away.
> Perhaps you might give them some respite.
> Be kind to these central states
> To bring peace to the four quarters.

"This is treating the people with leniency. And further,

> Do not permit deceit and indulgence
> In order to rein in the wicked.
> You should stop the robbers and villains
> Who do not respect civilized conduct.

"This then is disciplining the people with strictness. There
is another passage in which harmony is used to bring
peace to the world:

> Pacify the distant reaches
> And win over those close at hand
> To secure the throne of our king.

"And again there is another song that speaks of the highest
harmony,

> Neither anxious nor remiss,
> Neither inflexible nor indulgent,
> He carried out the work of governing unhurriedly,
> And every manner of good fortune befell him."

When Zichan died and Confucius heard about it, he wept
for him and said, "His love was our legacy from the ancients."

In the *Spring and Autumn Annals of Master Lü* (Xu Weiyu 1955):550,
cooking as the art of contextualizing is described in the following terms:

> In combining your ingredients to achieve a harmony (*he*
> 和), you have to use the sweet, sour, bitter, acrid, and the
> salty, and you have to mix them in an appropriate se-
> quence and proportion. Bringing the various ingredients
> together is an extremely subtle art in which each of them
> has its own expression. The variations within the cooking

pot are so delicate and subtle that they cannot be captured in words or fairly conceptualized.

217. The Dingzhou text has "A petty person is difficult to serve."

218. The *Analects* discusses *shanren* 善人 several times: see also 7.26, 11.20, and 13.11.

BOOK 14

219. See 6.5.

220. Compare 8.13.

221. See also 4.9. The *Zuo Commentary to the Spring and Autumn Annals* Xi 23 (compare Legge V:187) has a relevant passage in which Duke Wen of Jin settles in the state of Qi, takes a wife, accumulates wealth and property, and giving himself up to the good life, is unwilling to travel anywhere:

> On arriving in the state of Qi, Duke Huan of Qi gave Duke Wen of Jin to wife a woman who managed an estate of twenty chariots. The duke found great satisfaction in this arrangement, but his followers disapproved, and were about to leave. They discussed the situation in the shade of the mulberry bushes. There was a concubine tending the silk worms who reported the conversation to Madame Jiang. Madame Jiang put her to death, and said to the duke: "You have grand ambitions to travel the world. I just put to death someone who overheard them."
>
> "I have no such ambitions," protested the duke.
>
> "Go!" she insisted. "By cherishing your home here and finding such contentment you in fact are destroying your name."
>
> The duke was unwilling to leave, so Madame Jiang conspired with Zifan, and getting her husband drunk, she had him sent on his way. When the duke returned to his senses, he grabbed a spear and chased after Zifan.

222. Following D. C. Lau (1992).

223. The Dingzhou text has "someone who has boldness."

224. This reference to personally engaging in farming is a counterweight to other passages in which Confucius seems to denigrate such occupations.

225. This passage illustrates the one that precedes it. *Yong* 勇, often translated "courage," but more properly, "boldness," by itself is not virtue.

226. Compare 12.24.

227. The "people" and the "lord" are implicit in the terms *ai* and *zhong*. Yang Bojun (1982):147 cites the *Guoyu* "Luyu" as a footnote to this passage:

> If the people work hard, they will be thoughtful, and if thoughtful, the proficient heart-and-mind will grow therefrom; if they are idle, they will be corrupt, and if corrupt, they will forget about being proficient, and if they forget about being proficient, the dissipated heart-and-mind will grow therefrom.

228. The *Zuo Commentary to the Spring and Autumn Annals* Xiang 31 (compare Legge V:565) has a complementary passage:

> In the twelfth month, Beigong Wenzi was in attendance on Duke Xiang of Wey in travelling to the state of Chu to comply with their alliance with Song. While passing through the state of Zheng, Yinduan went to Feilin ("Yew Woods") to requite them with gifts. He followed the etiquette proper to inviting his guests, and used the appropriate language for requiting gifts. Wenzi entered the capital to pay Wey's respects. Ziyu served as go-between, Feng Jianzi and Zitai Shu welcomed the guests. When the official visit was finished and Wenzi took his leave, he said to the Marquis of Wey, "Zheng observes ritual propriety (*li* 禮). This will be her good fortune for several generations, and indeed will keep larger states from encroaching. The *Book of Songs* says,
>
> > When the weather is hot
> > Who can go without bathing?
>
> "Observing ritual propriety is to governing what bathing is to hot weather. With bathing saving one from the heat, what is there to worry about?"
>
> In his administration of the government, Zichan selected the able and employed them. Feng Jianzi was able to be decisive on important matters; Zitai Shu (Shi Shu) was an outstanding talent and a man of letters; Gongsun Hui (Ziyu) was able to understand the workings of the neighboring states, to distinguish rank, nobility, and talent in the clans and houses of their ministers, and further, he was good at drafting official proclamations; Pi Chen was

an able advisor, although those plans laid in the country-side were successful while those laid in the cities were not.

When his state of Zheng was going to have dealings with the other various lords, Zichan would ask Gongsun Hui about the workings of the neighboring states, and moreover, would get him to prepare some draft proclamations. With Pi Chen he would drive out into the country-side and seek his advice on what should be done, and reporting all of this to Feng Jianzi, he would get him to make the final decision. With affairs thus in order, he would turn them over to Zitai Shu for implementation in coordination with his official guests. It was for this reason that Zheng rarely failed in its diplomacy, and Beigong Wenzi was to say of Zheng that it observes ritual propriety.

229. Yang Bojun (1982):148 interprets this as an expression of contempt.

230. In service to the parallel structure of this passage, and considering 14.16 and 17 in which Guanzhong is described as authoritative (*ren* 仁), we have amended this passage by reading *ren* 人 as *renren* 仁人. Compare these passages to 3.22 where Confucius 'expresses a somewhat different opinion about Guanzhong.

231. See the *Zuo Commentary to the Spring and Autumn Annals* Zhuang 8-9 (compare Legge V:83–84). The story is that the people of Lu put Prince Qiu and his tutor to death, while Guanzhong asked to be taken prisoner.

232. The Dingzhou text does not repeat the phrase.

233. The Dingzhou text does not have "the people."

234. According to Waley (1937):185, Duke Huan was responsible for stemming the tide of the Di barbarians from the north.

235. For this event, see the *Zuo Commentary to the Spring and Autumn Annals* Ai 14 (compare Legge V:840):

> On the day *jiawu*, Chen Heng of Qi assassinated his ruler Ren at Shuzhou. Confucius fasted for three days, and then petitioned three times that Qi be attacked. The duke replied to him, "It is long since that Lu has been weakened by Qi, so if we were to attack them, what do you think would happen?"
>
> "Chen Heng has assassinated his ruler," responded Confucius, "and half of the people of Qi are disaffected.

With the Lu forces augmenting this half of the Qi population, Lu can take the victory."

"You go and report this to the Ji Sun clan," said the
duke. Confucius took his leave, and said to someone,
"Having held rank below the high officials at court, I had
no choice but to speak up."

236. Compare 14.35.

237. Compare 12.1 and *Xunzi* 2/1/32.

238. *Huainanzi* 1/5/10 has a passage which serves as commentary here:

> The average lifespan of man is seventy years, but with all
> our choices and goals, we regret every day what we did the
> day before and in this way we reach the end of our life.
> Thus, Qu Boyu, at fifty years of age, realized that he was
> wrong at forty-nine.

See also *Zhuangzi* 71/25/51 and 75/27/10. The final comment by
Confucius is ambiguous. Either he is condemning the envoy for not being discreet in talking about his lord, or he is praising the envoy for
"telling it like it is."

239. See 8.14. Alternatively, "unless you have office, you don't get to
plan policy."

240. Words are cheap—if you have the position, you have the responsibility.

241. Compare 9.29.

242. There is a similar passage in 1.16. See also 1.1 and 15.19.

243. Compare *Daodejing* 63.

244. *De* 德 means both beneficence and gratitude—actually, it characterizes the situation of both giving and getting. It also entails "excellence" as the consequence of this situation, as we find in the preceding
passage.

245. Compare *Daodejing* 70:

> My words are truly easy to understand
> And truly easy to act upon,
> Yet in the world no one is able to understand them
> And no one is able to act upon them....
> Only because of ignorance do they not recognize me.
> Those who recognize me are rare;
> Those who model themselves on me are revered.

246 This passage seems to refer to the prior passage that an-
nounces that the way (*dao* 道) does not prevail in the world.

247. See 14.35.

248. *Songs* 34. Compare Legge IV:53.

249. This refers to King Wu Ding of the Shang who reigned for fifty-nine years. See Legge III:466. The question of the length of the mourning period is raised several times in this text. See 17.21.

250. The Dingzhou text has "It was not only three . . . ," with the text breaking off at this point.

251. Compare *Mencius* 3A2 translated in note 202 above.

252. Compare 13.4.

253. The "peers (*ren* 人)" here is contrasted with "the people (*baixing* 百姓)," and refers to a particular class of people. See 1.5.

254. There is a story in the *Book of Rites* (*Liji*) 4.69/30/6 about Yuanrang. On the death of Yuanrang's mother, Confucius went to help with the funeral arrangements, and, finding Yuanrang singing by the coffin, pretended not to hear him.

255. The Dingzhou text has "I have seen him as lord (*jun* 君)," which is probably a textual corruption for the graphically similar (*ju* 居), translated here as "sitting."

BOOK 15   256. See 5.15 for another reference to Kong Wenzi. The *Zuo Commentary to the Spring and Autumn Annals* Ai 11 (compare Legge V:826) has a related passage:

> Kong Wenzi was about to attack Taishu, and went to Confucius for advice. Confucius said to him, "I have studied the use of ritual vessels, but I have never heard anything about arms." He withdrew, and ordered his carriage harnessed for his departure, saying, "The bird chooses a tree to roost; since when can the tree choose the bird?"
>
> Wenzi hurriedly detained him, saying, "I was not asking your advice for my own sake, but to prevent the troubles that are befalling our state of Wey." Confucius was going to stay, but when an envoy from Lu came with a ceremonial monetary gift to summon him, he returned home.

257. Compare 4.15.

258. The performative force of "to know (*zhi* 知)" means that it is not simply a cognitive understanding, but something done.

259. This is the earliest instance of what is usually taken to be a Daoist idea, "nonassertive action (*wuwei* 無爲)."

260. See 14.25 for Qu Boyu.

261. The Dingzhou text does not have "first."

262. According to Yang Bojun (1982):164, the Xia calendar began with the first day of spring, and was convenient for the farmers, while the Zhou calendar began with the first day of winter.

263. See 3.25 and 7.14.

264. Waley (1937):196 notes that the words to these songs are preserved in the *Book of Songs*, and hence what Confucius is objecting to is specifically the music. The examples show a concern to use the resources of the people well, but not at the expense of the important life forms: observing ritual propriety and playing music. Hence the ornate Zhou cap, and attention to music.

265. This passage is repeated in 9.18.

266. See also 18.2 and 18.8.

267. The received text begins this passage with "the exemplary person," and then ends the passage by repeating it. We follow the Dingzhou text in omitting the first instance of this expression.

268. Compare 5.12 and 12.2.

269. The Dingzhou text does not have the reference to "I": "When it comes to other people, who should you praise or blame?" Compare 14.29.

270. Perhaps the idea is that one should have others proof their work. It would thus connect with the following passage.

271. The Dingzhou text has these two phrases in the reverse order, beginning with "Where everybody celebrates a person . . ." Compare 13.24.

272. "Having gone astray (*guo* 過)" continues the "way" metaphor. The *Hanshi waizhuan* 3.17/19/23 has a similar passage in which Confucius says, "Having gone astray, to get right back on track, is to never have strayed at all." See also *Guliangzhuan* Xi 22 for a very different turn on this passage.

273. Compare 2.15.

274. Neither hunger nor salary enter into the equation.

275. Compare 1.12.

276. The Dingzhou text has "swimming/wandering (*you* 游)."

277. In *Mencius* 7A23 it says:

> Mencius said, "Take care of the fields under cultivation and go light on taxes, and you can make the common people prosper. If the people consume their stores at the proper time and expend them in accordance with ritual propriety, their stores will be inexhaustible. The people

cannot live without fire and water, yet were you to knock on anyone's door in the evening asking for them, no one would deny you. This is because there is more than enough to go around. When the sage governs the world, provisions are as abundant as fire and water. For when provisions are as abundant as fire and water, how could anyone among the common people be perverse?"

Even though fire and water are vital, they can be dangerous; authoritative conduct is even more vital, and will never be dangerous.

278. Compare *Xunzi* 104/29/6ff which makes a sophisticated case for the position that "filial piety (*xiao* 孝)" is not simply doing as you are told.

279. Compare 7.7.

BOOK 16 280. We follow D. C. Lau in reconstructing this passage.

281. This "screen of reverence" is the screen used in the court of the Lu ruler. Because, on reaching this screen, the Lu subjects demonstrate their reverence for the ruler, it is called the "screen of reverence." "Within the screen of reverence" refers to the Lu ruler. At this time, Ji Sun had taken over the reins of government, and was in a power struggle with the Lu ruler, knowing that the Lu ruler wanted to deal with him in order to recover his political authority. On this account he was afraid that Zhuanyu would take advantage of its strategic location to help the Lu court. As a preemptive strike to maintain his strength, he therefore attacked Zhuanyu. In this passage, Confucius is very critical of the intentions of Ji Sun.

282. Here Confucius is condemning the current situation where political power in the state has devolved first to the powerful clans, and then to the household ministers of those same clans. Power must be articulated through patterns of deference, and there can only be one center.

283. The Dingzhou text just has "ritual propriety."

284. These "natural propensities" would include both one's natural abilities and the specific conditions into which one is born such as family and community. After all, *sheng* 生 means "birth, growth, and life." What *sheng* does not reference is some a priori category of understanding or wisdom. In 7.20 Confucius denies that he himself belongs to the first category.

285. Do both of the sayings in the preceding 16.11 passage apply to Bo Yi and Shu Qi, who would only do what they felt was appropriate, and who eventually died for what they thought they should do? These passages should be read together with 5.23, 7.15, and 18.8.

BOOK 17

286. Yang Huo was a household steward in the House of Ji.

287. Yang Huo's ploy was that Confucius would have to come and thank him. A fuller report of this encounter occurs in *Mencius* 3B7:

> Gongsun Chou asked Mencius, "What is the meaning of the fact that you do not go and seek interviews with the various feudal lords?"
>
> Mencius replied, "In ancient times, if one was not in service as a minister to a state, one did not seek an interview with its lord. Duangan Mu climbed over a wall to avoid such an interview; Xie Liu bolted his door and would not open it. But this is taking things too far. If pressed by one of the feudal lords, one may have an interview with him. Yang Huo wanted Confucius to come and see him, but did not want others to think that he had no sense of ritual propriety (*li* 禮). When a minister gives a gift to a scholar-apprentice (*shi* 士), but the scholar-apprentice is not at home to personally receive it, it is incumbent upon him to go to the minister's home to pay his respects and express his gratitude. Yang Huo waited until Confucius was out, and then presented a steamed suckling pig at his home; Confucius waited until Yang Huo was out, and then went to pay his respects at the minister's residence. One might ask: On this occasion, since Yang Huo had in fact first paid his respects to Confucius, how could Confucius have refused to go and see him? Master Zeng said, 'It is harder to cringe and smile obsequiously than it is to irrigate the garden in the heat of summer.' Zilu said, 'To have to speak with someone you do not want to, and further, to have to take on a humble look in his presence—I would find such conduct unthinkable.' From such reports we can see how exemplary persons (*junzi* 君子) cultivate their character."

The point here is twofold. First exemplary persons do not put themselves in situations where protocol requires them to defer to people they do not respect. Secondly one does not speak on the responsibilities of others.

See also The *Zuo Commentary to the Spring and Autumn Annals* Ding 8 and 9 (Legge V:765ff).

288. The Dingzhou text has *sheng* 生 for *xing* 性, but this is common in editions of the classical texts.

289. See 6.14. Ziyou was the local prefect.

290. The contrast is one of proportion: a string quartet at a picnic.

291. This story as reported in the *Zuo Commentary to the Spring and Autumn Annals* Ding 12 has Gongshan Furao revolting against Lu, but he does not call Confucius to join him. In fact, in this account, by this time Confucius is Minister of Justice, and sends people to defeat him.

292. Bi was the Ji family stronghold.

293. *Xing* is literally "walking," and by extension, "carrying into practice," continuing the "way (*dao* 道)" metaphor.

294. Waley (1937):211 notes that *shi* 食 means both "to eat/food" and "to receive an official salary," as we saw in 15.38. The Dingzhou text for 15.32 has *shi* 食 as a variant for *lu* 祿, "to receive an official salary," which is found in the received text.

295. Compare 8.2.

296. There is one version of the *Analects* in which 9 and 10 are one passage, but the Dingzhou text and several of the others have them separated. See also 16.13.

297. See *Mencius* 7B37 in explanation of this rather laconic remark, translated in note 86 above. Mencius then adds his own commentary to it. Such a village worthy is overdetermined in the sense of form and regularity so that he is plausible to those who would look to him as a model, yet the creative element necessary for his personalization and renewal of the exemplary role is absent. He has no blood. He is a hypocrite because he has nothing of quality to contribute on his own. Confucius is given the last word in this passage, summing up his concerns about the corrosive influence such a "model" can have on the quality of the culture.

298. Although there is good textual evidence that this passage should be "he is desperate that he will not be," all of the received texts are without the negative, *bu* 不. But D. C. Lau and Yang Bojun reference numerous texts that cite this passage with either the *bu* or *fu* 弗 negatives. In fact, the text makes sense both ways. It might also mean that "he is desperate that he will be" appointed to office, being aware of his own shortcomings.

299. Repeated from 1.3.

300. Purple is a mixture of red and blue, where red is a pure color. It seems that as early as the *Zuo Commentary to the Spring and Autumn Annals* Ai 17 there is a record of purple already taking the place of red as the color of the nobility's dress.

301. See 15.11 above, and *Mencius* 7B37 translated in note 86 above.

302. Translating *shu* 述 as "to follow the proper way" enables us to maintain the "path (*dao* 道)" metaphor. See 7.1.

303. Ru Bei appears in the *Book of Rites* (*Liji*) 21.41/113/12 where he is sent to Confucius by Duke Ai to learn about mourning rituals.

304. The commentator Ma Rong (79-166) cites the calendrics chapter of the *Zhoushu* 周書 which states, "In spring we take fire from the elm and willow trees, in summer from the jujube and apricot, in late summer from the different kinds of mulberry bushes, in autumn from the oak and *you* tree, and in winter from the sophora and sandalwood."

305. See 14.40.

306. In *Mencius* 3A2, ministers object to the three-year mourning period advised by Mencius by claiming that it has not been the norm. See note 202 above.

Both Caiwo and Confucius argue by appeal to a cycle, although the cycle is longer for the latter.

307. *Bo* 博 and *yi* 弈 are board games. The first was played with dice, and was a method of divination. See Li Xueqing (1997). The second was an ancestor of *weiqi* (which later became the game *go* in Japan).

308. The Dingzhou text has "Zilu inquired, saying, . . ."

309. Following Waley in relocating the character "replied (*yue* 曰)" to this phrase.

310. The Dingzhou text has passages 23 and 24 as one passage.

BOOK 18   311. These were all persons who had a role in the life of Zhou, the last infamous ruler of the Shang. The Viscount of Wei was the elder brother of Zhou who was born while their mother was still a concubine of Di Yi. It was because their mother was installed as the official consort by the time of Zhou's birth that it was Zhou who inherited the throne. The story is recounted several times in the *Lüshi chunqiu* (Xu Weiyu 1955):1083.

> The Viscount of Ji was Zhou's uncle. He sent Zhou into a rage with his remonstrances, and was subsequently enslaved.
>
> Bi Gan was also an uncle. When he remonstrated with Zhou, Zhou responded by saying that he had heard that sages have seven openings in their hearts. He then proceeded to find out if Bi Gan was indeed a sage.

312. The Dingzhou text has "persons (*ren* 人)" rather than "authoritative persons (*ren* 仁)."

313. See 15.14 and 18.8.

314. Confucius did not achieve any exalted political position during his lifetime. Hence Waley (1937):218 suggests that this chapter is "legendary": "The Confucius who ranked above the head of the Meng family is already well on the way to apotheosis."

315. The term *ren* 人 here cannot be read as "people"—it must refer to the upper classes of kinsmen. See 1.5 and 14.42.

316. Ji Huanzi was the father of Ji Kangzi, the head of the Ji clan that appears throughout the *Analects*. He was a high minister who usurped power in Lu from the reign of Duke Ding until the first year of Duke Ai, dying two years later.

317. This same madman of Chu also appears in *Zhuangzi* 19/7/4, where he observes that exercising impositional authority is anathema to effecting social order:

> Shoulder-Us went to see the madman, Carriage Groom. The mad Carriage Groom asked him, "What has Beginning-Midday been telling you?"
>
> Shoulder-Us replied, "He told me that when a ruler on his own initiative lays down the formal instruments of government, who would dare disobey or remain unreformed by them!"
>
> The mad Carriage Groom observed, "This is a ruffian's kind of excellence (*de* 德). As far as its bringing proper order to the world, it would be like trying to walk across the ocean, or trying to drill one's way through a river, or trying to make a mosquito carry a mountain on its back. When the sage (*shengren* 聖人) governs, does he govern the external? He straightens himself out before he does anything, and is concerned precisely with being able to go about his own business—no more, no less.

Compare Graham (1981):95. Yang Bojun (1982):193 points out that recluses appearing in the *Analects* are named for their occupations: for example, the "gatekeeper" in 14.38. Here, then, Jie Yu, "carriage groom," is both a name and occupation.

318. The phoenix is an auspicious omen that is seen when sagely government prevails.

319. A similar elaboration of this passage appears in *Zhuangzi* 12/4/86; Graham (1981):74–75.

320. Perfect rhyme between *qin* 勤 and *fen* 分.

321. See a similar account about Confucius and Zilu in *Zhuangzi* 71/25/33; compare Graham (1981):109.

322. See also 5.23, 7.15, and 16.12.

323. See 15.14 and 18.2.

324. The Dingzhou text has "But I am different in how I employ the people."

325. Nietzsche says that "evil men sing no songs." It is difficult to keep good music and bad government together.

326. Compare the *Zuo Commentary to the Spring and Autumn Annals* Wen 18 in which a similar phenomenon of the birth of twins is recorded. "Doubles" are auspicious in a Chinese world. Note that the names of the twins are rhymed in the archaic pronunciations.

BOOK 19

327. The Dingzhou text has these two phrases in reverse order. Compare 1.6.

328. *Xunzi* 17/6/48; Knoblock 1:229 describes the Zizhang school:

> Their caps bent and twisted, their robes billowing and flowing, they move to and fro as though they were a Yao or Shun—such are the base Ru of Zizhang's school.

329. Compare *Mencius* 3A2 translated in note 202 above.

330. Compare 1.11. The real accomplishment here is on the part of the father who made it easy for the son.

BOOK 20

331. *Mozi* 27/16/57 and *Lushi chunqiu* (Xu Weiyu):363 say that this was a prayer for rain that Tang made because of a drought that occurred after his defeat of Jie, the last ruler of the Xia dynasty.

332. These four rhymed sentences are attributed to King Wu, founder of the Zhou dynasty, probably on the enfeoffment of Jiang Taigong of Qi.

333. See 18.8.

334. A version of this passage also occurs in 17.6.

335. Compare *Mencius* 2A2 in note 119 above. Just as "words (*yan* 言)" and "ritual propriety (*li* 禮)" are modes of discourse, so "the propensity of circumstances (*ming* 命)" has to be understood analogously as a discourse.

Dingxian 定縣, also known as Dingzhou 定州, is a prefecture in Hebei province just a few hours outside of Beijing. During the Han dynasty, this territory fell within the fiefdom of Zhongshan 中山, and over time many ancient kings and noblemen came to be buried in the sprawling hills surrounding the central walled fortification, Dingxiancheng 定縣城. Tombs dating back to the Han dynasty have in recent decades been discovered in this area. The initial excavation of what has come to be called Dingxian Tomb #40—a tomb identified with Liu Xiu 流修, King Huai of Zhongshan 中山懷王, who died in the third year (55 BCE) of the reign of Emperor Xuan of the Han 漢宣帝 —began in May 1973, and was completed by December of that year.

Sometime probably towards the end of the Western Han (202 BCE– 25 CE), the tomb was plundered by grave robbers, and the bamboo strips contained in it were burned and thrown into disarray. Most of the strips were severely damaged and broken, and the fragments remaining were heavily scorched from the fire, making the work of deciphering and transcribing their contents particularly taxing. Along with remnants of a book knife, a rectangular inkstone, and a small copper water pot, there were traces of ashes from silk, suggesting that some silk manuscripts had also been included among the funerary objects, but unfortunately had been destroyed.

In 1974, the contents of the find were sent to the Ministry of Culture for preservation and restoration. It was not until August 1981, however, that the long-awaited summary description of a cache of bamboo strips was published in an issue of the archæological journal *Cultural Relics* 8 (*Wenwu* 文物). But there had been good reason for the delay.

In the middle of 1976, a team of scholars who had worked on the Mawangdui silk manuscripts set to work on identifying the partial texts and piecing their contents together. They began by transcribing the characters from the bamboo strips onto notecards, one card per strip, assigning them a sequential identification number. The reconstruction process was halted by the devastating earthquake at Tangshan just a month into the project. Even though the find had been meticulously attended to, somehow the wooden chest into which the strips had been transferred was overturned, and yet again the strips were not only thrown into disarray, but suffered further considerable damage. With eighty percent of the job done, work on the cache of strips stopped.

In 1980, another reconstruction team was commissioned under the direction of the distinguished scholars Liu Laicheng 劉來成 and Li Xueqin 李學勤, and the project of recovery continued. Relying heavily upon the notecard transcriptions for the sequence, location, and order of the strips, the reconstruction of the *Analects* was the first order of business, comparing what had been recovered with the existing text. At the same time, every effort was being made to identify and copy the characters as they occurred on the original strips. By the time of the 1981 report in *Cultural Relics* 8, the basic work of reconstruction had been completed, and out of an unpromising heap of broken and charred bamboo strips, the team was able to report on the remnants of eight classical works: *Words of the Ru Lineage* 儒家者言, *Duke Ai Inquires about Five Ways of Being Appropriate* 哀公問五義, *The Biography of the Grand Tutor* 保傅傳, *The Grand Duke* 太公, the *Wenzi* 文子, *A Record of the Visit of Liu Ding, King of Liuan, to the Court of Emperor Xuan of the Han in 56 BCE* 六安王朝五風二年正月起居記, some divinatory materials that are by and large unintelligible, and, not least important, the new manuscript of the *Analects* 論語 .

For some undisclosed reasons, the reconstruction work was again halted, and it was not until 1993 that Liu Laicheng was able to complete the *Analects* portion of the project, with Li Xueqin making the final evaluation.

Some of these texts contain materials already found in the early corpus. For example, *Words of the Ru Lineage* discusses such Confucian virtues as deference, filial piety, propriety, and living up to one's word, often appealing to the words of Confucius and his disciples. Much of this text is to be found scattered among the late Warring States and early Han texts such as the *Shuoyuan* 說苑 and *Kongzi jiayu* 孔子家語 .

Duke Ai Inquires about Five Ways of Being Appropriate overlaps with the *Xunzi* 荀子 , *Dadai liji* 大戴禮記 , and the *Kongzi jiayu*, although textual variants suggest that the latter three texts are perhaps drawing from different redactions of these received texts.

Although *The Biography of the Grand Tutor* shares text with the *Xinshu* 新書 of Jia Yi 賈誼 and the *Dadai liji*, it also contains some passages not seen elsewhere.

In the dynastic bibliographies, there are many works listed under the title of *The Grand Duke*, and it is difficult to determine from which manuscript or manuscripts the remaining contents have been copied. There is much text here that has not been seen before.

The text recovered from the *Wenzi* has rekindled the historical debate over the relationship between this text and the mid-first century BCE *Huainanzi* 淮南子 , close as it is to the *Huainanzi* in content. Almost all of what has been recovered from the fragments can be located in different parts of the present *Wenzi*, although the participants in the fragments of dialogue are different. Consistent with the court bibliography in the *History of the Han,* the Dingzhou *Wenzi* has Wenzi as teacher who is being asked questions by a King Ping of the Zhou 周平王 . The received text, on the other hand, has the teacher Laozi 老子 being asked questions by the student Wenzi, certainly less appropriate given that texts are usually named for the teacher rather than the student. From the recovery of the partial text, first published in the December 1995 issue of *Cultural Relics*, we can confirm against much earlier speculation that at least at 55 BCE a *Wenzi* existed. A plausible scenerio is that the *Wenzi* was edited out of the powerful *Huainanzi* and circulated after its compiler, Liu An 劉安, was executed for treason, and his works banned.[1]

A Record of the Visit of Liu Ding, King of Liuan, to the Court of Emperor Xuan of the Han in 56 BCE is a travelogue of the journey to Chang'an and an audience with the emperor, providing the names of places visited, distances, and a description of life along the way, as well as the gifts, clothing, and food witnessed at the court.

The more than 620 surviving strips and fragments, with 7,576 characters identified as the *Lunyu* or *Analects of Confucius,* amount to a bit less than half the length of our received text. As whole strips, they would have measured 16.2 cm long and 0.7 cm in width with 19 to 21 characters per strip. The bundle of these strips was tied together with silk thread at either end and in the middle of each strip. The imprint of these threads, which themselves were burned or have long since rotted away, has facilitated the process of textual reconstruction. While sixty to seventy percent of the contents of certain books among the twenty which comprise the *Analects* have been recovered, other books are much more fragmentary. For example, only one strip of book 1, with just 20 characters has been recovered, while 694 characters of book 15—about seventy-seven percent of the received text—are extant. There are also fragments of ten slips of the kind that are usually found at the end of a book, recording the number of sections and characters contained in the book, but it is impossible to determine to which books the slips belong, the number of characters originally included in any particular book, or the original order of the books themselves.

This Dingzhou *Analects*, dating from prior to the entombment in 55 BCE, predates the *Marquis Zhang Analects* 張候論 compiled by Zhang Yu 張禹 (d. 5 BCE), that became the standard text of Eastern

Han and beyond. Zhang Yu compiled his text from the *Analects of the State of Lu* 魯論 and the *Analects of the State of Qi* 齊論 to instruct Emperor Cheng of Han 漢成帝 (r. 33–7 BCE). As mentioned in the Introduction, prior to the recovery of the Dingzhou fragments, the earliest known edition of the *Analects* was the extant fragments of the Xiping text engraved in stone 熹平石經, circa 178 CE. The received text as we have it today is a version of the *Marquis Zhang Analects*. The late Eastern Han scholar, Zheng Xuan 鄭玄 wrote his famous commentary on the *Analects* by comparing the *Marquis Zhang Analects* with the still extant *Analects of the State of Qi* and the *Analects from the Estate of Confucius* 古論 . Although Zheng Xuan's important commentary was lost early on, recent finds primarily in Western China have enabled scholars to piece together about half of its original form.[2]

Not only is this Dingzhou text the earliest example of the *Analects* ever discovered, it belongs to an age in which at least three different versions of this text were still in circulation: the *Analects of the State of Lu*, the *Analects of the State of Qi*, and the *Analects from the Estate of Confucius*. The process of transmission inevitably entails the introduction of variant characters, simplified and mistaken characters, and inadvertent omissions, as well as interpolations by misguided but well-intended editors. It was hoped at the time of this first detailed report that the recovery of such an early redaction of the *Analects* would shed light on the history of this central classical text, and that it would resolve some of the questions that surround its early transmission.

In the May 1997 issue of *Cultural Relics*, about a quarter of the reconstructed text was revealed to the scholarly world for the first time, complete with textual notes and an introductory essay on the condition of this specific text. This was followed in July of the same year with a book-length publication of the text and textual notes in their entirety. It is that 1997 publication which informs our present translation.

Some scholars, such as D. C. Lau, would contend that among the pre-Qin classics, the *Analects* found its canonical form relatively early and did not change much subsequently. Even so, when comparing the text found at Dingzhou with the received text, there are some significant differences. For example, in the division of the books into passages, often the number of passages contained in any one book as recorded on the final strip does not correspond to the number contained in the received text. Further, the passages are not always divided up at the same place. What the Dingzhou text takes as two passages, the received text at times takes as one; what the Dingzhou text takes as one passage, the received text may take as two or even three. If we consider variant characters and grammatical particles, almost every sentence in every passage recovered is different in some way from the received text. Said another way, in a reconstructed text that in quantity is less than half of the received version, there are more than 700 places in which the Dingzhou edition differs from the received text, constituting some ten percent of the text itself. What we cannot tell from the recovered text is the original order of its chapters or the chapter titles, although some strips that seem to have titles and character counts were included in the find, and have been appended to the 1997 publication.

We have indicated in the individual notes to our translation those several places in which the Dingzhou text has provided important clarifications and alternative readings for the text. Beyond these specific passages, we can make some generalizations about the nature of this document.

First, the Dingzhou text is most probably a version of the *Lulun*—the *Analects of the State of Lu*—a version of this text which, prior to this find, had been thought lost. That some of the variants we find in the Dingzhou *Analects* are distinctively from the Lu version is corroborated by the recovered Zheng Xuan commentary. Further, Liu Laicheng, in his introduction to the 1997 publication of the Dingzhou *Analects*, reports that it is probably no accident that a memorial of the statesman, Xiao Wangzhi 蕭望之 (109–46 BCE), was found in this same tomb, although it is not listed in the inventory of texts. Xiao Wangzhi was not only a champion of political reform, but a scholar associated with advocating a set of orthodox texts, the *Analects of the State of Lu* being among them.

There are several features of an early pre-edited redaction of this text that are prominent in the Dingzhou find. In comparison with the received texts, often "root" characters are used without the classificatory signific element: 主 for 社, 中 for 仲, 間 for 簡, 狀 for 莊, 卷 for 倦, 辟 for 譬, and so on. On the other hand, less frequently the fuller version of the characters is used: 智 for 知, 輿 for 車, 壹 for 一, and so on. There is the use of loan words: 迷 for 彌, 說 for 悅, 房 for 防, 年 for 佞, 音 for 陰, for example. There is a seeming economy of grammatical particles— 矣, 而, 者, 乎, 也, and so on—with the received text being considerably fuller. This is not always the case; the Dingzhou text on occasion has the fuller version. Sometimes synonyms are used: 奚 for 何, and vice versa, 通 for 達, for example. The text respects imperial taboos, using 國 for 邦.

These many features of such an early version of the *Analects* provide us with a clearer understanding of the nature of the differences that obtained among competing redactions, offering us a new vantage point from which to anticipate the ensuing process of editing and collating the received versions.

NOTES TO APPENDIX I

1. The contemporary scholar, Ho Che Wah 何志華 (1998) has offered this speculation in a recent article. The "execution" of the King of Huainan in 122 BCE as a traitor to the throne likely had a numbing effect on the circulation of the philosophical text that bore his name, at least throughout the long reign of his executioner, Emperor Wu (d. 87 BCE). Ho reasons that, to keep in circulation some of the content of the valuable but proscribed treatise, some of its contents were appropriated, edited into a second volume, and circulated as the *Wenzi*. In a literary culture in which it was common for one text to borrow freely and liberally from another, the kinship between the suspended *Huainanzi* and its close cousin, the *Wenzi*, would not necessarily draw official

condemnation, especially given the conflicted relationship Emperor Wu had with his literary uncle.

2. See Makeham (1997) for a thorough examination of these materials.

Language and the Vagaries of Translation

Despite the manifold advances made during the present century in such fields as linguistics, cross-cultural studies, artificial intelligence, and cognitive science, the art of translation is still just that: an art—and thus, we suspect, it will always remain. If so, then even the most linguistically disciplined comparativists, armed with state-of-the-art translation-assisting programs, will continue to fear that their results will merely be one more verification of the famous *Tradduttore, traditore*: "translators are traitors."

Our own fears about the vagaries of translation are heightened by the fact that while we have had training in formal linguistics and in Chinese philology, our disciplinary home is philosophy, which is why it is on the philosophical significance of the Analects that we have focused our attention in this translation. As a consequence, our interpretation of what the text is about philosophically has influenced strongly our translation of it. The eventful, dynamic, and relational reading we give to early Chinese thought and the language in which it is written is regularly reflected in our translation. Most other translators of the *Analects* have assumed a more essentialistic and conservative Confucius, more concerned with constancy than with change. Both views are clearly in evidence when translations are compared. Consider the concluding section of 1.11, first by James Legge:

> If for three years he does not alter from the way of his father, he may be called filial.

Then Arthur Waley:

> If for the whole three years of mourning he manages to carry on the household exactly as in his father's day, then he is a good son indeed.

Raymond Dawson, in the same vein:

> If for three years he makes no change from the ways of his father, he may be called filial.

And finally, D. C. Lau:

> If, for three years, he makes no changes to his father's ways, he can be said to be a good son.

Our own version:

> A person who for three years refrains from reforming the ways of his late father can be called a filial son.

The first four standard translations suggest that if the son remains constant in following his father's way for three years, he will continue doing so thereafter; simply maintaining the *status quo*. Legge in his commentary is explicit on this:

> It is to be understood that the way of the father had not been very bad. An old interpretation, that the three years are to be understood of the three years of mourning for the father, is now rightly rejected. The meaning should not be confined to that period. [1]

The emphasis in this passage as we understand it is on reforming the ways of the father only after having fully embodied and understood them, and then only with due deliberation. Our translation implies that the son must first honor the ritual traditions seriously, but then must re-appropriate them for himself, and in the course of time, attune them to make them appropriate to his own particular circumstances.

Philology will not entirely settle the matter, for *gai* 改 has been conventionally rendered as "to change," "to alter," "to correct," "to amend," or "to reform," and the negative *wu* 無 can thus equally be linked to *gai* as "does not alter," "makes no change" or "refrains from reforming." We hedge and say philology will not "not entirely" decide the case because translating *gai* as "change" in this instance is within the semantic tolerance, although it might not be sufficiently specific to convey the intended meaning. That is, "change" is very real in the "eventful" world of classical China, and hence is expressed in many different ways, *gai* being only one of them. A translation of this passage needs to distinguish among several different senses: 1) *bian* 變 is to change gradually across time, 2) *yi* 易 is to change one thing for another, 3) *hua* 化 is to transform utterly where A becomes B, 4) *qian* 遷 is to change from one place to another, and 5) *gai* 改 is to correct or reform or improve upon *x* on the basis of some other standard or model *y*.[2]

Although we attempt an adequate translation of this passage based upon our understanding of the language, we also consider the passage philosophically. The important philosophical concern here is that the classical Confucian sense of order is processional and hence provisional. As we have suggested in the Introduction, a ritually constituted community requires that the values of the tradition be internalized and *personalized*. This need to "re-form" the inherited order is made explicit when Confucius says, "It is the person who is able to broaden the way, not the way that broadens the person" (15.29), and "In striving to be authoritative in your conduct, do not yield even to your teacher" (15.36). This philosophical consideration not only disallows the conservative reading that would have the son simply replicating the ways of his deceased father, but further would make such a son who only replicated the ways of his father something less than filial.

In our opinion, therefore, translation and interpretation are inextricably linked. No words, or strings thereof, carry with them any precise cognates in another language, and dictionaries, etymological or otherwise, can seldom function as the final arbiters. For example, believing that the Chinese had heard the word of God from the Patriarchs, Leibniz did not cavil at Matteo Ricci's uses of *shangdi* 上帝 or *tian* 天 for the Christian "God." Nicolo Longobardi, Ricci's successor at the China mission, however, was convinced the Chinese were out-and-out materialists, and therefore insisted on a neologism (*tianzhu* 天主 "Heaven's Lord") to translate "God." These differing interpretations were proffered over three hundred years ago, and with the growth of sophistication of Chinese studies since then, most sinologists today would probably agree that Longobardi's interpretation was superior to Ricci's. (Ricci might concur; after all, it was he who first introduced *tianzhu*.[3]) But only a part of this consensus is attributable to increased scholarly sophistication in Chinese studies. The important point is that sinologists are no longer Christian missionaries (there are a few exceptions) and consequently the question of how consonant, or not, Chinese views are with Christian views is simply no longer asked when translating.

Moreover, the interpretative views translators bring to their work are not confined to the beliefs expressed in the Chinese object language; they also have interpretative views on how and what the object language—and target language as well—expresses and can express, as we have already suggested in the introductory section on philosophic concerns. Consider, for example, the views of Angus Graham, perhaps the most distinguished sinologist/philosopher of this century. In his *Later Mohist Logic, Ethics and Science* he well cautions:

> The danger of imposing his own categories on the thought of other cultures is one which no investigator can finally escape. The most fundamental of such categories are those implicit in the structure of the language in which we think. . . .[4]

Graham felt that this interpretative problem was in fact so overwhelming that until we come to terms with it fairly, we must allow that "none of us yet knows classical Chinese."[5] And Graham set himself the task of investigating those differing "implicit structures" between the Indo-European languages and classical Chinese as integral to the project of learning the language.

But this is interpretation, and disagreements arise. Immediately after the passage quoted above, for example, Graham puts forward the interpretative claim that the later Mohists "discovered" the sentence—about which, more below—and then went on to translate the Chinese ci 詞, usually translated "phrase," as "sentence/proposition."

Chad Hansen disputed Graham's claim: the later Mohists did not discover the sentence, and they did not use ci as a technical term to be translated "sentence/proposition"; ci should continue to be rendered "phrase."[6] Now given both Graham's and Hansen's knowledge of the later Mohist texts, and of Western philosophy of language and logic, how do we account for these differing renderings of ci?

The answer is twofold. At one level, Graham and Hansen hold different views on how and what early Chinese thinkers thought about language and, at another level, they themselves hold different views about the nature of the Chinese language. Their differences are minimal, but not inconsequential, evidenced in their (at times) differing translations—which are, of course, based on their interpretations.

What these examples suggest (and they could be multiplied a hundredfold) is that when we speak of interpretation or exposition necessarily accompanying translation, we are not simply speaking of what is expressed *specifically* in the object language of the work under consideration. Our translation does not impose a singular reading of the English text; the *Analects*, in both the Chinese and the English languages, is too rich for that.

Rather do the fundamental interpretations that must guide translation have to do with, first, what the metaphysical presuppositions of the users of the object language were, and second, the nature of the object language itself, and to a lesser extent, the nature of the target language as well. Many translators do not make their interpretative views on these matters explicit, and it is understandable why they do not. Metaphysical views, and views of language, are seldom given to us explicitly. Virtually every native speaker of English can be said to have an ontological commitment to the distinctions between mind and body, subjective and objective, facts and values, cognitive and affective, and so forth. Of course most of these people have never received explicit instruction in how to carve the world of experience in these ways, and many of them are probably not even altogether sure of what it means to have an "ontological commitment." Similarly, although we are aware that human languages show great variety in their phonetic, syntactic, and semantic properties, it is difficult to imagine that they might not all be used in the same way, and for the same purposes, as we "use" our own language. (See the Introduction, pp. 33–36.)

For these reasons, it is perhaps not out of place for philosophers to essay translations of texts of great philosophical significance, for philosophers are obliged to make explicit, and to argue explicitly for, basic views that are all too frequently taken for granted—presupposed—by other translators anxious to get on with their work.

We do not at all wish to denigrate the efforts of our predecessors; without them we could do nothing. But neither in linguistics nor sinology nor philosophy have our predecessors spoken in a single voice. On the contrary, they have too often contradicted each other, both within and between the differing disciplines. In order to take sides among these predecessors where necessary, and in order to defend the interpretative views reflected in this translation where they disagree with any or all of them, we must first address a number of questions pertaining to the nature of human language, the relation between speech and writing, and say more about the specific nature of Chinese writing as we see it.

In addressing these questions, we also hope to break out of the circularity, at least to some extent, of simply arguing from specific interpretation to specific translation, and back again. That is to say, we believe that readers of this translation of the *Analects* will give it credence in proportion to the credence they give to our account of language, speech, and writing in general, the Chinese written language in particular, and to the cosmology we have described for all who employed this written language.

The Classical Chinese Written Language

For a number of excellent reasons, most linguists take speech as their primary focus of investigation, with writing decidedly secondary. Some linguists with a different agenda have lamented this focus on speech:

> ... [T]he primacy of speech position is not seriously challenged within contemporary linguistics, and its basic tenets continue to permeate most language related research.[7]

The bias toward speech, however—if bias it be—is well motivated scientifically. In the first place, of the 3000+ dialects spoken in the world today, less than a fifth of them have written forms. It follows immediately that speech offers a richer database for linguistic generalizations than writing, or speech/writing combinations.

Those linguists who wish to focus more on writing do so because of their commitment to the belief that language is first and foremost a system of communication and that written languages surely communicate no less than their oral forms. Most of them further believe writing is speech in visible form. A large number of passages in the *Analects* begin with the formulaic *ziyue* 子曰, "The Master said," but because there are no punctuation marks in classical Chinese, we must ask if whatever follows *ziyue* is a literal transcription of speech, or a paraphrase of it, or a method of transmitting ideas in a written language which existed in important ways independently of the spoken language.

In turning from theories of language to theories of communication, a Western bias is evident at the outset because in asking about the relation of speech to writing, research has been conducted, and communicative theories developed, focusing on the *sender* of information. Unfortunately, it is not the only paradigm from which a science of communication might develop, natural though it might appear at first blush. For example, June Ock Yum has argued cogently that

> Confucianism has also contributed to East Asian communication patterns of process orientation, differentiated linguistic codes, indirect communication, emphasis, and receiver-centered communication. In contrast, North American patterns of communication represent outcome orientation, less-differentiated linguistic codes, direct communication emphasis, and sender-centered communication.[8]

Yum offers several arguments for her position, but details aside, the most disturbing part of her view is that purported scientific models of communication—and derivatively, language—based on the receiver might be as different from those based on the sender as heliocentric and geocentric models of astronomy are different from each other, and they may be incommensurable to boot.

In examining the language of the *Analects*, we have made a point independent of Yum that raises a related consideration about the role of agency. We have suggested that the classical Chinese language generally, rather than being "sender" or "receiver" centered, seems to be situation-centered, where situation has privilege over agency. This point is made explicit in several ways, "things" defaulting to "processes" in paronomastic definitions being one of them. Further, a term such as "bright (*ming* 明)" does not primarily mean perspicacity on the part of the agent, or resplendence on the part of the object, but both. That is, "brightness" is first situational, and then derivitively associated with subject or object. The examples we have given are that an expression such as *de* 德 does not mean "beneficence" or "gratitude," but both, and *xin* 信 does not mean "trust" or "confidence," but again both. *De* characterizes a generous situation, and *xin* characterizes a fiduciary situation.

Thus, just as receiver-centered theories of communication might differ from sender-centered ones, so too might theories of language differ depending on whether the spoken or written forms are taken as fundamental. Consider, for example, this difference between verbal and transcribed human languages: whereas there is a naturalness to the former, the latter is certainly less so. There is a specific sense in which *all* written languages can be said to be nonnatural or artificial. Parents and elders give children very few phonological, syntactic, and semantic lessons, yet the children learn the grammar of their native language rapidly and efficiently; not being formally taught, the grammar of native languages can be said to be learned naturally, and largely independent of intelligence and motivation. Learning to read and write, on the other hand, requires a good deal of explicit instruction, the mastering of certain instruments, training of the eye and hand as well as the ear and vocal organs, and practice in relying on language alone to communicate without benefit of extralinguistic aids such as gestures, facial expressions, and so on. Learning to read and write requires a great deal of motivation as well.

Given these arguments, it might well be asked why any linguist would wish to attend carefully to written forms of language. One answer is straightforward: it is the means by which the dead "speak" directly to us. Our present ruminations on the human condition are enhanced by being reminded by John Donne that "No man is an Island," and they are deepened when we are obliged to attend to Thoreau's claim that "The mass of men lead lives of quiet desperation." The former, although written, was meant to be delivered orally, as a sermon; the latter, although surely a "sermon" in its essentials, was not.

These examples (and countless others: Homer, Shakespeare, and so on) should suggest that written language should be viewed as a transcription of speech, with the image of courtroom stenographers uppermost in mind (at times, "listening" to themselves). Unfortunately, this response leaves open the question, basic to linguistics, of whether what is transcribed is basically phonetic in character (sound), or semantic (meaning), or some combination of the two.

Unlike all other linguistic scripts, the Chinese writing system has an unbroken history of more than three thousand years. Even today, at least a few of its characters are written pretty much as they were at the outset, as noted in our Introduction: those representing the sun, moon, human, door, and so on. This unique genealogy must be at least partially responsible for the frustration many nineteenth-century Protestant missionaries to China felt when attempting to transmit the gospel; not a few of them claimed that Chinese writing had to be the invention of the Devil because of the seeming impossibility of translating "The Good Book" without great distortion of meaning, as an earlier quote from a missionary suggests.

Even today, sinological linguists do not agree on what name to give the symbols that comprise Chinese writings (although they no longer give any credence to their having originated in the Nether World). The eminent scholar John DeFrancis has catalogued the terms sinologists have suggested for written Chinese symbols, and the descriptive list is a rather long one: "pictograph," "ideograph," "ideogram," "phonogram," "logograph," "lexigraph," "morphemic," "morphographic," "phenosemantic," "logosyllabic," "word-syllabic," and "syllabograms."[9]

Most of these scholarly differences of opinion—quite often heatedly debated—hinge on whether the characters are seen as basically phonetic or semantic in nature, and derivatively, whether these characters are to be construed as syllables, morphemes, or words. Without entering into the technicalities of these arguments, we will simply refer to the written symbols by their ordinary name of "Chinese characters" and we will also follow ordinary English usage in describing the writing system as a "language."

Our own thesis was sketched in the Introduction: the classical written Chinese language—the language in which the *Analects* was composed—is unique, being sharply distinct not only from all non-Sinitic languages but from spoken Chinese as well (ancient and modern), and that the differences between the two Chinese languages are of greater linguistic and philosophical significance than has been generally noticed.

The distinguished philologist Bernhard Karlgren reports on the separate nature of the Chinese written and spoken languages:

> Thus China has, on the one hand, for many centuries had a literary language which is short and terse and understandable, only through the ideographic script which clearly keeps every single word distinct from all others, a language which, on the whole, remains just as it was formed before the beginning of our era. On the other hand, China has a spoken language or, more correctly, many languages, based on different dialects which in their characteristics differ considerably from the language of literature.[10]

The separation between the spoken and written languages appears to be temporal as well as grammatical, going back to the late Shang dynasty of circa 1200 BCE. The earliest forms of Chinese writing extant are the oracle bone inscriptions, and these inscriptions deserve at least a brief mention herein because they indicate that the written language had a life of its own, independent of the spoken language, even during the earliest historical period of Chinese civilization, that is, more than a millennium before the *Analects* was composed.

The oracle bones used in Shang divination are cattle scapula and turtle plastrons that developed cracks when heated. The patterns of the cracks were interpreted as responses to specific divinatory messages which at some point were inscribed on the bones and shells. The lexical units of these messages were incised on the hard surfaces with knifelike instruments. Several features of these characters and inscriptions merit our notice.

In the first place, a little more than three thousand different lexical items have been isolated, and some half of these have been translated. The classifications of the characters which define the later classical language are largely present in the Shang inscriptions, indicating that we are already dealing with a mature language.[11] This does not preclude the fact that many of the thousand-plus characters that have been identified thus far (excluding those which seem to be used only as proper names) are importantly pictographic and ideographic in construction. That is, they are either direct pictures of a tree, horse, man, hand, meat, or mountain; or, they are a combination of such pictures to represent a concept, such as hand, meat, and "offering up" together representing "to sacrifice (*ji* 祭)." These characters are thus to be interpreted basically as representations of objects and ideas respectively, and although they would likely have some relationship to the pronunciation of these same objects and ideas, they are not merely representations of these sounds. David Keightley, reflecting on the insurmoutable problem of pronunciation of Shang graphs, has observed:

> Since there is no evidence of rhyme in the oracle inscriptions, the traditional and even modern approach to their study has been resolutely graphemic.[12]

Consequently, we have morphological as well as phonetic support for considering the early written forms to have their own communicative function without having been transcribed speech; at this stage, much information was communicated visually.

As Karlgren has noted in his reflections on the history and the nature of the written Chinese language:

> In this way the Chinese script in its first stage was not phonographic, analyzing how the word sounded in its different components, but ideographic, picture writing, in which a sign indicated a whole word, and moreover not its *pronunciation* but its *meaning*.[13]

The expressive nature of the original Chinese graphs is often hidden by the standardized version of the language presently in use. In fact, time spent with the early artifacts—oracle bones, bronzes, and even the bamboo slips dating now as early as the Warring States period (403–221 BCE)—is an important reminder of the visual power of the early characters in communicating meaning.

Another factor which suggests an independent life for the classical written language at a very early stage of Chinese history is that the excavated inscriptions are written on divinatory or other materials that are religious, not secular, in nature. That is to say, the archæological materials at hand show clearly that whatever other uses it might have had, early writing was intimately bound up with ritual religious practices. Consequently the development of the written forms must have been under the direct and powerful influence of extralinguistic factors, especially the religious and other beliefs of the early Chinese people—which is not, after all, very surprising. The written characters, for instance, may have been thought to possess magical qualities which it would have been defiling and even dangerous to apply regularly in nonreligious contexts, accounting for a general lack of secular inscriptions in the early materials that have been unearthed. (Admittedly the latter inscriptions could have been written on less durable artifacts.) Less speculatively, a clear indication of the religious and nonverbal influences on the written forms can be seen on those shells where the oracular message was inscribed with the characters written in one form on one side of the center seam of the plastron, and their mirror-image form on the other—after the fashion of a dominant artistic theme, the *taotie* 饕餮 masks. No *linguistic* reason seems to be of any relevance in attempting to account for this fact.

Further, in addition to religious and ceremonial features the process of incising the characters on bones and shells was a fairly laborious task; it surely was not simply a way of taking dictation. Dictation would be unnecessary in any case because speech tends to have a high degree of redundancy which there is no need to replicate in a written language that is not isomorphic with the sounds of speech, especially when that language is capable of transmitting much information by visual means. To make a terrible pun, only the "bare bones" of the oracle message would have to be inscribed for the message content to be later cognizable.

Moreover, it is not difficult to imagine these highly abbreviated linguistic forms becoming models for all written composition over a period of time, because knowledge of the medium was probably handed down carefully from initiates to novices, along with other religious rituals. As the social utility of the written symbols came to be exploited in less religious contexts, one can hardly suppose that the scribes invented wholly new patterns to perform the newer functions (if they had, a knowledge of classical Chinese would not be very helpful for learning to read the oracle inscriptions); rather would it be expected that the patterns employed in early ritual observances were important determinants of the later symbolic patterns.

During this lengthy secularization period, teachers and students came slowly to replace initiates and novices, but the linguistic curriculum seems to have remained intact, and classical Chinese certainly did remain the medium of the few and not the many. Not being the clear reflection of speech, which was used by everyone, it continued to be esoteric and used by the literati. We can also see that the written standards and models were kept by them; little attention is given to the fact today, but the written patterns found in the Shang materials continued to be exemplified in the classical literature throughout the period of its paramountcy, a time span of thirty-five centuries. The assumption that there is a direct line between the linguistic patterns found on the oracle bones and the classical literature that emerged from these beginnings is generally correct.[14]

This is not to say that the written language remained the same— indeed, once under way, it evolved rather dramatically. Karlgren delineates what he takes to be four significant evolutionary stages in this process:

> . . . first, simple pictographs; then, ideographic compounds; then again, phonetic loans; and finally, improved phonetic loans, i.e., compounds made up of phonetic and signific.[15]

Karlgren tells the story of how the early Chinese written language evolved. The movement from characters representing specific objects and ideas to the use of more or less homophonous "loan words" to do the work of abstract ideas was a critical juncture. For example, the pronunciation of "to come" was similar to "barley," and hence the character for "barley (*lai* 來)" would be written to represent this abstract idea, counting on the intelligence of the reader to make the connection. This loan method enabled the culture to increase the number of characters importantly, but at the growing cost of ambiguity and a demand on the reader to decode the script. Also, there were only a relatively small number of homophonous terms available that could be used in this way. Another stage was necessary.

Ideographs joined two ideas or pictures to make a new character, so that "sun (*ri* 日)" and "moon (*yue* 月)" could be combined to make "bright (*ming* 明)." And loan words using a character that had a similar sound had expanded the vocabulary. A proliferation of characters began when scribes combined these two notions, constructing new characters by using a similar sound as the phonetic element, and a classifier as the semantic significator. For example, the pictograph for "square (*fang* 方)" could be used as the phonetic representative of other words which had a similar pronunciation, and then a semantic component could be added to distinguish among them: "to speak (*yan* 言)" could be added to construct the character, "to ask (*fang* 訪)," and "metal (*jin* 金)" could be added to construct the character, "kettle (*fang* 鈁)."

Of course, this process was not always systematic. For example, in the construction of the character "one hundred (*bai* 百)," obviously "one (*yi* 一)" is meaning indicative, yet this character is classified under the "signific" "white (*bai* 白)," which is clearly the phonetic element.

This final stage in which the phonetic and the semantic components of the characters both had important relevance was already under way by the late Shang, as the method is attested on the oracle bones, and further, an extensive vocabulary was already available at the beginning of the first millenium BCE when early poetry flourished.[16]

This description of the Shang writing is far too brief and simplified, but three factors should stand out in any interpretation. First, the archæological evidence suggests important and fundamental differences between spoken and written Chinese; second, the same evidence suggests that many extralinguistic considerations influenced the independent development of the latter; and third, linguistic considerations were visual (semantic) as well as sometimes oral (phonetic) for most of the lexical items, giving the written language a definite form, structure, and vocabulary of its own over thirty-three hundred years ago. Intimately tied to religious and other beliefs, classical Chinese thus seems to have been importantly distinct from its verbal sibling at birth; and it grew up the same way.

One of the greatest obstacles to appreciating the basically nonverbal nature of literary Chinese is the fact that most of the characters today are not purely pictographic or ideographic, but rather are compounds—composed of a classifier indicative of the meaning of the character, called the "signific," and another element which is supposed to signal its pronunciation, the "phonetic" (Chinese *xingsheng* 形聲 category). As mentioned earlier, these phonograms are now classified as constituting approximately ninety percent of the 45,000+ entries in a Chinese unabridged dictionary. Their heritage is a long one, for in the twelfth century a dictionary of 24,200 characters categorized almost 22,000 of them as phonograms. As early as the first century CE, the etymological dictionary *Shuowen jiezi* with its 9,353 characters was made up of roughly 2,000 picto- and ideograms and 7,000 phonograms.

The high percentage of phonograms in later Chinese does not, however, affect adversely the argument that classical Chinese is sharply distinct from the spoken language and not basically a transcription of it. What then is the relation between the spoken and the written languages? A point that Karlgren makes with great emphasis is how the written language was fixed, and hence developed an increasing independence of the ever changing spoken language:

> It is true that it was to a considerable extent phonetic when the great category of characters were created (the great majority of the really current ones were created during the first millennium B.C.) which consist of a "significant" and a "phonetic." But it soon ceased to be a properly phonetic script, for it was not possible, as in a language with alphabetic spelling, to let the gradually changing pronunciation be reflected in the script, and modify the spelling accordingly. The Chinese characters were fixed once and for all in their composition, and could not be changed in this respect.[17]

The consequence of this separation between the spoken language and the written script, beginning in classical times has been that:

> The literature is a product for the eye, and not for the ear and tongue, as a spoken language. It lives its own life as a kind of independent phenomenon that is parallel with the spoken language.[18]

A number of scholars have focused on the phonograms, however, and consequently have not given sufficient notice to the semantic properties of the graphs, dismissing the use of such terms as "ideographs" to denote them. John DeFrancis, for example, says that:

> It should be apparent that there is much justification for considering the Chinese script to be basically—that is, more than anything else—a phonetic system of writing.[19]

Similarly, William Hannas maintains that:

> We can dismiss the fanciful notion that the units are icons of objects and concepts in the real and psychological worlds, i.e., that the symbols are pictographic.
>
> We also reject the untenable assumption that Chinese characters are "ideographic," that is, relate to meaning directly without the intervention of language.[20]

There are a number of problems with this construal of the Chinese character as fundamentally phonetic in nature when applied to the classical period, not least among them being the implication that Chinese scholars of language have, throughout history, done their job badly. Thus DeFrancis claims that while written Chinese is indeed a phonetic syllabary, it is "a very poor one"[21]; Hannas too claims the primacy of phonetic content for the writing system, and then notes it does the job "poorly."[22]

Even lacking any knowledge of modern Western linguistics, it is hard to believe that for over two thousand years, Chinese scholars were in any way confused about their own language(s). Until the present century under the influence of Western languages, Chinese dictionaries employed a semantically organized system of classification of the graphs, as well as those organized by tones and finals. These semantically arranged dictionaries, classifying characters according to their "radicals" or "significs," were necessary because one could not use the rhyme dictionaries to locate a character the pronunciation of which one did not know.

Thus, the existence of a large number of characters which may properly be called "phonograms" does not establish that classical Chinese was fundamentally a transcription of speech. If brief written forms could convey—by visual or other means—the relevant information to be transmitted, then, as noted earlier, there would be no need to represent all of the sounds made when that information had been conveyed orally. The point is a general one, and is also applicable to alphabetic written languages. The grammar of English, for example, is not well reflected in the "grammar" of newspaper headlines because the latter is a significantly abbreviated representation of the spoken language. In this case, the desire is for brevity, and the price paid is increased ambiguity (which makes the analogy with classical Chinese, we think, a good one). Consider the contrasting images conjured up by a headline some years ago from the sports page of a Seattle newspaper: SALMON BITING OFF PUGET COAST.

Even more importantly, the severe separation of the semantic and phonetic elements in a character seems questionable conceptually and misleading methodologically for early classical Chinese, for in the case of many lexical entries, what is called the phonetic element is actually (and sometimes solely) meaning-indicative, and in all such cases the ostensible phonogram will consequently be formally indistinguishable from an ideogram. It is not difficult to see why this should be so. Remember the very great number of homonyms in Chinese, so great that there is no unique written form for any common phoneme. In fact, after centuries of a process in which sounds were simplified, not counting the permutations permitted by the use of tones, there exist now only about 420 different syllables in modern Mandarin. Thus the inventive scribe seeking a character to represent a new vocabulary item might have had from three to a hundred different forms to pick from, all of which were pronounced almost exactly the same. On what basis would the scribe pick one over another? Surely it would be a semantically motivated choice. For instance, if he wanted to represent in written form the sound /wu/ which meant "to lie and deceive," "to slander," he would obviously use the pictogram denoting speech (yan 言) as the radical element of the compound character. And among the many lexical items pronounced /wu/, the scribe might have a range of homophones from which to choose. "To not have 無," "martial 武," "do not 毋," and "sorcerer 巫," for example, would all be pronounced the same. He might rather creatively pick the character wu 巫 which approximates "sorcerer" in meaning to be the phonetic element, especially if he remembered that sorcerers were usually considered to be suspicious folk in ancient China and were not to be trusted. Thus the character *wu* 誣 meaning "to lie and deceive" would be represented in written form as "the words of a sorcerer"—yet be classified among the phonograms and not the ideograms. Whether or not, or probably, to what extent, the concept of "phonogram" requires modification is beyond the scope of our present concerns; in any event we can admit that phonetic considerations played a role in determining the structure of many Chinese characters, and still maintain that the language of the *Analects* is not transcribed speech. The burden of proof must rest with those linguists who have assumed that it is.

There is still another important reason why the current existence of a large class of Chinese phonograms should not mislead us into the belief that the classical written language was more or less a transcription of speech. In the earliest stages of the development of the written language, there are very few phonograms to be found, especially if obvious proper names are discounted; as noted earlier, the majority of the characters identified from among the three thousand that have been recorded from Shang inscriptions are either pictograms or ideograms. Particularly, the increased use of phonograms during the first centuries of the Han dynasty coincided with the greatly increased contacts between the new imperial Chinese and the peoples of Central Asia and India. The need to reproduce, in Chinese, words from many foreign languages led naturally to the greater utilization of straightforward phonetic representation in the introduction of some new lexical items. But these non-Chinese terms were incorporated—sinicized—into linguistic patterns which were already well established.

Thus, during the formative period when patterns were being established which were to become standard—that is, when the great literary tradition was being developed—while phonograms surely played a role, it can be argued that the written forms were dominated linguistically by semantic rather than phonetic or syntactic considerations, with a focus on the visual more than on the oral features of the written forms. It is therefore not surprising that the linguistic structures of written and spoken Chinese are significantly dissimilar. No one can deny that over time, each language has had a profound influence on the other, or that some of the influences date back to antiquity; the present point is that the genealogy of the divergence appears to be equally ancient.

It may be objected at this time that our linguistic arguments are not conclusive and that too much weight has been given to meager archæological evidence in our premises. Perhaps the relative unimportance of phonograms and the nonverbal structure of the oracle-bone writings is peculiar to the religious and ceremonial nature of the artifacts and materials that have been unearthed. It might be argued, in other words, that what has been preserved on the bones and turtle shells is the fairly restricted vocabulary of religious language found on ritual objects, and, consequently, the rich symbolism and lack of correspondence to speech patterns are to be expected and are to be explained by reference to the specific religious beliefs and practices of the Shang people. Further, the objection might continue, a vocabulary of less than three thousand terms, applied only in religious contexts and often with unusual orderings, surely does not constitute an adequate base from which to generalize about the entire range of the language and its literature.

Linguistic arguments with respect to the Shang inscriptions may never be altogether suasive on either side, although David Keightley's foundational work on those inscriptions is supportive overall of our uniqueness thesis.[23] But the arguments do not need to be ironclad in the present instance because the basic pictographic/ideographic, and nonverbal features of classical Chinese are not confined to the Shang writings, nor even to the ritual bronze inscriptions of the Western Zhou period. On the contrary, and most importantly, the features of *wenyan* that have been emphasized herein are characteristic of the entire early classical literature, all of which came to be removed, linguistically at least, from the context of purely religious ritual symbolism, and from the spoken language. It may seem implausible that a rich and varied literature and literary tradition could grow around an initial inventory of some 3,000 vocabulary items, but such was indeed the case. The *Book of Songs*—the oldest and most revered of poetic works in China, in which phonetic features are many and varied—is one of the five Confucian classics; it has exerted an incalculable influence on all later poetic forms and styles, yet itself contains fewer than 3,000 different characters in the 305 poems that comprise it. The *Chun Qiu* or *Spring and Autumn Annals* has only 950 and so on. The *Analects* itself has 2,200 different lexical items. Further, as late as circa 213 BCE when Li Si attempted to standardize the variant written forms of characters by introducing the "lesser seal (*xiaozhuan* 小篆)" script, the number of terms standardized is supposed to have been slightly over 3,000.

We thus have a number of good reasons for seeing the classical written language as not just a poorly done transcription of the spoken language, but rather as a distinct, visually oriented medium of communication. At the early and formative stages of its development there is considerable evidence to show that the written forms were strongly influenced by cultural factors and their own internal structure, and relatively little evidence to show that they were similarly influenced as much by the spoken tongue. Up to this point, however, we have dealt almost solely with the phonetic and semantic features of the languages in building a case for the uniqueness thesis, and something must also be said about classical Chinese syntax, because the relation of symbols to each other obviously plays an essential role in the communicative process, and it is here that perhaps the greatest differences between the spoken and written languages make their appearance.

The Classical Chinese Language: Syntactical Considerations

Our skepticism begins when we seek a descriptive account of classical syntax, for we are quickly bombarded with negatives: Chinese has no tenses, no cases, no gender, no inflections, no plurals, no prefixes or suffixes; there are no "parts of speech" apart from context; and so on. All of these statements are true, but not particularly illuminating for the person seeking an outline of syntactic structures except insofar as they intimate that relatively few such structures will be found.

Second, although Chinese is an analytic language, order is not rigidly fixed in classical writing; reading the *Xunzi* is very different from reading the *Analects*. When this fact is coupled with the observation that every Chinese character has several meanings and can belong to several word classes, we can appreciate why there are few general statements about the grammatical relations of terms in classical Chinese relative to those we have for other languages. To take only a trivial example from English, the statement that articles precede rather than follow their nouns is intended to cover all articles and all nouns in all contexts. (And we do not have difficulty locating nouns in English because of the standard ordering noun phrase–verb phrase.) When exceptions to statements of this kind are found, they must be accounted for by other factors or else the generalizations will have to be modified or abandoned. In classical Chinese, on the other hand, the exceptions are usually more numerous than the cases covered by the generalizations; hence, it is difficult to state a nontrivial necessary condition for grammaticality in *wenyan*.

The issue deserves closer attention. There has been much linguistic work done on the classical language, but the conclusions that have resulted from this research differ crucially from the grammatical generalizations mentioned earlier. We do not get universal statements, but rather statistical correlations of the following form: in context A, character x {serves as a/means} y n% of the time. This statement-form does not correlate a particular meaning or function uniformly with a context. On the contrary, even in the same linguistic environment a character may occur, for instance, 40 percent of the time as a noun, 30 percent as a modifier, and 30 percent in other forms. Similarly for meaning, we do not have generalizations that link contexts with meanings, so we are not able to say that in such-and-such an environment a particular character is to be translated one way and in some other specifiable context it must be translated another way. The best we can say is that in a certain context the character will have this one meaning or grammatical function roughly five out of ten times. These probability-type statements are highly useful in helping to interpret Chinese texts, but it should be clear that they are not the stuff from which grammars are made. A proffered rule/principle that covers only a fraction of the cases would be quickly dropped as a hypothesis, and the fact that there is agreement in number between subject and verb in standard English would not be useful descriptively or linguistically if it only occurred some of the time.

The student of classical Chinese then, does not come to master the language by mastering its grammatical rules, for in the sense that syntactic rules are of uniform regularity, very few such rules can be found (there are some, of course, especially involving the particles). Rather it appears that the neophyte must memorize written patterns of symbols unique to a text or set thereof, which may and usually do differ more or less from the patterns found in other texts. Good Chinese students will memorize the poems of the *Book of Songs*, for example, and thereby "internalize" the patterns of characters exhibited in that classic. Similarly, they will memorize the *Analects*. But it is not the case that they generalize syntactic rules of classical Chinese in a basic way from these two sources; on the contrary, they appear to learn one set of patterns from one source, and another distinct set from another source. Further, neither these nor any other sets of written patterns will, we believe, fully exemplify the grammatical rules of the language spoken by the reader.

This is not to say that the reading student is totally without linguistic cues in attempting to interpret new passages, but only to point out that unlike written languages which are intended to represent the sounds of speech, many of the cues are not primarily phonetic or syntactic. In English, case markings, tense, affixes, position, and so on, all provide strong interpretative clues to the reading of a passage even when the meaning (semantic content) of key terms is not known. The nominalization of 'true' in English is clearly marked by the suffix -th. Similarly, the sentence "the preeves clithe away" will be interpreted as being made up of the (unknown) plural noun-form "preeves" and the purported verb "clithe." Thus, even though very few of us would know what preeves might be, at the least we would expect them to be objects in some sense; that is, we would interpret the term substantively: our question would surely be "What are preeves?" not "How do you preeve?"—the form our question would take for "clithe."

In classical Chinese, on the other hand, phonetic and syntactic cues of this kind are not regularly available to the reader; again, it is almost wholly an analytic language. Context provides the basic setting for the interpretation of most passages, aided less by syntax or phonetics than by semantic information. For instance, nominalization is not affix-marked in Chinese, nor is it consistently indicated by position or the particle 者 . Nevertheless, if a student came across, say, the term *shan* 山 which means "mountain," he would undoubtedly read it substantively no matter what its position in the passage; only if all efforts to interpret the passage failed with *shan* read as a topic would the reader try to interpret it verbally or as a modifier. But this circumstance is not so much due to any feature of the Chinese language as it is to the nature of the extralinguistic world: mountains are indeed substantial, and except to a geologist, they are not easily seen as events or actions; hence, terms which denote mountains will be read as the (or a) topic (noun) of a passage rather than as part of the comment (verb). Similarly, the character *jian* 見 , which is usually translated as "to look," (an eye walking), would be construed first in a verbal, active form and only secondarily as denoting a sight, view, or vision. In many situations, of course, this kind of information might be of only limited assistance to the reader, but in the absence of standard syntactic cues, any assistance at all is better than none, which is why we have emphasized the visual elements of Chinese characters. If the interpretative cues are significantly semantic in classical Chinese, then the visual forms of the graphs are linguistically significant if they thereby convey semantic information. To people who work with alphabetic languages this point is perhaps obscure, but it is actually a simple one. Chinese pictograms are almost always simple pictures, as noted earlier, of objects—trees, hands, doors, horses, or mountains. Consequently we formulate a heuristic rule for interpreting difficult passages: in the absence of contextual evidence to the contrary, read pictograms as nouns or topics. Similarly, because ideograms portray the interactions or relations between objects, or are an extrapolation therefrom, the analogous heuristic would be: interpret ideograms first as comments if a clear reading is thereby obtained. The fundamentally pictorial quality of written Chinese is hard to appreciate today because most of the characters are highly stylized. As noted earlier, however, such was not the case during the formative stages of the language; the evidence shows that in their early forms many of the characters, while conventional in one sense, nevertheless resembled fairly closely what they represented. And there were often many variants of the same character. Further, when we examine the bamboo and silk manuscripts being recovered in the recent archæological finds, we must conclude that the characters are "drawn" rather than "written." And, as noted in the introduction, the Chinese penchant for parallelism in structuring their writing also aided interpretation of passages.

In addition to carrying its own linguistic weight, the semantic component of classical Chinese therefore had to perform functions which are more commonly served by the phonological and syntactic components of the grammars of other languages. That is to say, the less the grammar of a language conveys information, the more the lexicon must provide it. This is one more premise warranting the conclusion that classical Chinese is a unique linguistic medium. Enough should have been presented thus far to at least generate skepticism for the too easily accepted assumption that classical Chinese is simply the transcribed version of the early spoken language. With these minimum linguistic warrants for the thesis in hand, let us turn briefly to a few of its more philosophical implications.

The Chinese Language: Some Philosophical Considerations

Our views of the nature of classical Chinese are relevant to an ontological dispute among contemporary scholars of language concerning what there is in the linguistic universe. Following the pioneering work of Noam Chomsky, generative linguists, and a few philosophers and social scientists (including Henry Rosemont, Jr., a member of this collaboration), maintain that the great surface differences—phonetic, syntactic and semantic—between natural human languages obscure the far more significant similarities that bind them together at a deeper level, that is, Universal Grammar (UG).[24] Indeed, in his more recent work, Chomsky holds that linguistic research will probably prove most fruitful if conducted on the basis of the hypothesis that there is only a single human language, articulated in many varied dialects.[25]

Other scholars (including Roger Ames, the second member of this collaboration), however, seem to have a preference for Ockham's razor over Plato's beard, consistently exhibiting skepticism about purported rules/principles of UG. At times, classical Chinese has been invoked as warrant for such skepticism. George Steiner, for example, following the work of the linguist Yorick Wilks, has said:

> Classical Chinese (and what other evidence have we?) seems to
> have no need of our noun-and-verb structure. How, then, can we
> assign to it innate grammatical properties obviously patterned on
> our own habits of syntax?[26]

Steiner (and Wilks) make their case too strongly: classical Chinese has *some* "need" for syntactic structure, and exhibits this need with particles and word order. But the more general, (if not obvious) claim is substantially correct: classical Chinese does not unambiguously express grammatical relations, such relations being considered a basic feature of UG (and would seem to be a feature of all natural human languages). But Steiner, Wilks, and others (such as Ames) should not take heart from this point, because the uniqueness thesis does not imply that the theory of UG is mistaken, but rather that classical Chinese is simply not a valid counterexample to it. That is, if natural languages are to be equated with spoken languages, classical Chinese is probably not an appropriate example or counterexample for *any* linguistic theory of natural languages. Fortunately, for this collaboration at least, Chomsky is an argument postponed.

We underscore this point about the difference between classical Chinese and natural languages because the Sapir-Whorf hypothesis of linguistic relativity is also associated at times with the Chinese language.[27] According to this hypothesis, the structure of their native language determines, to a significant extent, the way people structure their experiences and view of the world, from which it may be inferred that members of two distinct and divergent language groups "look" at the world in fundamentally dissimilar ways. Something like this hypothesis, as noted at the outset, is often used explicitly or otherwise to justify an inference from a particular feature of classical Chinese to a purported feature of Chinese conceptual capabilities. With respect to the way in which worldviews are sedimented into languages, Friedrich Nietzsche observed:

> The strange family resemblances of all Indian, Greek, and German philosophizing is explained easily enough. Where there is an affinity of languages, it cannot fail, owing to the common philosophy of grammar—I mean, owing to the unconscious domination and guidance by similar grammatical functions—that everything is prepared at the outset for a similar development and sequence of philosophical systems; just as the way seems barred against certain other possibilites of world-interpretation.[28]

Our own view is that the classical Chinese language surely influenced the way the Chinese experienced the world (as we have sought to describe in the Introduction), and that the nature of the classical language provides us with many real clues as to the way in which people lived and thought in ancient China. Such claims, however, need to take into account the non-natural and unique qualities of the classical written language. Whatever the final judgment on the Sapir-Whorf hypothesis, it should not be invoked without qualification, for such an invocation would be appropriate only where the languages compared cross-culturally were spoken languages.

A related implication of the uniqueness thesis concerns the so-called lack of development of logic in early Chinese thought. If we may oversimplify basic formal logic for purely illustrative purposes, it is roughly of two kinds: a study of the relations between whole sentences which are connected by disjunctive, negative, or conjunctive terms, formalized today in the sentential or propositional calculus; and also the study of the relations between two or more whole sentences which share at least one term, as exemplified in Aristotelian syllogistic and the predicate calculus. What these two studies have in common is a focus on the relations between declarative sentences, and more specifically, between sentences of the topic-comment kind; and of course, both systems are truth-functional. Most spoken Chinese sentences will fit into this category, but the uniqueness thesis suggests that the early written forms will fit into it only by being significantly disfigured. Therefore, there is no good reason to expect sentential or predicate logic to be reflected in Chinese classical philosophical writings on a major scale.

In such a light, the ancient Chinese philosophers do not have to be seen as either contemptuous of or oblivious to logical requirements, or as possessing some inscrutable logic of their own.[29] When important for their instructional concerns, they simply employed regularly a certain subset of semantic relations which were not particularly emphasized in the bulk of Western philosophical writings (which is one reason many Western philosophers have said that the Chinese weren't "really" philosophers).[30]

But while some of these differences in logical emphasis may be accounted for on purely linguistic grounds (once logical—that is, truth-functional—relations are made explicit), not all of them can. The differences between early Chinese and Western philosophers run deep, extending beyond grammar. While there is a clear logic and reasonableness to the Chinese *Weltanschauung* reflected in their classical language, we do not wish to suggest an overtly *logical* or *rational* ordering of their views, or their language (there are no close equivalents for either "logic" or "rational" in the lexicon of the *Analects*). It is for this reason that we have emphasized *æsthetic* order.

The distinguished historian of China John King Fairbank observed that for a Chinese thinker "... to question the Confucian virtues would have been to deny the existence of the written characters which expressed them."[31] That is, for Chinese philosophers to doubt the existence of an abstract quality was tantamount to their doubting the existence of the character naming that quality which was staring them in the face. At first glance it appears this view is suggesting that the Chinese tended to confuse symbol with reference, but that is surely to miss the point. (The visual properties of the characters certainly gave them a concreteness which would probably prove a match for the most hardened of epistemological skeptics; it is difficult to doubt that a picture is a picture of *something*.) The linguistic and logical evidence we have advanced thus far, however, is in further support of our claim that the Chinese concern was not so much with ontology or epistemology as it was with the relations among and between objects, events, and qualities. Of course, authoritative conduct (*ren* 仁) must, in some sense, "exist"; as noted earlier, the character for 'human' (*ren* 人) is one of its elements, and humans surely exist. More interesting and absorbing for the Chinese thinkers seem to have been the questions of how and why *ren* 仁, *yi* 義, and other moral qualities were related to each other, to human beings, to society, and to nature; when fitting, harmonious relationships were proffered, they must needs have had a strong *æsthetic* dimension.

We are not the first to have called attention to an æsthetic order in Chinese. Over a hundred and twenty-five years ago the sinologist S. Wells Williams said:

> If there are serious defects in Chinese, the language also possesses some striking beauties. The expressive nature of the characters, after their component parts have become familiar, causes much of the meaning of a sentence to pass instantly before the eye, while the energy and life arising from the brevity attainable by the absence of all inflections and partial use of particles add a vigor to the style, that cannot be reached by any alphabetic language.[32]

If, however, a purely logical order is imposed on a language and thought patterns that has these significant æsthetic dimensions, clearly "something will be lost in translation." In his *Mencius on the Mind*, published in 1932, the late Cambridge scholar I. A. Richards used the task of understanding the *Mencius* as an occasion to pioneer a novel technique for comparative studies. In so doing, he rehearsed many of the questions we have addressed in this translation, and offered his remedy. For Richards,

> The problem, put briefly is this. Can we, in attempting to understand and translate a work which belongs to a very different tradition from our own, do more than read our own conceptions into it? . . . To put it more precisely, can we maintain two systems of thinking in our minds without reciprocal infection and yet in some way mediate between them?[33]

Like Graham, Richards surmises—we think correctly—that if "analysis" is introduced as the methodology for understanding *Mencius* (or the *Analects*) as a text, or any concept in it, it smuggles in with it a worldview and a way of thinking that is alien to the tradition itself. We cite him at some length:

> Our Western tradition provides us with an elaborate apparatus of universals, particulars, substances, attributes, abstracts, concretes, a generality, specificities, properties, qualities, relations, complexes,

accidents, essences, organic wholes, sums, classes, individuals, concrete universals, objects, events, forms, contents, etc.

Mencius, as we have seen, gets along without any of this and with nothing at all definite to take its place. Apart entirely from the metaphysics that we are only too likely to bring in with this machinery, the practical difficulty arises that by applying it we deform his thinking . . . The danger to be guarded against is our tendency to force a structure, which our special kind of Western training (idealist, realist, positivist, Marxist, etc.) makes easiest for us to work with, upon modes of thinking which may very well not have any such structure at all—and which may not be capable of being analyzed by means of this kind of logical machinery.[34]

Seen against Richards's claim, our own analysis of the semantic properties of classical Chinese is not meant to tell the reader how to impose a logically ordered reading on the Chinese texts, but merely to point out that they are not *il*logical or *ir*rational, very different from our own patterns of language and thought though they might be. With proper apologies to Pascal's shade, a Confucian might paraphrase him as saying: "The heart-and-mind has its reasons, which the mind alone realizes not."

The failure to give the Chinese tradition its difference is thus nowhere more evident than in the language which has been used to translate it and the lexicon that has emerged to bridge the cultural divide.[35] From the initial encounter with China in the late sixteenth century, and particularly in the scholarship that has developed over the last century, the classical Chinese corpus has been carefully studied by philologically sophisticated translators with adequate and sometimes exceptional language skills. But the translations of Chinese philosophical writings over the last century have had very little impact on philosophy as practiced in Europe and the Americas. To be sure, a significant part of the blame for this sorry state of affairs lies with the philosophers themselves, far more parochial than they would wish to admit.

Translators, however, cannot evade their own responsibility for this situation, for they have employed in their translations a large number of key terms that have been central in the history of Western philosophy, with the result that the Chinese texts seem to be little more than very naïve versions of what Western thinkers have been doing for the past twenty-five centuries. Thus, because most philosphers have consequently not entertained the Chinese tradition as "philosophy," they have made little contribution to the introduction of Chinese thinking in the West. And given that philosophy as a discipline is responsible in the academy for articulating the broad strokes of a tradition's worldview, we have necessarily paid a penalty in the quality of our understanding of Chinese culture for this indifference.

The greatest hurdle confronted by any Western humanist in attempting to use the "translated" Chinese materials, both textual and conceptual, lies only minimally in the phonetic, phonological, or syntactic properties of the translated materials, but maximally in the lexicon which informs it. Not only is the semantic significance of the core philosophical vocabulary inadequately appreciated, but, further, by appealing uncritically to terms saturated with Western connotations, a foreign worldview overwhelms these humanists, persuading them that they are on familiar terrain where they are likely not.

Simply put, our existing uncritical formula for translating the core philosophic vocabulary of Chinese philosophy is freighted with a metaphysics which is not Chinese, thus perpetuating the pernicious cultural reductionism rehearsed above. Consider the "stock" translations of the following terms: *tian* 天 : Heaven; *you/wu* 有無 : Being/Nonbeing; *dao* 道 : the Way; *xing* 性 : human nature; *ren* 仁 : benevolence; *li* 理 : principle; *qi* 氣 : primal substance; *shi* 實 : reality; *yuzhou* 宇宙 : universe; *zhi* 知 : knowledge; *taiji* 太極 : Supreme Ultimate; *shifei* 是非 : right/wrong; *li* 禮 : ritual; *zhi* 志 : will; *yi* 一 : unity, the One; *jing* 精 : essence; *yi* 義 : righteousness; *lei* 類 : category; *ming* 命 : fate or Fate; *shan* 善 : good; *zui* 罪 : sin; *yin/yang* 陰陽 : negative cosmic principle, positive cosmic principle; *wuwei* 無爲 : doing nothing.

When, for example, we translate *tian* as "Heaven" with a capital "H," like it or not, we invoke in the Western reader a notion of transcendent creator Deity, along with the language of soul, sin, and afterlife. When we translate *ming* as "fate" (or worse, "Fate"), we conjure forth notions like irrevocability, predicament, tragedy, and teleology—notions which have little relevance for the classical Chinese tradition. When we translate *ren* as "benevolence," we psychologize and make altruistic a term which originally had a radically different range of sociological connotations. Being altruistic, for example, implies being selfless in the service of others. But this "self-sacrifice" implicitly entails a notion of "self" which exists independently of others and that can then be surrendered—a notion of self which we believe is alien to the world of the *Analects*; indeed, such a reading transforms what is fundamentally a strategy for self-realization into one of self-abnegation.

Uncritical assumptions about universal "humanity" as a category, and the fear in some quarters that too much difference leads to incommensurability, have disguised and obscured the radical degree of difference we owe the Chinese in observance of their distance from the West as a radically different order of humankind. An alternative inventory of presuppositions has been at work in the growth and elaboration of Chinese civilization, and the failure on our part to excavate and acknowledge this difference in our translations has rendered the Chinese worldview deceptively familiar. When an alternative philosophic tradition is made familiar and, at the same time, is adjudicated on the basis of Western standards of evidence that are foreign to it, it can only be an inferior variation on a Western theme. (Thus once again: Chinese writings aren't "truly philosophical.")

We are caught up in a vicious circle. The Western philosopher's ambivalent attitude toward the Chinese tradition and the consequent reluctance of philosophy as a discipline to legitimize the Chinese tradition as an area of philosophical inquiry are traceable at least in part to the nonphilosophical translator's inability to identify and respect fundamental cultural differences, and the consequent impoverishment of the Chinese lexicon. And the inadequacy of the translated lexicon is in important measure due to the marginalization of ethnography and history in the positivist's methodology-centered program, thereby precluding professional philosophical interest in Chinese culture. The Chinese texts can be neither interesting nor philosophically significant when reduced to the cultural importance of a tradition other than its own.

From this reflection, it becomes clear, at least, that the existing formalistic translation of these terms puts at risk a great deal that is philosophically significant. Choices of how to resolve this translation problem are several, and yet all have real limitations. The easiest and most common move has led largely to our contemporary situation—we search our inventory of philosophical terms and select that equivalent recommended by our own cultural interests and experience. We consult the dictionary, and on the basis of the multiple meanings provided, decide that in some cases *shen* 神 means "human spirituality," in other cases it means "divinity"; in some cases *xin* 心 means "heart," in others, "mind." What has not been properly noticed is that this approach often resolves ambiguity at the expense of equivocation and cultural bias. The smoothness of an English translation is interrupted if the reader is required to surrender entrenched assumptions which distinguish between the human being and God, or between the cognitive and affective aspects of the human experience.

A second option available to us in translating Chinese philosophy is to muddle through, attempting to do justice to as many of the different connotations as possible by providing novel terminological equivalents: the "heart-and-mind" and *pneuma* gambit. This effort sometimes leads to clumsy and puzzling neologisms, and sometimes, for the better informed, into an unexpected audience with Philo Judæus. On the positive side, given the relative unfamiliarity of these new terms, they sound a warning that we have entered a different philosophical landscape. To the extent that we can rely upon our readers to exercise their imaginations, these neologisms might even bring some novel complex of meanings into relief. Unless done carefully, however, such attempts at semantic honesty will impress impatient readers only as mystifications.

A third methodological approach, with much to recommend it, would be to take the key twenty-plus terms in the Chinese lexicon of philosophical import, provide initial glosses, and thereafter merely transliterate them. While this approach would make greater demands on readers, it would reduce markedly the number of questions begged in the translation and exposition.

To some, this approach may appear to be simply the laziest way out of a difficult problem. But "ritual" has a narrowly circumscribed set of meanings in English, and *li* 禮 an importantly different and less circumscribed set. Just as no Indological scholar would look for English equivalents for *karma, dharma,* and so on, perhaps it is time to do the same for classical Chinese, the homonymity of the language notwithstanding. We have begun that task by including romanization with our translation of philosophical terms, and by refusing to translate at least the problematic notion of *tian,* as a beginning to the appropriation of Chinese terms into the English language. We do so because we believe Western scholars, especially philosophers, must become more sensitive to what Confucius had to say *in his own terms*—quite literally so.

In sum, we hope that readers will see that our views of languages in the abstract, of written "language" in general and of the Chinese written language in particular, and our views of how the ancient Chinese thinkers may have viewed their language—with attendant cosmological presuppositions—are all geared to a *re-* rather than a *de-*construction of the *Analects.* We know that even when taken together our linguistic evidence, and logical and ontological arguments, may not be fully persuasive, yet we simultaneously believe that they provide at least reasonable warrants for the way we have utilized the principle of logical charity in our translation to steer between the Scylla of rational unintelligibility and the Charybdis of logical and philosophical naïveté. While some of our views of the Chinese language and Chinese thought are mutually reinforcing (a more gentle expression than "circular"), it should be clear that much of what we have said about the former will or will not hold up independent of the accuracy of our views of the latter.

Philosophy is the only intellectual discipline which takes the definition of its subject matter as a basic element of its subject matter. Throughout the twentieth century, philosophy has been defined in the English-speaking world as an attempt to clarify thought. But in the ordinary, everyday use of the word "philosophy" in English, it signifies a way of coming to terms with a world not of our own making, and philosophers are generally considered to be those who envision different "worlds" with which we can come to terms. We believe the *Analects* offers us just such a different world, and have therefore construed our translation and commentary as a philosophical enterprise.

In the end, it may turn out that the art of translation is far too important to be entrusted to philosophers, but we thought it imperative to try.

NOTES TO APPENDIX II

1. For citations to Legge, Waley, Dawson, and Lau, see note 1 to the Introduction.

2. A failure to make this "reforming" sense of *gai* clear has led to some classic misunderstandings in translating important texts, one of the most glaring perhaps being a passage in *Daodejing* 25 which describes *dao* 道 as 獨立不改, translated almost uniformly as "it stands solitary and does not change." This translation "does not change" is hard to square with the line which follows: 周行而不殆: "Pervading everything and everywhere it does not pause." The meaning here is not that *dao* "does not change," but being the *sui generis* totality of all there is (*wanwu* 萬物), it is not open to reform by appeal to something external to it.

3. On this debate, see the "Terms Controversy" chapter in Cook and Rosemont (1994) which contains references.

4. Graham (1978):25.

5. Graham (1990):359.

6. Hansen (1992):45ff.

7. Leonard Scinto, quoted in Hannas (1995):1.

8. June Ock Yum (1988):374.

9. DeFrancis (1984):71–74.

10. Karlgren (1949):57.

11. Keightley (1978):59.

12. Keightley (1978):67. No less provocative in his later than in his earlier work, Keightley has recently advanced the claim that while many of the oracle bone graphs did have a phonetic dimension that cannot be ignored for interpreting them, he also suggests that the earliest forms of the graphs—at least some of them—were abbreviated and stylized representations of even earlier iconic sculpture and drawing. See Keightley (1996).

13. Karlgren (1949):9. In a recent work, Boltz (1994) flatly contradicts Karlgren on this score, insisting that there are *no* phonetic-less Chinese characters. Unfortunately, while Boltz offers keen insights on a number of graphs and their development, his sweeping general claim requires a hypothesis which it would be difficult to falsify—hence our suspicion of the claim. A more careful and detailed critique of Boltz's claims is in Handel (1999).

14. Keightley (1974):65–66.

15. Karlgren (1949):15.

16. See Karlgren (1923), (1926), and (1949) for a full account of this fascinating story.

17. Karlgren (1926):39.

18. Karlgren (1926):41.

19. DeFrancis (1984):111.

20. Hannas (1995):6.

21. DeFrancis (1984):97–100.

22. Hannas (1995):1.

23. Keightley (1978). The following several pages follow Rosemont (1974).

24. Rosemont (1978.)

25. Chomsky (1993):47–48.

26. Steiner (1969):233.

27. Whorf (1956):esp.134–60.

28. Nietzsche (1966):20.

29. For a more detailed discussion of logic in ancient China, see Rosemont (1974).

30. Especially the paradigmatically rational (logical) Kant. After referring to the philosophy of Laozi as a "monstrosity," Kant goes on to say ". . . Chinese philosophers strive in dark rooms with eyes closed to experience and contemplate their nihility." Kant (1981):79.

31. Fairbank (1962):66.

32. Williams (1888) Vol II:370–71.

33. Richards (1932):86–87.

34. Richards (1932):91–92.

35. The next several pages follow Lin Tongqi, et al. (1995).

Ahern, Emily (1981). *Chinese Rituals and Politics*. Cambridge: Cambridge University Press.

Allan, Sarah (1979). "Shang Foundations of Modern Chinese Folk Religion," in *Legend, Lore and Religion in China*, ed. Sarah Allan and Alvin P. Cohen. San Francisco: Chinese Materials Center.

Ames, Roger T. (1999). "Human-centered Spirituality in Classical Confucianism," in *Confucian Spirituality*, ed. Tu Wei-ming and Mary Evelyn Tucker. New York: Crossroads Press.

————— (1998). "Death as Transformation in Classical Daoism," in *Death and Philosophy: Reflections on Mortality*, ed. Jeff Malpas and Robert Solomon. London and New York: Routledge.

————— (trans.) (1993). *Sun-tzu: The Art of Warfare*. New York: Ballantine.

Bodde, Derk (1938). *China's First Unifier: A Study of the Ch'in dynasty as seen in the life of Li Ssu (280?-208 BC)*. Leiden: E. J. Brill.

Boltz, William (1994). *The Origin and Early Development of the Chinese Writing System*. New Haven: American Oriental Society.

Boodberg, Peter (1953). "The Semasiology of Some Primary Confucian Concepts," in *Philosophy East and West* 2:4.

Brooks, E. Bruce, and Taeko Brooks (1998). *The Original Analects*. New York: Columbia University Press.

Chan, Wing-tsit (ed.) (1986). *Chu Hsi and Neo-Confucianism*. University of Hawaii Press.

—— (1969). *Neo-Confucianism, etc: Essays by Wing-tsit Chan.* Hong Kong: Oriental Society.

Chomsky, Noam (1997). *Language and Thought.* London: Moyer Bell.

—— (1996). *Powers and Prospects.* Boston: South End Press.

Cook, Daniel J. and Henry Rosemont, Jr. trans. (1994). *Leibniz: Writings on China.* Open Court.

Creel, H. G. (1960). *Confucius and the Chinese Way.* New York: Harper Torchbooks.

Dawson, Raymond (trans.) (1993). *Confucius: The Analects* Oxford: Oxford University Press.

—— (1981). *Confucius.* Oxford: Oxford University Press.

DeFrancis, John (1984). *The Chinese Language: Fact and Fantasy.* Honolulu: University of Hawai'i Press.

Dewey, John (1920). *Reconstruction of Thinking.* New York: New American Library.

Dubs, H. H. (1929a). *Hsun-tzu: The Moulder of Ancient Confucianism.* London: Probsthain.

—— (1929b). "The Failure of the Chinese to Produce Philosophical Systems," in *T'oung Pao* 26.

—— (trans.) (1928). *Hsun-tzu.* London: Probsthain.

Fairbank, John King (1962). *The United States and China.* New York: Viking Press.

Fingarette, Herbert (1983). "The Music of Humanity in the Conversations of Confucius," in *Journal of Chinese Philosophy*, 10.

—— (1972). *Confucius: The Secular as Sacred.* New York: Harper and Row.

Fung, Yu-lan (1953). *A History of Chinese Philosophy*, 2 volumes,. trans. D. Bodde. Princeton: Princeton University Press.

Graham, A. C. (1990). *Studies in Chinese Philosophy and Philosophical Literature.* Albany: State University of New York Press.

—— (1989). *Disputers of the Tao.* La Salle: Open Court.

————— (1978). *Later Mohist Logic, Ethics and Science*. Hong Kong: Chinese University Press.

Hall, David L., and Roger T. Ames (1998). *Thinking From the Han: Self, Truth, and Transcendence in Chinese and Western Culture*. Albany: State University of New York Press.

————— (1995). *Anticipating China: Thinking Through the Narratives of Chinese and Western Culture*. Albany: State University of New York Press.

————— (1994). "Confucian Friendship: The Road to Religiousness," in *The Changing Face of Friendship*, ed. Leroy S. Rouner. Notre Dame: University of Notre Dame Press.

————— (1987). *Thinking Through Confucius*. Albany: State University of New York Press.

Handel, Zev (1999). "In Defense of *huiyi*: The Case for the Phonetic-less Character" (a review essay of William Boltz, *The Origin and Early Development of The Chinese Writing System*), in *China Review International*.

Hansen, Chad (1992). *A Daoist Theory of Chinese Thought*. Hong Kong: Oxford University Press.

Hannas, W. C. (1997). *Asia's Orthographic Dilemma*. Honolulu: University of Hawai'i Press.

————— (1995). "The Cart and the Horse." Georgetown University. Unpublished ms.

Hebeisheng Wenwu yanjiusuo Dingzhou Hanmu zhujian zhengli xiaozu 河北文物研究所定州漢墓竹簡整理小組 (1997). *Dingzhou Hanmu zhujian Lunyu* 定州漢墓竹簡論語. Beijing: Wenwu chubanshe.

Ho Che Wah 何志華 (1998). "Chutu Wenzi xinzheng 出土文子新證 (New evidence from the *Wenzi* excavated at Ding County)," in *Sino-Humanitas* No. 5.

Ivanhoe, P. J. (1993). *Confucian Moral Self-Cultivation*. New York: Peter Lang.

Jensen, Lionel (1998). *Manufacturing Confucianism*. Durham, NC: Duke University Press.

Jingmen Muncipal Museum 荊門市博物館 (1998). *Guodian Chumu Zhujian* 郭店楚墓竹簡. Beijing: Wenwu chubanshe (Cultural Relics Press).

Kant, Immanuel (1981). On History, trans. L. W. Beck. Indianapolis: Bobbs-Merrill.

Karlgren, Bernhard (trans.) (1950a). *The Book of Documents.* Stockholm: Bulletin of the Museum of Far Eastern Antiquities.

—— (trans.) (1950b). *The Book of Odes.* Stockholm: Bulletin of the Museum for Far Eastern Antiquities.

—— (1950c). *Grammata Serica Recensa.* Stockholm: Museum of Far Eastern Antiquities.

—— (1949). *The Chinese Language: An Essay on its Nature and History.* New York: The Ronald Press Company.

—— (1926). *Philology and Ancient China.* Cambridge, MA: Harvard University Press. (Reprinted 1980, Philadelphia: Porcupine Press.)

—— (1923). *Sound and Symbol in Chinese.* London: Oxford University Press.

Keightley, David (1996). "Art, Ancestors, and the Origins of Writing in China," in *Representations* 56, Fall.

—— (1990). "Early Civilization in China: Reflections on How it Became Chinese," in *Heritage of China: Contemporary Perspectives on Chinese Civilization,* ed. Paul S. Ropp. Berkeley: University of California Press.

—— (1978). *Sources of Shang History: The Oracle-Bone Inscriptions of Bronze Age China.* Berkeley: University of California Press.

Knoblock, John (trans.) (1988–1994). *Xunzi: A Translation and Study of the Complete Works.* Stanford: Stanford University Press.

Lau, D. C. (trans.) (1992 revised edition). *Confucius: The Analects (Lun yü).* Hong Kong: Chinese University of Hong Kong Press.

—— (trans.) (1984). *Mencius.* Hong Kong: Chinese University of Hong Kong Press. First published Hamondsworth: Penguin, 1970.

Lau, D. C. and Roger T. Ames (trans.) (1996). *Sun Pin: The Art of Warfare.* New York: Ballantine.

Lau, D. C. and Chen Fong Ching (1992). *A Concordance to the Shuoyuan.* Hong Kong: Commercial Press.

—— (1992). *A Concordance to the Liji.* Hong Kong: Commercial Press.

———— (1992). *A Concordance to the Hanshih waizhuan.* Hong Kong: Commercial Press.

———— (1992). *A Concordance to the Huainanzi.* Hong Kong: Commercial Press.

———— (1992). *A Concordance to the Yi Zhoushu.* Hong Kong: Commercial Press.

Legge, James (trans.) (1960 rep.). *The Chinese Classics,* 5 volumes. Hong Kong: University of Hong Kong.

———— (trans.) (1885). *Li Chi.* In the Sacred Books of the East series, vols. 27 and 28. Oxford: Clarendon.

Leys, Simon (trans.) (1997). *The Analects of Confucius.* New York: Norton.

Li Xueqin 李學勤 (1997). "Bojuzhan yu guijuwen 博局占與規矩紋 (Divination by Gambling, and the TLV Design)," in *Wenwu* 文物, no. 1.

Lin Tongqi, Henry Rosemont, Jr., and Roger T. Ames (1995). "Chinese Philosophy: A State of the Art Essay," in *The Journal of Asian Studies,* August.

Lynn, Richard John (trans.) (1994). *The Classic of Changes: A New Translation of the I Ching as Interpreted by Wang Bi.* New York: Columbia University Press.

Makeham, John (1998). "Between Chen and Cai: *Zhuangzi* and the *Analects*" in *Wandering at Ease in the* Zhuangzi, ed. Roger T. Ames. Albany, State University of New York Press.

———— (1997). "The Earliest Extant Commentary on Lunyu: Lunyu Zheng zhi zhu," in *T'oung Pao,* LXXXIII, 260–99.

———— (1996). "The Formation of LUNYU as a Book," in *Monumenta Serica* 44, 1996.

Munro, Donald (1969). *The Concept of Man in Early China.* Stanford: Stanford University Press.

Nietzsche, Friedrich (1966). *Beyond Good and Evil,* trans. Walter Kaufmann. New York: Vintage.

Pound, Ezra (trans.) (1954). *The Confucian Odes.* New York: New Directions.

———— (trans.) (1951). *Confucius: The Great Digest and Unwobbling Pivot.* New York: New Directions.

Raphals, Lisa (forthcoming). "A Woman Who Understood the Rites: Confucius on Ji of Lu," in Bryan Van Norden (ed.), *Essays on the* Analects of Confucius.

————. (1998). *Sharing the Light: Representations of Women and Virtue in Early China.* Albany: State University of New York Press.

Richards, I. A. (1932). *Mencius on the Mind.* London: Routledge and Kegan Paul.

Rosemont, Henry, Jr. (1999). "Tracing a Path of Spiritual Progress in the *Analects*," in *Confucian Spirituality*, ed. Tu Wei-ming and Mary Evelyn Tucker. New York: Crossroads Press.

———— (1996). "How Do You Learn to Be Religious?" in *Cultural Dynamics* 8.2.

———— (1995). "Why the Chinese Economic Miracle Isn't One," in Z *Magazine* (October).

———— (1991). *A Chinese Mirror.* La Salle, IL: Open Court.

———— (1978). "Gathering Evidence for Linguistic Innateness," in *Synthese* 38.

———— (1974). "On Representing Abstractions in Archaic Chinese," in *Philosophy East and West* (January).

Ryle, Gilbert (1949). *The Concept of Mind.* London: Hutchinson.

Schuessler, Axel (1987). *A Dictionary of Early Zhou Chinese.* Honolulu: University of Hawai'i Press.

Schwartz, Benjamin (1985). *The World of Thought in Ancient China.* Cambridge, MA: Belknap Press.

Shaughnessy, Edward L. (trans.) (1996). *I Ching: The Classic of Changes.* New York: Ballantine.

———— (1993). "*Shang shu* 尚書 (*Shu ching* 書經)," in *Early Chinese Texts: A Bibliographical Guide*, ed. Michael Loewe. Berkeley: The Society for the Study of Early China.

Sima Qian 司馬遷 (1959). *Shiji* 史記 (Records of the Historian). Beijing: Zhonghua shuju.

Sivin, Nathan (1965). "Chinese Alchemy and the Manipulation of Time," in *Earlham Review* I.

Steele, John (trans.) (1917). *I-Li*. London: Probsthain.

Steiner, Ralph (1969). "The Tongues of Man," in the *New Yorker*, November 15.

Takeuchi, Teruo (1965). "A study of the meaning of *jen* advocated by Confucius," in *Acta Asiatic* 9:57–77.

Tu Wei-ming (1997). "Chinese Philosophy: A Synopsis," in *A Companion to World Philosophies*, ed. Eliot Deutsch and Ron Bontekoe. Oxford: Blackwell.

—— (ed.) (1996). *Confucian Traditions in East Asian Modernity*. Cambridge, MA: Harvard University Press.

—— (1985). *Confucian Thought: Selfhood as Creative Transformation*. Albany: State University of New York Press.

—— (1979). *Humanity and Self-Cultivation: Essays in Confucian Thought*. Berkeley: Asian Humanities Press.

Twitchett, Denis, and Michael Loewe (eds.) (1986). *The Cambridge History of China V. I: The Ch'in and Han Empires (221 BC–AD 220)*. Cambridge: Cambridge University Press.

Ullman, B.L. (1969). *Ancient Writing and Its Influence*. Cambridge MA: MIT Press.

Veith, Ilza (trans.) (1972). *The Yellow Emperor Classic of Internal Medicine*. Berkeley: University of California Press.

Waley, Arthur (trans.) (1938). *The Analects of Confucius*. New York: Modern Library.

—— (trans.) (1937). *The Book of Songs*. London: Grove Press.

Watson, Burton (trans.) (1963). *Hsun Tzu: Basic Writings*. New York: Columbia University Press.

Whorf, Benjamin (1956). *Language, Thought and Reality*. Cambridge, MA: MIT Press.

Wilhelm, Richard (trans.) (1961). *I Ching, or Book of Changes.* Translated by Cary F. Baynes. Princeton: Princeton University Press.

———— (1931). *Confucius and Confucianism.* New York: Harcourt, Brace, Jovanovich.

Williams, S. Wells (1888). *The Middle Kingdom.* 2 volumes. New York: Charles Scribner's Sons.

Wright, Arthur (ed.) (**1953**). *Studies in Chinese Thought.* Chicago: University of Chicago Press.

Xu Weiyu 許維遹 (1955). *Lushi chunqiu* 呂氏春秋. Peking: Wenxue guji kanxingshe.

Xunzi 荀子 (1950). Harvard-Yenching Institute Sinological Index Series, Supp. 22. Peking: Harvard Yenching Insitute.

Yang Bojun 楊伯峻 (trans.) (1980). *Lunyu yizhu* 論語譯注. Beijing: Zhonghua shuju.

Yum, June Ock (1988). "The Impact of Confucianism on Interpersonal Relationships and Communication Patterns in East Asia," in *Communication Monographs*, December.

Zhou Zhongling 周踵靈, Shi Xiaoshi 施孝適, and Xu Weixian 許惟賢 (eds.) (1982). *Han Feizi suoyin* 韓非子索引. Peking: Zhonghua shuju.

Zhuangzi 莊子 (1947). Harvard-Yenching Institute Sinological Index Series, Supp. 20. Peking: Harvard Yenching Insitute.

Roger T. Ames is a professor of Chinese philosophy at the University of Hawai'i. He is a translator of Chinese classics, and the author of several interpretative studies of classical Chinese philosophy, including *Thinking Through Confucius* (with David L. Hall). His translation, *Suntzu: The Art of Warfare*, is recognized as a landmark of contemporary Chinese military and philosophical studies.

Henry Rosemont, Jr., is the author of *A Chinese Mirror* and the forthcoming *A Confucian Alternative*, and has edited and/or translated six other works, including (with Daniel J. Cook) *Leibniz: Writings on China*. He is George B. and Wilma Reeves Distinguished Professor of the Liberal Arts at St. Mary's College of Maryland.